MADONNA/WHORE

THE MYTH OF THE TWO MARYS

by
Doris Tishkoff

1663 Liberty Drive, Suite 200
Bloomington, Indiana 47403
(800) 839-8640
www.AuthorHouse.com

7/06

First published by AuthorHouse 02/20/06

ISBN: 1-4208-9767-5(e)
ISBN: 1-4208-9765-9 (sc)
ISBN: 1-4208-9766-7(dj)

Printed in the United States of America
Bloomington, Indiana

This book is printed on acid-free paper.

For permission to use Edvard Munch's Madonna for the cover design of this book*, I am grateful to The Munch Museum, Oslo Norway, The Munch Ellington Group, and the Artists Rights Society (ARS), NYC.

All New Testament quotations are taken from *The New English Bible,* Oxford University Press/Cambridge University Press, 1971.

This book is dedicated to WIN, Women In Need, an organization in New York City that provides shelter, support, and hope to single mothers and children who are struggling to maintain family and dignity in the face of overwhelming obstacles.

ACKNOWLEDGEMENTS

It would be difficult to cite all those who contributed in some form to this book over a period of years. To begin, thanks to my son, Will, for replacing my creaky old computer with a modern, updated version, and to my good friend Finn Hakansson without whose encouragement this book might never have seen the light of day. I am most grateful for the generous help of Sarah G. Epstein who contributed so much to my understanding of Munch and graciously shared both her research and materials from the Epstein Family Collection of Edvard Munch Prints and Lithographs with me. Similarly, I am indebted to Professor Rowan Greer of Yale Divinity School and Professor Ben Page of Quinnipiac University for their warm collegiality and insights into the material on Jesus and the New Testament. Thanks to Professor Claudia Setzer of Manhattan College for reviewing the material on the New Testament in Chapter One of the manuscript. For invaluable technical assistance thanks to Professor David Valone of Quinnipiac for the hours he selflessly gave to get the Mss. into final form. Warm thanks as well to librarians at Amherst and Mount Holyoke Colleges, Yale Divinity School, and Quinnipiac University. Finally, thanks to James Clement van Pelt, who not only gently guided me through the mystifying maze of the computer, but gave so generously of his support, encouragement, and time in completing the final version of the manuscript.

CONTENTS

Preface		1
Chapter 1	In Remembrance of Her: Women and the Jesus Movement	5
Chapter 2	Mary the Mother	17
Chapter 3	Flesh of My Flesh	29
Chapter 4	They Are Like Angels in Heaven	47
Chapter 5	From Mother to Virgin	63
Chapter 6	The Many Faces of Mary	77
Chapter 7	Our Lady of Perpetual Inviolability	89
Chapter 8	This Heart of Stone	101

Chapter 9	Mary Magdalen	115
Chapter 10	"Some Call Her Love"	129
Chapter 11	A Confusion of Marys	139
Chapter 12	Mary Magdalen: Repentant Whore	147
Chapter 13	Mary Magdalen, Superstar	161
Chapter 14	From Whore to Courtesan	171
Chapter 15	'Tis Pity She's a Whore	187
Chapter 16	Modern Magdalens	197
Chapter 17	'The Great Social Evil'	211
Chapter 18	The Madonna/Whore Syndrome	229
Chapter 19	"I Don't Know How to Love Him"	243
Epilogue		257
Bibliography		267
End Notes		277
Index		299

PREFACE

Madonna/Whore: what is it and where did it come from? In simplest terms it means the ancient split between nice girls vs. bad girls, respectable wives vs. available sluts. In a religious sense it refers to Christianity's two most important women - Mary, mother of Jesus and without sin, Mary Magdalen, alleged prostitute and symbol of sin and woman's degradation. In sociological terms it describes society's age-old custom of putting women into two categories, one legitimate and honored, the other marginal and debased. In psychological terms it is the male conundrum of marrying the pure, trustworthy woman, while turning to the feral, exciting woman for sexual fulfillment.

In its origins the split is as old as the institution of marriage, for that's where it began. From time immemorial marriage had nothing to do with love, and everything to do with money, property, family. A virgin bride insured the integrity of the family, while a sexually experienced woman threatened it and might bring with her a trail of dishonor as well. Hence the dichotomy: potential wives conditioned to be modest, subservient, and asexual; women of the lower classes exploited as sex objects.

Yet the formula is not that simple, for sexuality is a driving and mysterious force that tends to make its own rules. When female sexuality is perceived as too powerful, its flip side can be a deep and abiding fear that manifests itself in a hatred for its perpetrator - not only the proverbial whore, but for women in general.

If such things might seem irrelevant in today's sexually permissive society, think again. Today as never before Christians are calling for a revision in the traditional portrait of the Virgin Mary and Mary Magdalen - partly because of the uproar caused by the Da Vinci Code, but also because women are taking their rightful place in the Church today. As to the psychology of Madonna/whore, clearly it continues to inhabit our collective unconscious. A case in point would be John F. Kennedy, a compulsive womanizer who before marriage confessed to a friend that, having had his fill of 'sexually traveled' women, he was searching for a virgin bride.[1] The wife he found became a legend for her beauty and elegance, yet her personal life was marred by pain caused by the dark obsession with 'forbidden fruits' that continued to haunt Kennedy until his death. More recently there was the embarrassment when baby-faced actor Hugh Grant was arrested for having sex in a car with a prostitute in Los Angeles, not to mention the revelations by the Beverly Hills Madam about her star studded, celebrity clientele.

Such things are no laughing matter, for in the wrong hands the potential for scandal can and has destroyed brilliant careers. Nor has our progressive society come to terms with the nitty-gritty of working women and the traditional segregation of roles. The strain to be perfect mother and wife in the image of the Madonna can be crushing on today's working women. Conversely, society still looks at women on their own with a jaded eye. Whether divorced, single, successful, or on welfare, they still remain somewhat suspect, as anyone who has ever lived in the heartland of the suburbs, or worked for a mainstream institution knows. As to women who turn the tables on their male colleagues, acting out male prerogatives of power and sexually predatory behavior, we have the killer/ monstrosities played by Glen Close in Fatal Attraction and Sharon Stone in Basic Instinct.

Still, one might ask, what does all that have to do with the religious paradigm of the Two Marys? To that I would answer: everything, for they remain the most pervasive icons of femininity in western culture, replete with an entire body of myth, fantasy, fiction, and delusion about the nature of woman. They inhabit our minds and our souls - men and women both - they burrow deeply into our subconscious to influence our notion of femininity and sexuality regardless of our religious beliefs.

Precisely because they are religious figures we either negate them or freeze them into rigid stereotypes that obscure their true origins. Yet their respective myths derive from ancient beliefs about women that pre-date Christianity, while even today they make manifest the catch 22 inherent to Christianity - the conflict between erotic and spiritual love that continues to haunt and divide the Church, especially in the wake of the sex scandals dogging the priesthood today. To seek them out in their original form demands that we examine the origins of Christianity and Jesus's own stance on women and sexuality—provocative and especially timely questions to which the answers lie buried beneath centuries of misunderstanding and religious dogma.

This book, however, is not meant to be either a religious or a feminist polemic. Rather, it is concerned with the way that the myths about the feminine polarity continually change and reinvent themselves in succeeding historical eras - not merely in the church, but in the secular world as well. In that sense, they pertain not only to the psychology of Madonna/whore, but also to political and legal issues such as divorce, welfare, and human rights.

For some, the most controversial aspect of the book will be its discussion of Jesus's attitudes toward women and sexuality - actually quite radical given the mores of his time. This was a man who genuinely liked and respected women, who included them in his teachings, who understood them, listened to them, even loved them, for compassion derives from love. His most remarkable parables about forgiveness have to do with women, and he refused to judge them by the harsh codes of the time - not even prostitutes, society's most degraded creatures. Above all, he never treated them as chattel, as even husbands were often wont to do.

Hopefully, then, this book will help us to better understand that subtle, often hidden paradox so destructive to relationships between men and women both. Apprised instead of a holistic model for modern woman, we might treat one another with the love and mutual respect manifested by Jesus himself.

CHAPTER 1

In Remembrance of Her: Women and the Jesus Movement

High noon just outside Sychar, a town in Samaria to the south of Galilee. A blazing sun has baked the parched earth around a well where the dusty, weary band of travelers—Jews traveling from Judea to Galilee—pause to rest. Legend has it that in ancient times this well belonged to the patriarch Jacob and his son Joseph, whom both Samaritans and Jews regard as their ancestors. Now the two groups have become bitter rivals, each respectively claiming the legitimacy of its God, its traditions, and its sacred temples, the Samaritans' being on Mount Gerizim, the Jews' in Jerusalem. Samaritans are said to have strewn human bones in the precincts of the great temple in

Jerusalem to defile it; Jews look down on Samaritans as a despised people. Pious Jews refuse to eat bread baked by Samaritan hands; merely to touch them is considered an impurity.

At midday the travelers are both hungry and thirsty, for their teacher and mentor, Jesus, has instructed them to travel without knapsacks, bread, money, or a change of clothing, and to depend upon hospitality for food, drink, and shelter. Leaving Jesus to rest at the well, the men go into town to seek food and water. The heat is intense, and when a local woman comes to draw water from the well, Jesus asks for a drink to slake his thirst. Shocked, the woman exclaims, "What! You a Jew ask a drink of me, a Samaritan woman?" (John 4:9)* To share her drinking vessel is to invite pollution.

Not only does Jesus drink, but he speaks to her of strange and wonderful things. If only she knew who he was, he might repay for her kindness with a "living water . . . always welling up for eternal life" (John 4:10-15). With that marvelous water she would never be thirsty again. Cynical at first, the woman finds herself drawn by this stranger's uncommon magnetism. She begs to receive the "living water," but Jesus tells her to go home and get her husband first. When she replies that she has no husband, Jesus commends her honesty. Having had five husbands, she now lives with a man to whom she is not married. Astounded at this uncanny knowledge of her past and present life, the woman recognizes Jesus as a prophet, perhaps even the long-awaited Messiah.

Eager to share this extraordinary news with the townspeople, she hesitates, for they will say that Jesus is a Jew. No matter, says Jesus; in time to come sectarian barriers will be dropped and true "worshippers will worship the father in spirit and in truth" (John 4:23). Not only does Jesus declare his message to be universal, but, moved by the woman's belief in him, he reveals his true self: "I am he, I who am speaking to you now" (John 4:25-6).

---

*All Biblical citations are taken from *The New English Bible,* Oxford University Press, 1971.

Returning from the town, Jesus's followers are "astonished" to find him talking with a strange woman, since pious Jewish men never spoke with women in public, not even a wife, "lest men should gossip."[1] Yet they accept Jesus's unorthodoxy, for Jesus has often broken with custom, offending even his followers by speaking, eating, and drinking with outcasts of various stripes, even the hated tax collectors. Nor does he always follow the letter of the law in regard to women. At a time when Orthodox Jewish men thank God in their daily prayers for having made them neither a slave nor a woman (as some Orthodox Jews still do today), and ancient law, as set down in Deuteronomy, holds that a menstruating woman contaminates everything she touches, beds and furniture included, Jesus does not exclude women from his teachings or judge them according to the harsh codes of the times.* Women are, in fact, drawn to him. Some become his most avid followers, join him in his travels, and help support his expanding entourage with money and basic necessities of life.

Soon a small group of curious townspeople arrives at the well. Amazed by Jesus's teachings, they affirm the woman's claim: "we have heard him for ourselves; and we know that this is in truth the Savior of the world." At their behest Jesus remains in the town for two days to continue his teachings (John 4:42).

Today some scholars dispute the authenticity of this story, but in the early Church the Samaritan woman was regarded as the first Apostle to the Gentiles. Certainly the story illustrates Jesus's disregard for powerful taboos. For one, he shares a drinking vessel and engages in conversation with a strange woman, a Samaritan ordinarily regarded by Jews as a reviled people. Moreover, the fact that she is living in adultery draws no

---

*We should keep the latter in mind. Such ideas were deeply ingrained in every society throughout the ancient Near Eastern world. Even in Egypt, where attitudes toward women were strikingly positive, women could not hold high civil positions or become scribes.

admonishment from Jesus. Indeed, perhaps it is his readiness to offer her grace, or forgiveness, that moves her so profoundly. Most important, by revealing his mission to the Samaritan Woman he underscores his accessibility to all who would believe in him—male or female, Jew or gentile, respectable or sinner.

Not coincidentally, the story of the Samaritan Woman is told by John, in whose Gospel we find several women strikingly close to Jesus: the wealthy sisters Mary and Martha of Bethany; Mary, the mother of James; and Joses, the mother of the sons of Zebedee. Some offer material support, such as Salome, the wealthy wife of a steward, and Joanna and Susanna who travel with the apostles and "provide for them out of their own resources." Others have been healed by Jesus, like Mary of Magdala, "from whom seven devils had come out," and women cured of seizures, possibly caused by epilepsy, neurasthenia, or mental disorders.

Although wealthy women often attached themselves to noted teachers whom they supplied with money, food and other necessities, Jesus's women followers were unique in various ways. For one, they shared in the deprivations—the fatigue, thirst, and hunger—of traveling from village to village in the blazing Galilean heat. And as Jesus's skill as healer spread, the crowd of sufferers—cripples, paralytics, the blind, epileptics, those possessed by demons that made them shout blasphemies, those covered with hideous sores caused by leprosy—grew larger and more insistent. At times the strain of teaching, debating points of law, baptizing, and healing seemed overwhelming. More than once Jesus sought relief from the pressing crowd, as when he embarked on a boat on the Sea of Galilee. At such times Jesus's women followers provided not only mundane needs, but also blessed repose.

Some even participated in the work at hand. Paul tells us that James, Jesus's brother, and the Apostle Peter were married and traveled with their wives when evangelizing. Biblical scholar

Dominic Crossan has also suggested that when Jesus sent missionaries out "in pairs" to heal and baptize, they were pairs of men and women, the latter being called "sister/wives" to give them respectability.[2] Later, as the movement spread, some women courageously traveled alone. One such woman was the amazing Thecla, who brought the 'good news' of the gospel to peoples in the most remote areas of Asia Minor.

Various stories are told of Thecla's unflinching courage. One legend claims that she was the first woman martyr, having been torn apart by lions in a Roman arena. Another asserts that she was miraculously saved twice—once from burning at the stake, once from the lions after she baptized herself and the animals refused to touch her. A close associate of Paul, by whom she was converted, legends about her have proliferated. One claims that she cut her hair and dressed like a man in order to do missionary work. According to another she eventually retired to a cave, where she lived as a hermit until the ripe age of ninety. There she healed many sufferers and inspired other women to become ascetics.[3] Today Thecla is virtually unknown. Nor would one guess that the disciples were not all bachelors or that Jesus's women followers played a significant role in his mission, so thoroughly have they been suppressed.

In part, the fault lies in a distorted view of women in antiquity as subservient, passive "doormats." In actual fact the households of the ancient Near East depended upon a dynamic partnership between husband and wife. Everyone, wives and children included, contributed to the productive power of the household, as did the extraordinary "capable wife" of Proverbs 31: "All her life long / She chooses wool and flax / And toils at her work / Like a ship laden with merchandise / She brings home food from afar." Mother, housekeeper, accountant, astute businesswoman who expands the family coffers through domestic or cottage industries, this woman, it would seem, never sleeps. Rising before sunrise, she puts "meat before the household," then sets about her "duties with vigour" as she spins and sews clothing for the family, weaves fine linen to make elegant sashes for sale to merchants, invests her profits in fields and vineyards. Trader, merchant, landowner and cultivator, "She is clothed in dignity and power / And can afford to laugh at tomorrow" (Proverbs 31:25).

The *Acts of the Apostles* are full of such women. For example, Tabitha, a seamstress from Joppa, made all the clothing for the members of her Christian community. So indispensable was she that when she took ill and was presumed dead, her distraught disciples sent word to Peter, who promptly came and resurrected her, for they could not survive without her. Another was Lydia of Philippi, whose native province was rich in the plants and mollusks that produced the deep, purple dye used to make the togas worn by the Roman upper classes. In Lydia's home city of Thyatira, slaves tended the great vats where the dye was boiled, its noxious odors seeping out of the cottage "factories" to pollute the surrounding air.[4] After the coveted purple cloth was weaved and dyed, it was sent out to Philippi, where Lydia acted as agent for its distribution all over southern Europe and the East. As an important importer/exporter, Lydia was a highly respected, central figure in the social and economic life of that most cosmopolitan of ancient port cities.

The Gospels, too, tell of strong, capable women active in the Jesus movement. Joanna was wife of a steward in Herod's household, and probably shared in the stewardship. Salome and Mary of Magdala may have been wealthy widows, the most propitious position for women, since marriage made them respectable, but widowhood made them independent. Widows might even manage the family business and properties on their own. According to a document of 126 B.C.E., a widow named Appollonia inherited an estate that included slaves, a vineyard, wells, wagons, a grain mill, and an oil press, all of which she managed on her own.

As to women of the Gospels, Mary and Martha of Bethany were especially close to Jesus. Two sisters from a distinguished and wealthy family, they often entertained Jesus as a guest in their comfortable home, located on the crest of the arduous, uphill road from Jericho, one hour's walk to Jerusalem. Once, after an especially busy period of teaching, Jesus stopped to rest there. Martha, the elder sister, warmly welcomed him, bustling about with domestic chores required by polite hospitality—washing of feet and hands, serving of food and drink. But Mary, the younger sister, seated herself at Jesus's feet—a position generally assumed by disciples of a great teacher—and listened intently to his words. Increasingly irritated, Martha finally protested that Jesus seemed oblivious to the fact that her sister had left her to do all the work alone: "Tell her to come and lend a hand" (Luke 11:41). Instead, Jesus gently chided his hostess for "fretting and fussing" over trivial things. Sanctioning Mary's truancy from "women's work," he says that she has "chosen [what] is best; and it shall not be taken away from her" (Luke 10:42).

This spare domestic drama has evoked endless interpretation; however, for our purposes we see that, once again, Jesus breaks with tradition. Not only is he on familiar terms with two unmarried women, but by teaching Mary he encourages her to neglect her domestic duties and to appropriate a man's role. Of course, the roles of Jewish women were expanding in the urban, Hellenized, more worldly class to which the sisters belonged. Yet, in general, Jews shared attitudes about women profoundly embedded throughout the Mediterranean basin.

Broadly speaking, the notion of women as physically, intellectually, or morally equal to men was utterly foreign to the mind of antiquity. Jews, however, had never engaged in the practice of exposure, abandoning unwanted female infants to the elements to die, nor did they sacrifice virgin daughters, as we know from the Old Testament story about Abraham and his son Isaac. Reverence for motherhood, the move away from polygamy and concubinage, and moral sanctions against extramarital sex also raised the condition of Jewish women, while ancient tradition elevated a feminine principle of wisdom known as *Sophia,* an intuitive wisdom that taps into the divine.

Nonetheless, in certain respects, especially in circles that adhered rigidly to ancient Jewish law, women were a separate category. Menstruating women were seen as defiling; contact between the sexes outside the immediate family was strictly prohibited; rules of modesty were enforced; and women were forbidden to study (customs still practiced by some Orthodox Jews today). But times were changing, as Jewish women of the urban and upper classes emulated their Roman neighbors, interacting with men socially and in the workplace. Such was the case with Mary and Martha of Bethany, who had a large circle of friends of both sexes. Especially striking is the tone of familiarity, even of reproach, they take with Jesus, most notably when he fails to respond to their urgent message that their brother Lazarus is mortally ill.

As the story is told by John, at that critical point in his ministry Jesus has become so controversial that, during a visit to the Temple in Jerusalem, his enemies hurl epithets of blasphemer at him, and even threaten him with stones. Quitting Jerusalem, he travels to the east bank of the Jordan River, where John is baptizing, followed, as always, by a throng. Despite an urgent message from the sisters imploring him to come at once to Bethany, he tarries there for two days—possibly because to pass through Jerusalem is still too dangerous. Not until four days after Lazarus' death does Jesus arrive at the outskirts of Bethany, to be met by a grieving Martha. When Jesus assures her that Lazarus will rise again, she assumes that he means on judgment day. Not so, says Jesus, for "If a man has faith in me, even though he die he shall come to life." Martha responds, "Lord I now believe that you are the Messiah." Once again, it is a woman who dramatically affirms her faith, even before the events of the crucifixion.

On learning of Jesus's arrival, Mary, too, rushes to meet him and falls at his feet weeping. So affected is Jesus by her sorrow that he too weeps—an astonishing display of emotion, and the only time in the New Testament that Jesus actually sheds tears. Arriving at the tomb, Martha's faith is again tested. When Jesus tells her to remove the stone sealing the entryway, she protests that the terrible stench could kill them. Jesus commands her to "have faith [in the] glory of God," and together they remove the stone. Uttering a loud cry, Jesus calls Lazarus to come forth, and the 'dead' man appears at the mouth of the cave, his body and face swathed in burial cloth (John 11:1-44).

The raising of Lazarus is the greatest of Jesus's miracles and a radical turning point in his ministry. Yet in the events leading up to that miracle, it is the sisters who are the central actors. Their grief, so poignantly shared by Jesus, moves him to act. Most important, Martha's confession of faith stands at the heart of the narrative, while Mary's weeping at Jesus's feet presages his most famous parable concerning sin and forgiveness—the story of the nameless woman who bathes Jesus's feet with her tears, dries them with her hair, and anoints him with precious oil.

Told in slightly different ways by all four Gospel writers, in Luke's Gospel the setting is the home of Simon the Pharisee, where Jesus has been invited to dine. Suddenly, a "woman who was living an immoral life in the town" rushes into the house carrying a small flask of precious oil of myrrh. Weeping copiously, she embraces Jesus's feet, kisses them, and bathes them with her tears. After drying them with her loose, flowing hair, she anoints them with myrrh, a ritual rife with layers of meaning. Shocked and repelled, Simon murmurs, "If this fellow were a real prophet he would know who this woman is who touches him, and what sort of a woman she is, a sinner" (Luke 7:37-40).

Actually, by custom the poor are allowed to enter a wealthy home in search of food. In this case, however, Jesus ignores deep-seated taboos and risks pollution, for only prostitutes appear in public with their hair loose. Yet, as Jesus reminds his offended host, this despised woman has provided common courtesies that Simon has neglected, perhaps because he failed to perceive the true stature of his guest. With genuine humility she has bathed Jesus's feet with her tears, as Simon did not. While Simon has offered no cordial kiss to his guest, she "has been kissing my feet ever since I came in." And while Simon has failed to anoint Jesus's head with oil, the woman has anointed his feet with the precious myrrh (Luke 7:45-6).

This dramatic episode becomes the launching point for one of Jesus's greatest parables on forgiveness and redemption. Two men, he says, are in debt to a moneylender. One owes 50 silver pieces, the other 500. After the moneylender forgives both debts, which man will love him the most? When Simon answers the man owing 500, Jesus points out that while Simon extended no courtesies at all to his guest, the woman provided them all. Thus:

> Her great love proves that her many sins have been forgiven; where little has been forgiven, little love is shown. Then he said to her; your sins are forgiven. Astounded, the guests ask: Who is this that he can forgive sins? (Luke 7:40-50)

Like other "sinners" whom Jesus refused to condemn, the episode goes to the very core of Jesus's mission: to bring the sick (whose illness was believed to be caused by some moral transgression), the outcast, the despised, the dispossessed, the poor and humble into His Father's kingdom. The fact that the woman is a sinner and possibly a prostitute makes Jesus's tolerance and forgiveness even more striking, for harlotry was considered a pollution so abominable as to be beyond redemption.

Matthew, Mark, and John, respectively, tell a slightly altered version of the story. In Matthew and Mark the setting is the home of Simon the leper, the place Bethany, the time Passover. The atmosphere is fraught with danger, for Jesus knows that his enemies are conspiring to bring about his death and tries to warn the disciples that in two days he will be handed over to the

Romans for crucifixion (Matt. 26:2). Thus, with death hanging in the very air, the ritual of anointment takes on a dark meaning that the disciples fail to perceive. Instead, they protest the cost of the precious oil, money which might have gone to the poor. Rebuking the disciples, Jesus praises the woman for comprehending what they do not—the imminence of his death. Moreover, in this version she anoints his head, not his feet, as did Old Testament prophets when anointing a king. For her recognition of Jesus as Messiah both evangelists pay a splendid tribute to that nameless woman, proclaiming "wherever in all the world this gospel is proclaimed, / what she has done will be told in remembrance of her" (Mark 14:3-9, Matt. 26:13).

Only in John is the anointing woman identified—she is Mary of Bethany, the same who wept at Jesus's feet in the raising of Lazarus. Here the setting is the house in Bethany. Lazarus sits among the guests, Martha serves them, and Judas protests that the money spent on the oil should have gone to the poor. Ironically, Judas fails to comprehend what Mary recognizes as the tragedy at hand, Jesus's imminent death. Although John omits the crucial ending — "in remembrance of her"— the point is clear. Although repeated three times, Jesus's prediction to the disciples of his death and resurrection falls on deaf ears. Only the anointing woman takes him seriously. For that, writes Dominic Crossan, she might be seen as the very first Christian, or at the very least "the supreme model of Christian faith." For only *she* believes in the resurrection even before it happens.[5]

Ultimately, too, it is Jesus's women followers who have the courage to follow along the pathway to Golgotha, to stand by the suffering man through the long, drawn-out agony, while the male "twelve or eleven" lock themselves behind bolted doors in fear of the authorities. Later, both Mark and John accord to Mary Magdalen the great honor of being the very first to bear witness to the resurrection. Yet the initial reaction of the disciples when she reports the great miracle is skepticism and outright disbelief.

What, then, has happened to those strong, brave women of the New Testament with their unshakeable faith? Today most of them are diminished in importance, or forgotten, or their identities have been merged. Most notably, the Magdalen has been conflated with the harlot who weeps and anoints and is forgiven and cleansed of sin. As to the others, their fate would be obscurity, for in the evolving Church women have been barred from leadership roles until only recently. Instead, the feminine face of the Church would coalesce into two principal figures—the Virgin Mary and Mary Magdalen.

Of the former we have heard nothing as yet. Yet in time to come she would rival her son as the powerful Queen of Heaven, a receptacle through the ages of Christian faith and prayer, the ideal of perfect holiness. It is to her, then, that we now turn.

CHAPTER 2

MARY THE MOTHER

Mary . . . is always and everywhere . . . in every human need and distress.

Queen of All Hearts: A Journal of Mariology

December 1531: a mountain trail in Tepeyac, Mexico. Breathing heavily, Juan Diego, a humble, newly baptized native, laboriously makes his way up the steep slope when he hears an unearthly music, like birds singing in heaven. Suddenly, a woman bathed in a light as brilliant as the sun appears. Dropping to his knees, he recognizes the Blessed Virgin and resolves to build a church on that very spot. In the face of his bishop's persistent skepticism Juan Diego perseveres alone. He is rewarded for his faith by further miracles—roses bursting into bloom in frosty December, the image of the Virgin outlined on his cloak. At last, the bishop concurs. A shrine is erected for Our Lady of Guadeloupe, a dark-skinned Madonna who understands Mexicans, their suffering and oppression, and protects them with fervid zeal. In 1810, when long years of exploitation by cruel and greedy overlords erupt into bloody rebellion, the revolutionists fight under her banner.[1] Today her image is everywhere—in every humble peasant home and in tourist shops for travelers who wish to bring something of the Mexican soul back to their native lands.

Winter 1793: San Raphael, capital of Santo Domingo (now the Dominican Republic). Toussaint Louverture, leader of the black slave revolt in French-occupied Haiti, is solemnly awarded the prestigious Order of Queen Isabella. A devout Catholic with a mystical bend, Louverture later retires to a secluded hill outside the city to meditate on such an honor conferred on a former slave. Suddenly, an African woman illuminated by brilliant light appears as trumpets sound a heavenly music. Scattering roses in his pathway, she says, "You are the Spartacus of the Negroes . . . you shall revenge the evil that has been done unto the people of your race."[2] Recognizing her as the Blessed Virgin, from that day on Louverture fights only under her banner, adorned with roses.

Well into our own century the Virgin Mary continues to make sporadic appearances, spawning shrines to which pilgrims—the sick, the lame, the suffering—painfully make their way in hope of a cure. Most famous are her visitations to humble peasant girls, Bernadette Soubirous of Lourdes and Lucia dos Santos of Fatima. More recently, in 1992 she appeared in Marlboro, N.J., to a local man, Joseph Januszkiewicz, on a warm summer evening in his garden. Ignoring the pleadings of the bishop of Trenton to allow time to authenticate the visitation, thousands of pilgrims immediately descended on the tiny suburb, causing chaos and massive traffic jams. Similarly, in 1995 in Pantano, Italy, a child raised his head from prayer to see a simple plaster figure of the Madonna shed bright red tears. Immediately, the once-sleepy port city forty miles northwest of

Rome became a booming tourist center, despite the fact that DNA analysis showed that the tears were made of human blood. And thanks to modern technology, anyone in West Hartford, Connecticut who desires a consultation with the Virgin can call a 1-800 hotline, posted next to her larger-than-life portrait on a giant billboard.

Clearly, for all our modern skepticism, the Blessed Virgin fulfills profound needs that modern science and technology cannot satisfy. As the Catholic Monthly Journal of Mariology, *Queen of All Hearts,* put it, "Mary . . . is always and everywhere, in every human need and distress."

Strangely enough, except in Luke's Gospel, Jesus's mother is an obscure, even marginal figure in the New Testament. The very first recorded reference to her comes from a letter of Paul to the Galatians dating some thirty years before the canonical Gospels: "God sent forth his son, born of a woman" (Gal. 4:4-5). For Paul, Jesus's humanity rests upon a fully human birth, yet he fails even to mention Mary by name. In fact, what little we know about her real person comes from tantalizingly brief fragments in the Gospels of Mark, Matthew, or John, while in Luke the leap from ordinary woman to a figure of mythic proportions is enormous. Nonetheless, on a few basic facts the Evangelists agree. Jesus came from a large family, with four brothers whose names are given and with sisters who, being mere women, have neither name nor number. Accounts in both Mark and Matthew also suggest that Mary's relationship to her son at the outset of his ministry was somewhat strained, that she shared the family's skepticism about his gifts and their fear that his notoriety would redound on them.

With good reason, perhaps, for the Romans watched the Galileans with an acutely nervous eye. Converted to Judaism somewhere between the eighth and seventh centuries B.C.E., they were ruled by the Herodian dynasty of kings, themselves recent converts to Judaism. In a day when travel was by foot or donkey, Galilee was somewhat remote from Judea proper, being a northern province surrounded by gentile districts. Its capital, Sepphoris, was a thoroughly Hellenized city of 40,000 that had an acropolis, a gymnasium, a bank, and thriving commerce with other great Mediterranean cities. Thanks to fertile soil and rich pasture lands, Galileans also enjoyed a measure of economic self-sufficiency. Reputedly proud and aloof, they spoke a bastardized, dialectical Aramaic, tended to neglect the purity laws, and often interpreted the law in an idiosyncratic way. Galilee may also have been the birthplace of the radical Zealots—to Rome a hot-bed of sedition and troublemakers to be closely watched. When rioting broke out after the death of Herod the Great, the Roman governor burned the capital, Sepphoris, to the ground. In such a climate Jews trembled with fear, being loath to bring the terrible wrath of Rome on their heads.

Yet here was Jesus, whose ministry began in earnest after the arrest of John the Baptist, almost crushed by throngs who came to hear him speak in the synagogues and the marketplaces, on hillsides, and beside lakes. Once, he fled the crowds by taking refuge in a boat on the Sea of Galilee, but the multitudes grew. Following him everywhere they fought to push through the crowds, to be close to him or touch his garments. A paralyzed man, desperate to be cured, had his friends break through the roof of a house where Jesus was teaching and lower him into the house on a stretcher. Touched by the man's faith, Jesus declared, "My son, your sins are forgiven," and the paralytic walked away (Mark 2:5).

Such a healing could be dangerous, for physical illness was believed to be a manifestation of a moral illness. Since only God could forgive sin, there were some who cried blasphemy. There was, too, Jesus's open embrace of reviled elements in society—tax collectors who milked their own people, lepers whose very breath exuded contagion, harlots whose beauty camouflaged their utter degradation. To consort with such people was (it was thought) to invite personal defilement. And there was Jesus's assault on the very cornerstone of society—the family and private property. Not only did Jesus ask his followers to give up their houses, fields, and vineyards and to share goods communally, he demanded that the rich make the ultimate sacrifice—to give all they had to the poor.

Jesus also employed a provocative, Socratic style of teaching in which disputations on the law might become heated debates lasting for hours. Like his contemporary, the great Pharisee sage Hillel, whose teachings have a striking resonance with those of Jesus, his interpretation of the law tended to be flexible and humane. A loving God, he insisted, would not want the poor to go hungry or the sick untended, even on the Sabbath. Nor did he support the ancient desert law of retribution, "an eye for an eye, a tooth for a tooth," for a people living under the crushing yoke of the Romans. Better to offer the other cheek to an aggressor, to give more than was demanded if sued for property, to go two miles if need be rather than one when conscripted into a labor force by the Romans.

Today we fail to comprehend how radical such teachings were in a society already fractured into a multitude of parties that argued and contended against one another. Even Jesus's own townspeople, the Nazarenes, had decidedly mixed feelings about his growing fame. On hearing about two of Jesus's most astonishing healings—the woman cured of hemorrhage of twelve years' duration (a condition that made her permanently unclean and thereby an "untouchable" to everyone around her), and the raising from the dead of a twelve-year-old daughter of Jairus, president of a synagogue, some of them reacted with suspicion and even hostility. Astounded by such reports about miracles and the brilliance of Jesus's teachings, they contended that such knowledge and skill in healing must come either from God or from Satan.

Where, they asked, did this man get his arrogance, for was

he not from humble stock, like themselves? How could this man, son of an ordinary carpenter, whose mother, father, brothers, and sisters they had known all their lives, claim such authority? Matthew tells us that on one visit to Nazareth some of the townspeople "fell foul of him" and even threatened to throw him off a cliff (Matt. 13:55-6). In response Jesus uttered the famous adage, "A prophet will always be held in honour except in his home town, and among his kinsmen and family". In Nazareth, his home town, the power for which he was so famous failed him; there only a few were healed. (Mark 6:4).*

Jesus's family, too, felt the sting of their resentment, for in a tightly-knit village community such things could redound on them. A particularly troubling rumor was that Jesus had great success in exorcising demons from the mad because he himself was possessed by Beelzebub—"He drives out devils by the prince of devils" (Mark 3:22). Consequently, on hearing that Jesus had come to Nazareth to teach, his mother and brothers "set out to take charge of him; for people were saying that he was out of his mind" (Mark 3:21). Clearly they were not part of Jesus's entourage, for a dense crowd surrounding the house where Jesus was teaching obstructed their way. In answer to a message asking him to come out and meet them Jesus responded: "Who is my mother? Who are my brothers? Fixing his glance on the close circle gathered about him, he replied rhetorically, "Here are my mother and my brothers" (Mark 3:33-35).

As always, Jesus's meaning here is ambiguous. Metaphorically speaking, he may have meant to acknowledge a "family" of believers. However, the Gospels offer other hints at alienation from his family. For one thing, Jesus's headquarters was in Capernaum, directly across the Sea of Galilee from Nazareth. For another, after the episode at Nazareth the family disappears from the Gospel narratives until the crucifixion. Even then, only in John is

*Possibly this passage is meant to convey indignation toward those Jews who rejected Jesus' message.

any family member present—Mary, his mother. And only after the crucifixion did Jesus's brother, James, become one of the disciples.

Indeed, Jesus repeatedly asked his followers to relinquish family ties. To a young man who wanted to bury his dead father before becoming a follower, Jesus responded, "Let the dead bury the dead" (Luke 9:59-60). After giving the disciples authority to heal, he tells them: "I have come to set a man against his father, a daughter against her mother, a son's wife against her mother-in-law; . . . no man is worthy of me who cares more for father or mother than for me . . . who cares more for son or daughter; . . . who does not take up his cross and walk in my footsteps" (Matt. 10:35-38).

Nor does Jesus ever speak of his natural father in the Gospel narratives. Rather, he repeatedly refers to his "heavenly father" using the affectionate Hebrew name *Abba.*[3] Possibly his father died before he began his ministry, for we hear only of his mother, brothers, and sisters. However, part of Jesus's radicalism was his rejection of the strict patriarchalism of late antiquity that made the father's authority absolute. Even a grown man was expected to accede to his father's will until the latter died—to act on one's own was in itself an act of rebellion.[4] But Jesus preached that all were equal in the eyes of God, for him the only true authority.

Such ideas were inflammatory, to say the least—politically dangerous and contrary to Jewish law. In earlier days disobedience to parents could be punished by public shame, exile, flogging, even stoning. Even in Jesus's day the law that a man is obligated to marry his brother's widow if she is childless was still observed by some Jews. To disrupt the family was a serious matter, yet the disciples left their families, their homes, and their occupations to follow Jesus. Clearly, for him the urgency of his mission precluded, if not superseded, the tightly knit family ties that were at the heart of Jewish society.

What, then, are we to make of the theology that has evolved around the person of Jesus's mother, a figure whose influence now rivals that of her son in strongly Catholic countries? To locate that persona we turn to the birth stories that open all four synoptic Gospels, keeping in mind that by the time they were written many Judeo-Christians were veering away from their Jewish roots. For Christian sects, especially, Jesus had become a manifestation of the divine, God briefly made man. Thus, parentage had become a doctrinal matter.

Both Mark and John, however, skirt the question of earthly parents altogether. Mark opens with Jesus's baptism by John the Baptist, after which a voice from heaven proclaims: "Thou art my Son, my Beloved; on thee my favour rests" (Mark 1:11). John is even more explicit: Jesus is "not born of any human stock, or by the fleshly desire of a human father, but the offspring of God himself. So the Word became flesh" (John 1:13-14).

Not so Matthew. In this, the most "Jewish" of the synoptic Gospels, Mary plays a subordinate role to Joseph, who traces his genealogy through Kings David and Solomon all the way back to Abraham. This Joseph also strongly resembles the dreaming Joseph of Genesis, for everything that happens is directed by angels who appear to him in dreams. First, having discovered Mary's pregnancy prior to their marriage, Joseph resolves quietly to revoke the marriage contract. But an angel appears in a dream announcing that "it is by the Holy Spirit that she has conceived this child." Thus, Mary fulfills Isaiah's prophecy: "The virgin shall conceive and bear a son and he shall be called Emmanuel" (Matt. 1:20-4).

Like other Old Testament virgin mothers of great figures, Mary is not a perpetual virgin, for the angel tells Joseph to "have no intercourse with her until her son was born." (Matt. 1:25). Rather, Matthew is concerned with establishing strong links to the Old Testament, while all manner of portents—including a brilliant star guiding astrologers to Bethlehem with gifts for the child king—identify the child Jesus as the great figure anticipated by Old Testament prophecies. Thus, an angel tells Joseph to leave immediately for Egypt (supposedly the birthplace of Micah, a great leader of the Jewish people) to avoid the slaughter of the innocents ordered by Herod Antipas, a reminder of the slaughter of the first born in the Passover story.* After Herod's death the dream angel tells Joseph to take mother and child back to Judea, thus fulfilling the ancient prophecy that the Son of God will be called out of Egypt. After this, Mary disappears completely from the text, even at the crucifixion.

Not so in John, a late Gospel infused with sophisticated Greek thinking and a mystical bend. Although Mary is not given the honor of virgin mother here, it is she who inaugurates her son's ministry by precipitating the miracle of the changing of water into wine at the wedding at Cana-in-Galilee.

When Mary tells Jesus that the wine for the guests has given out, he responds bluntly, "Your concern, mother, is not mine. My hour has not yet come." Mary orders the servants, "Do whatever he tells you.," and they fill the jars with water as Jesus instructs. It is wondrously transformed into wine. Thus, instead of serving the best wine first, as is customary, the bridegroom has "kept the best wine until now."

The story alludes to the familiar theme of first and last, recalling the teaching that even sinners may be the first to enter the heavenly kingdom if they have truly repented. But it is also Jesus's first great miracle, "the first of the signs by which Jesus revealed his glory and led his disciples to believe in him" (John 2:4-11). Afterward, Jesus's mother and brothers accompany him to Capernaum, but after that the family disappears from the narrative. Only at the crucifixion does Mary reappear, in company with Mary her sister and Mary of Magdala.

In the midst of his agony the dying man, catching sight of his grieving mother, commends her to his "beloved disciple," saying "Mother, there is your son", and to the disciple, "There is your

---

*A dangerous paranoiac whose father murdered two of his own sons.

mother" (John 19:26-7). Undoubtedly, this passage has more to say about a struggle for leadership than about family ties, for it implies that Jesus has given a mandate to the beloved disciple, possibly John himself. Nor does Mary appear at the tomb afterward, a rather strange omission. All told, in this Gospel she remains a somewhat marginal figure.

Mary's great moment actually comes in the *Gospel of Luke,* written some eighty or ninety years after the fact. Unlike the spare, bare-bones language of Mark and Matthew, Luke's style suggests a literate man fluent in Greek language and culture. Here Mary speaks in an ecstatic poetic language, while in her keen wisdom she resembles goddesses well-known to the Hellenized world—Athena, Isis, Ishtar. But Luke treats Mary like an ordinary mother as well, for after the required period of purification she presents her infant to the synagogue. Citing the law that "every male that openeth the womb shall be called holy to the Lord," Luke implies a natural delivery, thereby compounding the enigma of Mary as perpetual Virgin. (Luke 2:23).

Instead, Luke gives Mary a distinguished genealogy, establishing a matriarchal descent and links to miraculous virgin births in the Old Testament. There is Hannah (the Old Testament mother of Samuel), barren for many miserable years. She prays so ardently for a child that Eli, the priest, thinks she is drunk. When her prayers are miraculously answered, Hannah bursts into a poetry so exultant as to anticipate Mary's Magnificat, her finest moment in the New Testament. There is, too, the prophetess Anna, who "never left the temple, but worshipped night and day, fasting and praying," and, most important, Elizabeth of "priestly descent," also barren and postmenopausal (like Sarah, Abraham's wife) .

Elizabeth's prayers are answered when the angel Gabriel appears to her husband Zechariah, announcing that Elizabeth will bear a son, John, who will be "filled with the Holy Spirit." Six months later, Gabriel makes a similar announcement to Mary, a young girl betrothed to Joseph of Nazareth. At first Mary is incredulous, exclaiming that she is "still a virgin." But when Gabriel reminds her of Elizabeth's miracle she cries out: "Here am I—I am the Lord's servant; as you have spoken, so be it." Immediately, Elizabeth understands that Mary is destined to be "above all women," and the child in Elizabeth's womb leaps for joy. Mary then recites her glorious Magnificat:

> Tell out, my soul, the greatness of the Lord
> rejoice, rejoice, my spirit, in God my savior;
> so tenderly has he looked upon his servant,
> humble as she is
> For from this day forth
> all generations will count me blessed,
> So wonderfully has he dealt with me.
> The Lord, the mighty One.
>
> (Luke 1:26-49)

After this Mary appears again only once, in the only story that alludes to Jesus's childhood in the Gospels—that of the family's Passover pilgrimage to the Temple in Jerusalem when he is twelve. Traveling caravan-style in company with a large party of relatives and friends, they arrive at the great Temple, in whose labyrinthine mazes a boy might easily become lost. Sprawled over twenty-five acres, its colonnades are supported by massive stone pillars and columns fifty feet high. Inside its myriad courtyards, pilgrims from Egypt, Africa, Asia Minor, Babylonia, and Assyria jostle against one another, speaking in a babel of native tongues that recalls the cacophony of the ancient biblical city.[5]

Often, pilgrims would join a group and listen to a revered teacher expound on scripture and law. Apparently that is what the precocious boy does, for a day into the journey home Mary and Joseph suddenly realize that their son is missing. Distraught, they rush back to Jerusalem, searching frantically for three days. Finally they find their son in the Temple, surrounded by teachers amazed at the brilliance of his questions. When Mary scolds

Jesus for causing them such anxiety, Jesus's replies: "What made you search [for me]? Did you not know that I was bound to be in my father's house?"

Once again the implication is that Mary and Joseph are oblivious to their son's remarkable gifts. Yet back in Nazareth it is Mary who ponders the meaning of this extraordinary event: "Silently, his mother treasured all these things in her heart." After this she disappears once again from the text (Luke 41-52).

What, then, can we glean from the Gospel narratives about Mary? For one, all four agree that she had a large family that, like most families, may have had some internecine squabbles. Both Matthew and Luke affirm a divine conception—"she was with child by the holy spirit"—yet they acknowledge a large family with several siblings (Matt. 1:18-19). To add to the confusion, we are dealing with a text that has undergone various translations over the centuries. And therein lies one key to the enigma.

The word *parthenos,* while generally translated as virgin, had various meanings for both Greeks and Hebrews. On the one hand, it could refer to a man or woman who has never had sexual intercourse. However, the Greeks also used *parthenos* for the Hebrew words *na'arah* (girl), *almah* (young woman or maiden), or *bethulah* (virgin). This last term could also be used for an adolescent girl who conceives at the time of her first ovulation, before her periods actually begin. Hence a virgin mother.[6]

Even so, a slip in translation cannot explain how the Mary of the Gospels with her brood of children was transformed into an inviolate virgin. It would take 300 years—and a radical shift in Christian notions about the body and sexuality—before she was formally elevated to Virgin Mother at the Council of Nicaea in 325. From then on, however, it would be said, "If therefore a girl wants to be called a virgin, she should resemble Mary."

CHAPTER THREE

FLESH OF MY FLESH

"The two shall become one flesh . . ."

Genesis 2:25

Ironically, centuries would elapse before the cult of the Virgin Mary took root, and then not in Judea but in the Syrian branch of the Church, which has a deep-seated tradition of asceticism and celibacy. In fact, the notion of celibacy as a way of life would have been totally alien, even offensive, to Jews of Jesus's day, for the biblical injunction to "be fruitful and multiply" was at the heart of their attitude toward sexuality.

To be sure, certain fringe groups practiced celibacy, among them the Egyptian Theraputae, and the Essenes who lived in monastic-like communities in which either the entire community or an elect group remained celibate. Philo tells us that there was even a celibate female Jewish monastic community outside Alexandria in the first century, made up of

> aged virgins who have kept their chastity not under compulsion, like some of the Greek priestesses, but of their own free will in their ardent yearning for wisdom. Eager to have [wisdom] for their life mate they have spurned the pleasures of the body.[1]

Jesus, however, never made celibacy a requirement for his followers, while his position on marriage was so ambiguous as to confuse even his followers. On the one hand, Jesus taught that the imminence of the Kingdom took precedence over all earthly concerns, that in a time of crisis the most basic necessities, even the concerns of family, must be suspended. Yet, like his followers—ordinary farmers, fishermen, skilled artisans and their wives and widows—Jesus's attitude toward marriage and sexuality was shaped to some extent by the history and traditions of Jewish law, Jewish customs, and the teachings of the rabbis.

In ancient days the nomadic Hebrews, like others around them, regarded fertility as essential to survival. Old Testament patriarchs practiced polygyny and took non-Jewish concubines to produce as many children as possible, thereby making their clans powerful and giving their nomadic tribes a sharply ascending population curve. Even the powerful taboo against incest gave way to necessity when Lot's daughters had intercourse with their drunken father after all the males of their clan were wiped out. Their resulting pregnancies saved the population of Sodom and Gomorrah from extinction.

By late antiquity, however, polygamy and concubinage had given way to the overriding practice of monogamy and concern for the integrity of the family, a concern shared by Jesus, as evidenced by his uncompromising position on adultery and divorce. Sexual abstinence was not only a serious infringement of Jewish law, but also socially unacceptable. For girls, marriage was a rite of passage soon after puberty, while boys were expected to marry by age seventeen, or, at least, by age twenty. Unmarried men were regarded with profound suspicion. Not only were they unfruitful, but they might fall prey to defilement by adultery, to 'spilling the seed' or masturbation, or to the widespread homosexual practices of the Romans. So deeply instilled was the injunction to marry that the medieval sage Ben Azzai—who was, oddly enough, celibate himself—ruled that any Jewish man who failed in his duty to procreate is a murderer.[2] Even today, many Orthodox Jews marry outdoors under the starry sky as a reminder of God's promise to Abraham that his descendants would be "as numerous as stars in the sky."[3]

As for women, the greatest shame was to be barren; to avoid that catastrophe any trick of seduction might be used. In Genesis there is Tamar, twice widowed by two brothers, sons of Judah. When Judah refuses to give her his third son in marriage, Tamar disguises herself as a temple prostitute, seduces her father-in-law, and gives birth to twins. The widowed Ruth, daughter-in-law of Naomi, also contrives to seduce her wealthy kinsman Boaz, in whose fields she gleans. With Naomi's help she washes and perfumes herself and then creeps into the threshing hut where Boaz lies sleeping and into his bed. When Boaz awakens to find her there, Ruth begs him to "spread your skirt [to marry] over your servant because you are my next of kin."[4] Having spent the night with her, Boaz marries her even though Ruth is a Moabite and it is against the law. Eventually Ruth becomes the great-grandmother of King David, whose calculated seduction of the married Bathsheba provokes the wrath of the prophet Nathan.

Other Old Testament women resort to seduction to save the Jewish people from their enemies. Such a one was Jael, who lured the enemy general, Sisera, to a tryst in his tent. After plying him with liquor until he fell into a drunken stupor, Jael drove a tent peg into his neck, spilling his brains on the ground. Then there is Judith, a beautiful widow who saved the Jewish town of Bethulia from being sacked siege by the Assyrians led by their commander, Holofernes. Casting off her mourner's sackcloth, Judith bathed in perfumed oils, put on her most ravishing dress, wrapped her long hair in a turban, and adorned herself with glowing necklaces, earrings, bracelets, and rings. Making her way into the Assyrian camp, she won an audience with Holofernes, who invited her to a banquet. After the guests left, the drunken general collapsed on the bed, anticipating seduction. But Judith, assisted by her maid, beheaded him with his own sword, and her people were saved. Finally, there is Esther, whose beauty won the heart of the Persian king Ahasuerus. As queen she foiled the plan of the evil councilor Haman to massacre the Jews throughout the empire and confiscate their property. The glory of that day is celebrated yearly in the Jewish holiday of Purim.

For sheer eroticism we have Song of Songs, a hymn to erotic love derived from Egyptian love poetry. Theologians of every stripe have devised elaborate rationalizations to defuse its passionate dialogue of raw desire between a bride and bridegroom, making it an allegory for God's love for His people and for the Torah or for Christ's love for the Church. Yet its language of aching desire is too patently sexual to be denied. It remains an exquisitely graphic poetry of sexual longing:

> How beautiful are your sandaled feet
> O Prince's daughter!
> The curves of your thighs are like jewels
> Your navel is a rounded goblet
> That shall never want for spiced wine.
> Your belly is a heap of wheat
> fenced in by lilies.
> Your breasts are like two fawns,
> twin fawns of a gazelle
> and your whispers like spiced wine
> flowing smoothly to welcome my caresses,
> gliding down through lips and teeth

Song of Songs 7:1-9

Although Song of Songs clearly owes a debt to Egyptian love poetry of the period, a belief in sensuality as healthy and positive is intrinsic to Jewish thought to this very day. The revered Baal Shem Tov, the founder of Hasidism, taught that "it is better to serve the Lord in joy, without self-mortification. . . . Every Mitzvah or act of holiness starts with thoughts of physical pleasure."[5] Indeed, Jewish law and tradition stress the centrality of sexuality in marriage. The *katubah,* or marriage contract, states that a husband must provide food, clothing, and sexual gratification for his wife. Failure on any count is grounds for divorce, including neglecting a wife sexually. Rabbinic teachings recommend that married couples make love on the Sabbath and on holy days, even on Yom Kippur, the Day of Atonement, for marital sex is not merely a duty but a mitzvah, a good deed or sanctifying act.

Nor is erotic love ignored. According to the set of laws called *Onah,* a husband must provide his wife not only with reasonably regular sex but with pleasure as well. Any and all sexual positions are permitted as long as they culminate in vaginal sex. The influential Rabbi Yohanan argued that even anal sex is permissible if strongly desired, a solution to the problem of a menstruating wife.[6]

Midrashic writings hold that sexual love is a ladder one ascends to attain the higher rungs of spirituality. In that respect, wives are never to be forced; indeed some rabbis held that to force an unwilling or frightened wife is the equivalent of rape. Quoting Proverbs 19:2, the sage Rav Asi wrote, "One who presses the legs is a sinner," while Rabbi Yeshoshua ben Levi warned, "One who forces his wife in a holy deed will have dishonest children."[7] Much is also made of female orgasm; on this subject Jewish writings can be strikingly frank, even graphic. Husbands are urged to engage in foreplay and to gently coax their wives to a satisfactory climax, that "cry of joy in the night" referred to by the biblical Job when he cursed the night of his conception. A well-known treatise of the early thirteenth century, the *Iggeret ha-Kodesh* (Letter of Holiness), stresses that marital sex should be regarded as a holy act: "If we were to say that intercourse is repulsive, then we blaspheme God who made the genitals. . . . Marital intercourse, under proper circumstances, is an exalted matter."[8] The author warns husbands never to force their wives, but to put "her heart and mind at ease. . . . Speak words that arouse her to passion, union, love, desire and Eros . . . enter [her] with love and willingness so that she 'seminates' [has an orgasm] first."[9] If so, his wife will surely give him a son.

Wives also bless their progeny when they are active sexual partners. Rev Shmuel especially praised wives who ask their husbands for sex; their children will be gifted with wisdom. The great Talmudist Rav Hisda gave explicit advice to his daughters in the dynamics of desire: "When your husband caresses you to arouse desire for intercourse and holds the breasts with one hand and 'that place' [the vagina] with the other, give the breasts [at first] to increase his passion and do not give him the place of intercourse too soon, until his passion increases and he is in pain with desire."[10]

Little wonder that in the nineteenth century both Freud and Otto Rank believed that Jews were less sexually repressed than Christians. Rank even proposed that the healthier, more primitive sexuality of Jews could liberate Christians from the repression that lay at the root of "the sexual neurosis of civilization."[11] Yet the matter is complex, for, like Christianity, Jewish thought has never formed a seamless whole. Indeed, a harsh sexual Puritanism also runs through Jewish law and tradition, biblical as well as talmudic.

According to ancient purity codes set out in Leviticus, bodily fluids that create impurity include semen, menstrual blood, and discharges from childbirth and genital diseases. Menstruating or hemorrhaging woman defile anything they touch—clothing, a chair, or a bed. Similarly, a man with a prurient discharge of any kind defiles merely by spitting. Such a man, or one who has intercourse with a menstruating women, is unclean for seven days. In the extremity he can be excommunicated by "a casting out from his people."(Lev. 15:4-12)

Men are defiled by their semen, as are their clothing and sexual partners, but the impurity lasts only for a day or "until evening." After sex both partners must wash themselves and their clothing for purification, and the man is banned from the inner court of the Temple for one day after intercourse or nocturnal emission (Lev. 15:16-18). Menstrual pollution, however, requires purification in the *Mikvah,* the ritual bath. After both menstruation and childbirth women must purify themselves before entering the Temple or resuming sexual activity.

Such practices were widely observed in Jesus's day and well into the third century by some Christians as well. A letter from Dionysius of Alexandria to the Christian bishop Basiledes advises that menstruating women should not participate in the Eucharist, since they cannot be "perfectly pure both in body and soul" at such a time. Men defiled by nocturnal emission should follow their own conscience, preferably abstaining until the impurity is resolved.[12] The fifth-century Church Father Jerome held that the uncleanness of a menstruating woman could make mirrors dim and dogs rabid.

As Jews of the Diaspora clung to the Talmud, laws and customs governing sexual behavior became ever more complex. Orthodox women were required to shave their heads after marriage so as not to appear seductive to other men, and to wear some kind of head covering. Nudity became a no-no, as did touching of any erogenous zones beneath the neck. An ancient Talmudic writing warns that children will be visited with their parent's sin should they violate the prescribed sexual codes:

> Why are there lame children?
> Because [their fathers] turn over the tables [engage in intercourse from behind or with the woman on top].
> Why are there dumb children?
> Because they kiss that place.
> Why are there deaf children?
> Because they talk during intercourse.
> Why are there blind children?

Because they look at that place.[13]

Hence the practice by pious Jewish husbands of covering their wife's nakedness with a sheet with a hole strategically placed to permit penetration. During her unclean period when sex is prohibited, a wife is forbidden to make the bed in the presence of her husband for fear of tempting him. Certain Talmudic rabbis also devised rules for marital sex that would purge it of "animal" passion. Even today, in ultra-Orthodox sects (*haredim*), kissing or fondling below the neck is forbidden, sex takes place only in the dark, nightclothes should only be raised as much as is absolutely necessary.[14] Some pious Hasid men also wear the *gartel*, a special belt that symbolizes the separation of the lower sexual or animalistic body from its higher spiritual component.[15]

How, then, did these contrary sexual practices obtain in Jesus's time? As in all times, Jewish practice reflected, to some extent, the dominant culture in which they lived. Thus, Jews of late antiquity shared the widespread obsession with female virginity before marriage. On the wedding night it was incumbent on the husband to display the bloody sheet testifying to the bride's virginity, thereby preserving the family's honor. Jews and early Christians both shared the Greco-Roman aversion to sexual excesses, homosexual practices, or having sex before dark.* The Stoics in particular distrusted strong passions of any kind. Their belief that sex was for procreation, not pleasure, was absorbed not only into the teachings of the Church Fathers but into Rabbinic teachings as well. Even after Christians and Jews splintered into separate factions, they shared common attitudes toward sexuality, many of them fraught with ambivalence.

Both Jews and Christians of late antiquity regarded sexual restraint as a mark of moral superiority over their pagan

---

*Actually, homosexuality was a complex issue for Greco-Romans, being acceptable under certain conditions, but frowned upon when men (and women in Spartan culture) settled down to family life.

neighbors. But while Jews had dietary laws and circumcision to give them a separate identity, sexual purity became the primary way for some Christian sects to assert their singularity. And while some Orthodox Jews sought spiritual purity within marriage by divorcing sex from passion and sensuality, Christians elevated celibacy, which they institutionalized in convents and monasteries.

In the medieval period certain Jewish sages even taught a version of the Fall similar to Saint Augustine's conception of original sin. In the beginning, it was said, Adam and Eve in the Garden had been sexless creatures with genitals that behaved "like eyes or hands or other limbs of the body."[16] After eating the forbidden fruit they became ashamed of their nudity, yet now they were driven by physical desire—*yecer* (lust)—rather than the higher love of God (Gen. 4:1). One midrashric commentary on Genesis held that it was lust, not a desire for knowledge, that led them to eat the apple; the serpent, acting as agent for Satan, "went and poured upon the fruit the poison of his wickedness, which is lust, the root and beginning of every sin."[17] Crushed by his terrible loss, Adam cried out: "Lord, Lord, save me, and I will turn no more to the sin of the flesh."[18]

By contrast, the great sage Bal Shem Tov (whose contempt for empty ritual and arid law bears a remarkable similarity to Jesus's teachings) taught that physical desire and pleasure can be a pathway to love for the Torah and God. His disciple Menachem Nachum of Chernobyl, however, rejected the master's teaching. Echoing Augustine, Nachum warns that a husband "must use the arousal of love itself for the love of God . . . he may perform only for the sake of his creator . . . not seeking to satisfy his lust."[19]

To this day Orthodox Jews take precautions against temptation by strict segregation of the sexes. Men and women are separated by an opaque partition in Orthodox synagogues, and boys and girls are either taught in separate schools, or in coed schools seated only next to one of their own sex. School plays, mixed dancing, and even the most innocent touching between the sexes is forbidden. Girls wear long-sleeved, long-skirted dresses in public, even in the heat of summer; married women never appear in public without their head covered by a hat, scarf, or wig. To kiss or show physical affection toward their husbands is strictly forbidden, even in front of their children. In the musical *Fiddler On The Roof,* Tevye's wife is thunderstruck when he asks her, for the first time, "Do you love me?" In real life, for a woman to respond too enthusiastically to such a question would be a violation of her modesty.

All this has transpired since Jesus's death; indeed, the puritanical codes of the *haredim* would have been as foreign to him as their sidecurls, long black coats, and black hats. Yet the question of Jesus's position on marriage and sexuality leads us into a quagmire of contradiction, and the possibility of interpolations inserted at some later date. Despite his uncompromising position on divorce and adultery for both men and women, Jesus was shockingly tolerant of "wayward women." At a time when prostitutes occupied the most degraded position in society, he insisted that even they were not beyond redemption by a loving and forgiving God if they sincerely repented. At the same time he accepted a wife's adultery as the only legitimate cause for divorce.

Interestingly, when Jesus went into the desert for forty days before taking up his ministry, his temptations were not those of the flesh but of pride, the spiritual snare of believing that he was specially favored by God. Constantly the devil tries to force Jesus to put God to the test, to see if, in exchange for "all the kingdoms of the world in their glory," he will pay homage to Satan. Jesus does not budge, proclaiming, "God alone is to be worshipped" (Matt. 4:8-10). By contrast, when Anthony went into the desert Satan tormented him with visions of family, food, power, and, most agonizing of all, the sex appeal of beautiful and sensuous women. Jerome, too, fought against temptations of the flesh during his desert sojourn. Tortured by hallucinations in which bevies of sensual women appeared, "the fire of lust kept bubbling up before me when my flesh was as good as dead."[20]

As for celibacy, much confusion has arisen from Jesus's reference to those would become "eunuchs for the sake of heaven." Possibly he was referring to celibate sects such as the Essenes or the Theraputae. But teachers or *nabi* were not celibate, nor was Jesus an ascetic like John the Baptist, who wore nothing but rough camel skin, ate only locusts and honey, and made the desert his home. On the contrary, Jesus's taste for food, wine, and mixed company caused some of the Pharisees to accuse him of gluttony and drunkenness. So too the *Haberim*, Pharisees who set themselves apart by observing purity laws originally meant for the priestly castes, washing not only hands but cups, jugs, and copper bowls before every meal.[21] The great Jewish historian Josephus admired their pious ablutions, but Jesus viewed them with the same derision he had for all hollow shows of piety. For him, their real pollution lay in their role in collecting the hated agricultural tithes.

When the *Haberim* criticized Jesus and his disciples for eating with defiled hands, that is, not washing before eating, Jesus blasted their sterile rituals by quoting Isaiah: "This people pays me lip-service, but their heart is far from me . . . [they] make God's word null and void" (Mark 7:7-8). Turning the purity laws upside down, Jesus tells his followers: "Nothing that goes into a man from outside can defile him; no, it is the things that come out of him that defile a man" (Mark 7:15). Food, he says, passes through the body via mouth, stomach, and finally "out into the drain." But true purity is an inner state that has nothing to do with washing hands and utensils. True acts of defilement—fornication, theft, murder, adultery—"come out of a man's heart . . . these evil things all come from inside and they defile a man" (Mark 7:19-23).

Repeatedly, Jesus risked violating the purity codes, as in the case of the woman with "a flow of blood for twelve years." Desperate because of a condition that made her an untouchable condemned to total social isolation, she touched the hem of his garment in hope of a cure. Rather than rejecting her, Jesus called her a "daughter of Israel," healed her, and bid her be whole and happy (Mark 5:25-34). His healing of lepers generally took place from a distance, but Jesus did touch the hand of the risen Lazarus and thus risked violating the strict taboo against touching the dead.* Even his disciples were shocked by his tolerance and compassion for outcast women, even adulteresses and harlots.

In the case of the latter, Jesus saw society as the real sinner—the codes that often left widows, divorced, or otherwise unmarriageable women the option of starvation or prostitution. To them, as to the poor, the disfigured, and the leprous, he extended the compassion denied them by a heartless society. One of the most stinging insults Jesus leveled at the powerful, arrogant Temple establishment in Jerusalem was to say that on the day of reckoning, they would be inferior to tax gatherers and prostitutes. While priests and elders had turned away from the teachings of John the Baptist, a prostitute who had taken John's message into her heart would enter heaven before them (Matt. 21:31-32).

Nor does Jesus maintain the rampant misogyny of early Church Fathers who blasted the 'eternal feminine' for rendering men helpless in the face of desire. Rather, Jesus shifts the onus of blame to the man: "If a man looks at a woman with a lustful eye, he has already committed adultery with her in his heart" (Matt. 5:27-8). Responsibility, then, lies squarely on the man as seducer, an assertion as disquieting in the context of Jesus's social milieu as his attitude toward property and wealth.

Jesus's great parable on this issue, the woman taken in adultery, begins with a plot by some "doctors of the law . . . and

---

*The matter rests on whether Lazarus was already returned to life.

Pharisees." The plan is to trick him into repudiating the ancient law that condemns a woman caught in the act of adultery to death by stoning. Having found their "victim," they drag the terrified woman to the Temple where a crowd is listening to Jesus teach. Helplessly, she stands in the midst of her accusers, who are poised to execute the cruel sentence by pelting her with stones until she is slowly, agonizingly battered to death.

At first Jesus remains silent, hunched over the ground where he traces with his finger in the sand. The men demand to know his opinion. Slowly rising, Jesus responds: "Let whichever of you is free from sin throw the first stone at her," then calmly returns to his tracing in the sand. Silence reigns as, one by one, faced with their own culpability, the men mutely depart. When only he and the woman are left, Jesus asks, "Has no one condemned you?" She answers, "No one, sir." He replies, "Neither do I. Go, and do not sin again" (John 7:53-58).*

In this, as in other teachings, Jesus asserts that sexual sinners are not outside the realm of forgiveness, nor are they the lowest on the hierarchy of moral failings. For Jesus, unlike Paul and later the Church Fathers, for whom sex and sin are virtually synonymous, other than adultery the sins that most concern him are those of greed, hypocrisy, cruelty, neglect of the poor, a mind closed to the true meaning of the law which comes from a loving and compassionate God.

As for abstinence, nowhere does Jesus demand it as a way of life for his followers or as a requisite for entry into the Kingdom. Rather, his concern is with the sanctity of marriage and the abuse of divorce, the latter an exclusively male prerogative and the subject of intense debate between two schools of Jewish thought.

The great teacher Shammai held the traditional position that adultery was the only grounds for divorce. But the more liberal Hillel placed compatibility in marriage uppermost, for women as

---

*In *The New English Bible* this text is attached as an appendage or epilogue to the main text of the Gospel of John.

for men. Hillel went so far as to support a young girl's right of refusal, even if the marriage had been consummated.[22] Nor should husbands be trapped in an unhappy marriage. Instead Hillel supported the Mosaic tradition that gave husbands the right to serve a "bill of divorcement" which, theoretically, protected the wife by allowing her to remarry.

In actual fact, divorce generally meant poverty and social exile for wives, whereas husbands often found trumped-up reasons for a bill of divorce in order to remarry a younger or richer woman. With divorce becoming as easy for Jews as it was for Romans, it often caused untold misery for the cast-off wife. Even as late as the nineteenth century the abject misery of a wife being sued for divorce in a Rabbinical court is powerfully conveyed in *The Divorce Court,* a painting by the Russian-Jewish artist Jehuda Pen (Chagall's teacher). A plainly dressed but attractive young wife sits huddled in a chair, her body drooping, her head bent in shame, as the husband gesticulates wildly to the court in his recitation of her faults. For her the divorce is a sentence of privation and humiliation; for him it is a ticket to freedom and a new life.

In Jesus's time his critics seized upon this thorny issue as a means to entrap him. In Matthew they ask, Can a man arbitrarily divorce his wife "on any and every ground?"(Matt. 19:1-9) * Jesus astounded them, and his disciples as well, by rejecting divorce except for adultery, even in the case of a barren wife, a primary reason for divorce in Jewish tradition. At a time when peasant farms were being swallowed by wealthy Roman landlords, swelling the ranks of the poor and the dispossessed, Jesus clearly understood the vulnerability of a woman past her prime, or without a parental home to return to. For them divorce could mean poverty, social exile, the degradation of prostitution, even a death sentence. To him these abandoned women were also

---

*Also see Mark 10:5-12 .

God's children—the "lost sheep" to whom he was sent to minister.

Ultimately, Jesus drew on the Creation story in Genesis for his position on marriage and divorce: "a man shall . . . be made one with his wife; and the two shall become one flesh. . . . What God has joined together, man must not separate" (Matt. 19:5-7). Not only does Jesus sanction marriage here, he treats sex with reverence, as divinely ordained, not degrading. The sin, then, is not in sexuality, but in breaking the vow. Indeed, Jesus says that a man who remarries for any reason other than a wife's "unchastity" is an adulterer. This idea so astounds and confuses the disciples that they ask if it might be better to avoid sin by not marrying at all. To that Jesus replies that some men are "incapable of marriage because they are born so, or were made so by man" (i.e., eunuchs). Some, however, "have themselves renounced marriage for the sake of the kingdom of Heaven. Let those accept it who can" (Matt. 19:9-13).*

Rather than condemning marriage, Jesus's position is remarkably flexible, even psychologically astute in his acknowledgement that marriage may not be for everyone. Luke specifically mentions that the disciples had wives and children. Peter was certainly married; his wife is said to have traveled with him and possibly shared his martyrdom. Philip's wife and children are mentioned in the Apochrypha. Yet today one would think that the disciples were all confirmed bachelors. As for Jesus himself, the question is open.

For one thing, Jesus's life prior to his baptism by John is an insoluble mystery. What kind of life was it? Had he ever traveled to Sepphoris—only four miles from Nazareth—with his father as a youth? Was he exposed to its cosmopolitanism, its gymnasiums where young men exercised in the nude, its theaters and communal baths, its teeming diversity of people? What was it

---

*Possibly an interpolation.

that brought him to the desert and the cleansing waters of baptism? To those questions there are no answers. What Jesus's life was like before his meeting with John must always remain a closed book, open only to conjecture.

As to the crucial question of whether Jesus was married, we are once again wholly in the dark. What we do know is that individuals did not live outside a household in Jewish society of late antiquity. Marriage was obligatory for men and women both—for women just after puberty, for men at about age seventeen. To remain single was not an option. One would expect, then, that a man of Jesus's age would have had a wife, as did the great Rabbi Hillel, or, if not, was at least a widower. That a man in his thirties would be married was so taken for granted that it would not be worth mentioning.

Tradition did exempt Old Testament prophets from the duty to marry, and in certain exceptional cases a man might be excused to devote himself to study, or because of extreme poverty, but that was rare. Yet all this is conjecture, and an emotionally laden point of contention between those who seek the historical Jesus, and those for whom a divinity could not be tainted by such human dross as marriage and sexuality.

Of course one might argue that Jesus was no ordinary man, nor was his mission. One of the attractions of early Judeo-Christianity was Jesus's radical stance on the family. In Roman society, everyone—wives, children, slaves—was bound by the authority of the *pater familia* for their entire lives. Elder sons became independent only after the father died, and younger siblings could never hope to become autonomous. Marriages were arranged by parents who also chose their son's professions. Divorce was permitted, but only men could initiate it. For young girls in particular, conversion to Christianity offered a welcome option to the misery of a marriage totally against their will or inclination.

Among Jesus's Jewish followers, there was the climate of

despair that led away from normative family life. Not only were homes and farms being swallowed up by the rapacious great estates, but everyone lived under the Damocles' sword of the cruelty of Roman overlords. Rebels, whether Jews, slaves, or insurgents, suspected or real, were executed by crucifixion, a torturous, drawn-out death by dehydration and slow suffocation. After one rebellion thousands of victims hung from crosses that lined the Via Appia. At such a time the ethic of family rings hollow. Rather, Jesus's command to leave their homes, their farms, and their families reflects a desperation, a total commitment typical of messianic movements to this very day. When life becomes too oppressive, earthly possessions and ties seem intangible in comparison to the life to come.[23]

Jesus also made enemies amongst the powerful Jewish establishment in Jerusalem, infuriating them with his unceasing jibes at those who acted as Roman puppets, at the money changers and hawkers of sacrificial birds and animals who, for him, desecrated the sacred Temple. For them, Jesus's position on marriage offered yet another chance to entrap him. Supposing, they asked, the first brother in a family of seven dies, leaving his wife childless. As required by law, the next brother marries her. One after another the scenario is repeated with all seven brothers, until the wife also dies. Whose wife, then, will she be after the resurrection when all will rise from the dead? In both Mark and Matthew Jesus answers that at that time "men and women do not marry; they are like angels in heaven" (Mark 12:19-25, Matt. 22:24-30). But in Luke his response is more complex. While ordinary "men and women of this world marry," a certain few will be "worthy of a place in the other world and of the resurrection from the dead." That elite neither marry nor die, for "like angels; they are the sons of God" (Luke 20:35-37).

The difference is subtle but crucial, for Luke's notion of an elect who "live as angels" opens a door to a host of Christian men and women who would emulate them by adopting a celibate way of life. Yet the pathway to renunciation would be protracted and rocky indeed. For one thing, in the early Church those still tied to their Jewish roots frowned upon celibacy. Moreover, in the face of a plummeting population curve, the Emperor Augustus made celibacy illegal, while many converts were already married. Well into the fifth century it was taken for granted that priests were married and had families, and some even inherited their bishoprics from their fathers. Both St. Gregory Nazianzen and Bishop Julian of Eclanum were the sons of bishops; St. Patrick of Ireland was said to be the grandson of a priest.[24]

Those who dogmatically insisted on celibacy were regarded by some as fanatical, arrogant, and a threat to the married clergy.[25] Yet even as certain powerful factions denounced celibacy as unnatural and a detriment to the church, others advanced a theology that attached feelings of guilt and shame to erotic love. In their hands the Mary of the Gospels with her brood of children would be transformed into the model par excellence, not merely of female chastity, but of lifelong virginity as the pathway to heaven.

CHAPTER 4

THEY ARE LIKE ANGELS IN HEAVEN

"This gate shall remain locked."
St. Augustine

Even as the mighty Roman Empire began to crumble, rotting from within and without from corruption, greed, the lust for power, Christianity spread like a fast growing plant. Like Rome, it adapted itself to foreign soils. Traveling far and wide, Christian missionaries converted all manner of pagan peoples who brought their customs and beliefs with them. And the further Christianity moved away from its origins, the more it diverged from Jesus's original teachings, absorbing ideas and beliefs from Hellenism, the eastern mystery cults, Platonism, Stoicism, Epicureanism. In the ancient city of Antioch, Jewish synagogues, Christian churches, and Zoroastrian shrines stood side by side, each borrowing from the other.

By the second century hundreds of independent Christian sects existed; each one clustered around a particular leader, each one with idiosyncratic beliefs and gospels of their own that incorporated strange and bizarre stories about Jesus's life and teachings. Especially odd were the Gnostic sects (from *gnosis* or knowledge), who held the ancient Zoroastrian belief in a dual Universe—the higher, spiritual world of the good, the lower, earthly world of evil, constantly at war with one another. Extremist sects such as the Encratites, or Chaste Ones, and the Marcionites, held that the same warfare raged in human nature—between the spirit that ever aspires to the higher realm of the good, and the corrupt body that ever drags mankind into evil. Repelled by all things sensual, they saw the body as a "corpse with senses," and sex as "the devil's snare—the most powerful weapon in his arsenal against the soul."[1] Although such ideas were too harsh for mainstream Christians, they gradually crept into an evolving theology through the writings of influential leaders known as Church Fathers.

One such figure was Tertullian, a prolific third-century writer who had flirted briefly with the Encratites. Although Tertullian rejected their extremist views, he shared their abhorrence for sex and the body. For him, the Herculean struggle against the demands of the flesh was every bit as perilous as that of the Christian martyr's strife against Rome. Having had a brief taste of marriage, Tertullian knew of what he spoke, the better still to warn Christians, including his own wife, of the degradation of sex even within marriage.[2] When reminded that the patriarchs of the Old Testament married and even took concubines, he responded that "the new gospel" asked Christians to rise above the degraded mores of ancient times.[3] This would be no easy task, for obstacles abounded, the principle enemy being woman, with her alluring body and wily tricks. Like a prophet of old, Tertullian thundered: "YOU are the devils gateway; YOU are the unsealer of that tree, YOU are the first foresaker of the divine law [Eve] . . . YOU [who] so lightly crushed the image of God."[4]

In this Tertullian was not alone. It was rumored that Origen of Alexandria, fearing his own body as much as the wiles of women, submitted to castration at the age of twenty.[5] (This story was possibly an invention of Origen's archenemy, Eusebius of Caesarea.) Eventually, Origen believed, such drastic measures would be unnecessary, for in a perfect world Christians would be sexless like the angels. Then they would amend the Old Testament so that Abraham would no longer be called "*father* of Isaac, but by some other, deeper name."[6] Origen's writings became an apologia for the asceticism of the monastic movement as it evolved in the fourth century.

To be sure, Origen's alleged self-castration was widely regarded as an act of "heathen hysteria," the result of an unbalanced mind.[7] Yet an escalating chorus of voices joined in singing the praises of virginity, which they clothed in mystical veils. One such voice was Ambrose, bishop of Milan, who declared that sexual purity was precisely what elevated Christians above the despised pagans:

> This virtue [abstinence] is in fact, our exclusive property. The pagans do not have it . . . it is found nowhere else among living creatures . . . though we are no different than others in our birth, yet we escape the miseries of nature . . . only by virginity.[8]

Virgin women, he claimed, exuded a wholesome purity, a sweet odor that made "Christ . . . prefer the fragrance of . . . her garments . . . to all other perfumes."[9] Gregory of Nyssa agreed, comparing virginity to the fresh, sweet blossoms of spring, conferring an eternal youth that will never wither and decline as does a body debased by carnality.[10] John Crysostom, although eventually a strong advocate of marital sex, reminded Christians that Adam and Eve had been virgins in paradise where sexless angels were produced by parthenogenesis.[11] Had Adam and Eve not disobeyed, humans would have been reproduced in the same way.

Such views were bound to provoke a backlash. Opponents argued that Paul himself was married, that the "yokefellow" whom he addressed in letters was a wife left at home during his travels. Actually, whether Paul had ever been married is uncertain, but in his writings a wife is never mentioned. As to sexuality, despite his Jewish roots, Paul, a native of Tarsus, was clearly influenced by the Greek notion of the duality between body and spirit.

Exhorting Christians against the licentious behavior of their pagan neighbors, he warns that body and spirit must always oppose one another. While the higher, spiritual nature ever seeks "Love, joy, peace, . . . gentleness, self-control. ... (the) lower nature . . . [strives toward] fornication, impurity, and indecency; . . . envy, rage . . . drinking bouts, orgies." In that raging battle the higher nature must be the victor, for "... those who belong to Christ Jesus have crucified the lower nature with its passions and desires."[12]

Nor did Paul ever resolve his ambivalence about marriage. Ultimately it was the lesser of two evils. Those who lack self control, who "burn" with the fire of unrequited passion, should marry rather than commit the sin of fornication or masturbation. As to married converts, Paul advised them to remain so. True, marriage keeps one "busy with this world's demands," while a "virgin—indeed any unmarried woman" can devote herself entirely to God. Ultimately, Paul was torn: "I have no desire to place restrictions on you, but I do want to promote what is good, what will help you devote yourselves entirely to the Lord."[13]

Advising the Corinthian Church on the thorny matter of the "spiritual marriage'—the ambiguous situation in which a Christian man lived chastely with a virgin woman who cared for his needs—Paul applied the same formula:

> whoever is . . . determined in his heart to keep her as his virgin does well. In sum, he who marries his virgin does well, but he who refrains from marriage does better.[14]

Even Ambrose, that great apostle of virginity, shared that ambiguity. Citing Genesis 2:18 he writes, "It is not good for man to be alone," while Clement of Alexandria reminded Christians of the biblical injunction to "be fruitful and multiply."[15] Clement, in fact, regarded sex as a natural and necessary function, like eating and drinking. If food nourishes the body, sex propagates the race. Problems arise only from excesses.[16] Whether in eating, drinking, or in sexual passion, Christians should follow the golden mean, the "ideal of self-control . . . found among the Greek philosophers."[17] Striving for moderation in all things, at table a Christian should "burp gently, sit correctly, and refrain from scratching his ears."[18] In public they must not laugh or joke in a crude or abandoned way, and in the bedroom abstain from vulgar positions or violent passions, "for we have been taught not to 'take thought for the flesh' . . . and to 'walk decently as in the daylight' . . . not in reveling and drunkenness, not in chambering and wantonness."[19]

Moderation being antithetical to the nature of ordinary men and women, Ambrose and Jerome declared war against everything and anything that "tickles the sense and the soft fire of sensual pleasure that sheds over us its pleasing glow," including enticing foods and wines, even the casual touch of a woman's hand.[20] In this women could cooperate, making themselves plain and dressing in a "garb of penitence," for sex is highly addictive. Once the body knows sexual pleasure there is no turning back. "A dangerous fire is lust," wrote Ambrose, while Jerome remonstrated that "in view of the purity of the body of Christ, all sexual intercourse is unclean." "Matrimony," thundered Origen, "is impure and unholy, a means of sexual passion" no less defiling than prostitution, echoed Ambrose.[21]

Little wonder that Christianity would one day be blamed for casting a blanket of guilt and repression over sexuality. Yet, in truth, a deep-seated ambiguity about sex was rooted in the pagan world from which the Church Fathers came. The ancient Greeks, like others around them, considered sex and childbirth to be ritually polluting, and used the term *miasma* for a postpartum defilement. New mothers had to purify themselves before resuming life in the community. Indeed the Greeks were obsessive about female purity.

Literally from birth, Greek girls of the privileged citizen class were cloistered in strictly segregated women's quarters where no man, not even visiting relatives, could gaze on them. Married at puberty—age twelve to fourteen—to a total stranger, often an older, sexually experienced man, these child brides were often drugged with opium—crushed poppy leaves—to quell their terror on the wedding night. Even as wives they were conditioned to modesty: no brightly colored garments, jewelry, white powder, or red rouge, and absolutely no perfume—the mark of a whore! Nor should a wife behave like a whore in the marital bed where spouses made love only at night and in the dark. Nudity, too, was taboo—even prostitutes sometimes covered their breasts with bikini-type bandeaux during sex. As Xenophon put it, wives were for producing babies, prostitutes and mistresses for sexual pleasure.[22]

The Greeks had their reservations about male sexuality as well, the word for penis being *metula,* "little mind," an organ with a will of its own. Pythagoras warned that loss of semen depleted energy, particularly in summer heat, and athletes were advised to abstain before the Olympic Games. In this Aristotle agreed, for sex not only left a man fatigued, it could lower him to the level of brute animals. Plato, Xenophon, and Hypocrites all believed that too much sex could cause illness, insanity, even death. In *The Laws,* Plato wrote that sex hindered the quest for higher wisdom. The good citizen engaged in marital sex only for procreation, avoiding sex with other men or masturbation, that "wasting of the seed of life on a stony and rocky soil."[23] Epicurus, for whom pleasure was the absence of stress or pain, went even further, declaring, "Sex has never done a man good, and he is lucky if it has not harmed him."[24]

That axiom was certainly proven by the gross sexual excesses of Roman emperors such as Tiberius and Nero. Suetonius tells us that on the island of Capri Tiberius decorated certain rooms in his villa with his extensive collection of obscene and pornographic art, and imported young men and women who, "invented monstrous feats of lubricity and defiled one another" for his entertainment.[25] Tiberius' passion for young boys was insatiable: in his bath he employed young, barely weaned boys whom he called his "little fishes", who satiated his passion for oral sex as they swam between his legs. As for Nero, among his exploits were the deflowering of a Vestal Virgin, the castration of one of his youthful male lovers whom he "married" in a ceremony complete with a veil for the "bride," a dowry, and a great wedding procession, and, it was rumored, incestuous relations with his mother.[26]

Alarmed by a moral decline that was weakening the larger society, the Emperor Augustus passed laws to strengthen the family and curb sexual profligacy Stunned by the revelation of his own daughter's promiscuity, he exiled her to an isolated island where not even a male slave or animal was allowed to come near her. Men, too, might voluntarily abstain from sex. Apollonius of Tyana, the first-century wonder worker, allegedly took a vow of lifelong virginity, and Pliny the Elder, who perished at Pompeii in 79 CE, recommended that men emulate the constraint of elephants who mate only once every two years. Above all, the Stoics, whose influence on Christianity was profound, held that only by controlling the emotions could one conquer nature and its vicissitudes—sickness, death, grief, loss. The more the passions reign, the more the individual will be controlled by the object of his or her passions.

Sex being the most powerful of the passions, Stoicism grudgingly advocated sex within marriage, but with strict reservations. The great Stoic philosopher, Seneca, condemned not only adultery, but held that

> it is also shameful to love one's own wife immoderately. In loving his wife the wise man takes reason for his guide, not emotion. Resisting the assault of passion, he does not allow himself to be impetuously swept away in the marital act, for nothing is more depraved than to love one's wife as if she were an adulteress.[27]

Writing to his mother he warned,

> Do nothing for the sake of pleasure. . . . [S]exual pleasure has been given to man not for enjoyment, but for the propagation of his race. . . . [Take care that] lust has not touched you with its poisoned breath.[28]

For those who would no longer be ruled by passion, Seneca recommended celibacy.

Not coincidentally, Clement of Alexandria seems to echo Seneca when he warns that "One commits adultery with one's own wife if one has commerce with her in marriage as if she were a harlot."[29] In his treatise on marital sex Clement also warned against sex in daylight, with too much ardor, or resorting to various sexual positions, the sole purpose of sex being procreation, not pleasure.[30] *

Caesarius of Arles (470–542) went even further, creating a calendar for abstinence for married couples. Sex was forbidden on Sunday, during Lent, major feast days, during menstruation and pregnancy.[31] Of them all, however, it was the towering intellect of Saint Augustine, a figure with roots in the pagan world, who single handedly forged the Christian ethic of sexuality. A brilliant intellect, administrator and politician, Augustine understood that abstinence would never work for the masses. Rather, he saw the question of sexuality as standing at the very core of the human condition. Pouring his own

---

*The ancient Greeks had their own "Joy of Sex" in vase and wall paintings that depicted various sexual postures and variations, and were commonly displayed in citizen's homes.

anguished struggle to achieve and maintain chastity into his *Confessions,* Augustine gave us the first modern autobiography, and a discussion of sexuality so complex, profound and fatalistic as to augur modern, post-Freudian thinking.

Augustine, in fact, never wholly succeeded in resolving the tension between his sensual nature and his spiritual calling, holding that it was easier to renounce wealth, luxury, ambition, and fame than sexuality, for its fires can never be totally extinguished. After his conversion, to evade temptation he avoided all women, even his sister, for "they are the cause of hideous and involuntary erections in men."[32] Even the thought that he had sucked at his mother's breast in infancy tormented him, and in the dark of the monastic cell his body would play tricks on him—perhaps the dread "resurrection of the flesh'—an involuntary erection—or a nocturnal emission. At such a time Augustine would cry out, "Why, O perverse soul of mine, will you go on following your flesh?" Legend has it that in later life Augustine whipped himself nightly with chains to chastise the body that so stubbornly asserted itself.

Yet, until his conversion at age thirty-two, Augustine had been anything but an ascetic. Born in North Africa to a Roman father, Patricius, Augustine's mother, Monica, was a deeply religious Christian who prayed fervently for her son's conversion. Even in his teens Augustine had a longing to "love and to be loved" so intense as to precipitate a noxious rash over his entire body. At age eighteen he took a concubine whom, "wandering lust . . . brought my way," living with her in faithful monogamy for fifteen years. In 373 a son was born, the same year that Augustine became an *auditor* with the Manicheans, a Gnostic sect with a small elect who practiced celibacy. Increasingly torn between two worlds, he writes: "I, an unfortunate young man . . . would pray: "Lord, give me chastity and continence, *sed noli modo,* but not now."[33]

Eventually, ambition not religion led Augustine to abandon

his mistress. Having been appointed Professor of Rhetoric in Milan, his mother, Monica, pressured him into an engagement to a ten year old girl whose family had ties to Ambrose for the sake of his career. Heartbroken, Augustine's mistress returned to Africa, gave up their son, and swore she would take no other lover. The separation plunged Augustine into misery: "First there was burning and bitter grief; and after that it festered, and as the pain grew duller it only grew more hopeless." Years later he wrote that marriage is a matter of the heart, not of legality. A couple who live in faithful monogamy indefinitely might consider themselves married. But a man who abandons a mistress he loves and marries for the sake of rank and fortune commits adultery against his mistress. For that Augustine paid a price, for he declared that when his mistress departed, "my first youth was dead."[34]

Unable to wait until his bride reached the ripe age of twelve, Augustine took another mistress: "thus my soul's disease was nourished." His celibate friend Alypius urged him to follow his example as a remedy, but Augustine was not ready, for "[I] would be impossibly miserable if I had to forego the embraces of a woman." Yet celibacy offered a way out of a loveless marriage. Peter Brown has written that when, finally, he took that momentous step, "A deep sense of sadness lingered with Augustine for the rest of his life. Sexual love remained, for him, a leaden echo of true delight."[35] Yet, as his conversion deepened his antipathy to sexual desire and its aftermath, the memory of that youthful passion would take on a lurid hue. Years later, in his *Confessions,* Augustine suffered pangs of guilt for a relationship cemented not "according to the bright bond of friendship; rather, [by] the mists of slimy lusts of the flesh. . . . Both [love and lust] seethed together in hot confusion . . . in a whirlpool of shameful actions."[36]

In time, when Augustine became the powerful bishop of the African Church, that memory still haunted him. Although the

African Church never embraced virginity with the fervor of the Italian faction, led by Jerome and Ambrose, Augustine would put the stamp of his ambivalence on its position on sexuality and marriage.[37] Politically, Augustine understood that an expanding Church, by now wrapping its octopus-like tentacles about the Roman world, would atrophy if Christians did not beget more Christians. Nor was it realistic to expect the masses to give up the most basic of human drives.

But if marriage was a necessity, Christians need not debase themselves in "slimy lust," as did their pagan neighbors. Rather, Augustine brilliantly resolved the problem by incorporating ideas more akin to Stoicism than to those of Jesus and Jewish tradition. The bonds that cemented Christian marriage would be friendship and family concerns, not passion. Sex must be solely for procreation. Cleansed of the pollution of lust, Christian spouses might still be "as the angels in Heaven." No longer would a husband "hate in her [his wife] the corruptible and mortal sexual connection . . . [but] love in her what is human . . . what pertains to a wife."[38]

But how to impose such a discipline on the masses? For the curse of that primeval Fall was mankind's loss of free will. Men especially became enslaved by lust, for after the expulsion Adam's sexual organ no longer obeyed him, becoming erect with or without his compliance. Paul himself understood that terrible dilemma. In the *Epistle to the Romans* he writes:

> the law is spiritual, but I am not . . . I am unspiritual, the purchased slave of sin . . . In my inmost self I delight in the law of God, but I perceive that there is in my bodily members a different law, fighting against the law that my reason approves . . . bringing me into captivity to the law of sin which is in my members and making me a prisoner . . . Miserable creature that I am, who is there to rescue me out of this body . . . ?[39]

So, too, Augustine. Even after years of discipline and self-denial the old demons would return late at night, in the darkness of his cell In his agony he wrote of the stubborn independence of the male organ; "Even though it [lust] is restrained, it still moves."[40]

And therein lies the problem. If, like Paul, Augustine accepted marriage as a compromise, the dour legacy of Original Sin remained. In the blessed innocence of the primeval Garden there was no erotic desire, and sex was subject to "the bidding of the will." But thanks to Adam and Eve's blunder, "all nature was changed for the worse."[41] Now the farmer must labor ceaselessly, at the mercy of drought, flood, and pestilence. Mothers must bear their children in pain, infants might be born blind, deaf, or deformed as punishment for their parents' sins.[42] Ironically, Augustine was not entirely off the mark, for we now know that any number of illnesses, both mental and physical, are handed down genetically.

Not everyone subscribed to the Augustinian pessimism. John Chrysostum, although an ascetic in his youth, came to believe in love as the most potent force, "more tyrannical than any other tyrant." For him, Eros, or desire, works for the good of mankind, cementing marital bonds, smoothing out the storms and disappointments inevitable in any marriage.[43] What set Christians apart from the pagan Greeks and Romans was not the denial of Eros, but a belief in monogamy, restraint, companionship.

Chrysostum advised Christian husbands to treat their wives with an "an intense love," using gentle endearment, not force, to inspire obedience. He also had his own version of Original Sin—woman's inborn craving for money, jewelry, clothing, furniture, status.[44] From the very first night a husband must gently wean his wife away from that natural tendency, encouraging her to "dispose of money and crowds of servants and outward honors." Only then could she aspire to a holy life.[45]

In certain principles all parties were united. Christian spouses should comport themselves with modesty, practice restraint and fidelity, and husbands should abjure sex with boys, slaves, or concubines. Yet the fundamental dispute remained as to larger issues—the question of free will and the essential nature of humanity, whether we are born with a propensity for good or evil. Eventually, the debate coalesced around two opposing parties.

Roman and Palestinian factions mobilized around Chrysostum and a Roman monk named Pelagius. For the latter, a benevolent God had created mankind in His image. Sin was a matter of human choice, since a just God would not condemn all humanity for Adam and Eve's transgression.[46] To that, Augustine's faction countered that there is no innocence; to be human is to be tainted by Original Sin. Tempers flared on both sides, and riots broke out in Rome in 417. Two councils and a Pope supported Pelagius, but he lost in the end. In 418 he was excommunicated, stripped of office, and fined. He and all his supporters were exiled, and Augustine's doctrine of Original Sin became the official position of the Church on human nature and sexuality.[47]

Just as one enemy was vanquished, another rose to take his place. Bishop Julian of Eclanum, a small town in the south of Italy, condemned Original Sin as nothing less than insanity. Nature, he believed, is as benign as it is cruel. Pain, suffering, even death are part of the cycle of nature. Most important, mankind is free to choose good or evil, celibacy or chastity. (Julian himself had been briefly married.)[48]

With hindsight we might say that Julian anticipated Rousseau, while Augustine's conflicted, guilt-ridden soul seems post-Freudian, even existential. There is something compellingly modern about the notion of a subconscious force that renders a man as helpless in the face of impotence as in arousal. Humanity's curse is the futility of human will against powerful libidinous drives, or against the psychic demons that, in Augustine's own words, made his "soul . . . a rebel to itself."[49]

Ultimately, Augustine was victor in the great debate about Original Sin, the psychological effect of which remains to this very day.[50] For scholar Elaine Pagels, that notion of an inborn depravity is common to all religions as they try to rationalize pain, suffering, death, natural catastrophes.[51] Yet the obsession with sin and guilt that has gripped the Church in various times and places tends to divert from Jesus's striking tolerance, his open acceptance of human failings, his belief in a God whose magnanimous love embraces sinners who truly repent. In spite of this, the notion of Original Sin would cast a pervasive pall of guilt and shame over Western society for centuries.

Interestingly, pudenda, the word for the female genitalia, comes from the Latin *pudere,* to be ashamed. In the Middle Ages that sense of shame would erase the human figure from art, silence the sounds of music in the churches, foster a sense of personal guilt so profound as to create those macabre processions of flagellants, sinners who marched through towns and villages, whipping their backs until their flesh was raw and bloody.[52] In the confessional Catholics would wrestle on a more psychological level with the notion of sin and penance, while a rebellion against celibacy would play a major role in shattering the seamless garment of the Church during the Reformation. In our own day the debate about a celibate priesthood threatens the hegemony of the Catholic Church as does no other issue.

Most important, the doctrine of Original Sin negates the escape mechanism central to many religions and intrinsic to Jesus's own teachings—namely, that to sin is to be human. According to one school of Talmudic thought, a compassionate God understands that all who are human will make wrong choices at some time in their lives. The Hebrew word for sin is *hata,* "to miss the right pathway"; similarly, the Greek term means "to miss the mark." To do so is part and parcel of the human condition. Yet sinners need not despair, for to make a mistake is not to be fundamentally evil or flawed. One can voluntarily revert to the right path, the Hebrew word for repentance being *shuv,* to return. Having found the way once again, there is no need for self-recrimination or abuse. Rather, one takes strength, pride and joy in having returned by one's own volition.[53]

Yet the doctrine of Original Sin became central to the evolving cult of the Virgin Mary, as a bitter and fratricidal debate on the question of Jesus's humanity or divinity arose. Certain Gnostic sects such as the Docetists maintained that as pure spirit or "divine phantom" Jesus could not be tainted by Original Sin. The Gnostic Valentius went even further, holding that as son of a pure virgin, Jesus had never soiled himself with the filth of defecation. True, he ate and drank like everyone else, but "food was not corrupted in him, since he himself was not perishable."[54]

For mainstream Christians who held firmly to the Trinitarian principle of God, His Son, and the Holy Spirit, the problem of Jesus as both human and divine was resolved in the miracle of the virgin birth. If Jesus was a man who "was born, and ate and drank" like other men, thanks to the virgin birth he was born free of Original Sin.[55] For how, one Arnobius asked, could one even imagine Jesus as "born of vile coitus . . . a result of the spewing forth of senseless semen, as a product of obscene gropings?"[56]

Nor could his mother, Mary, have participated in such vulgarities. Inevitably the "party of virginity" seized the moment. In 381 at the Council of Constantinople, Mary, despite her large brood of children, was officially declared *virginus intactus*, a doctrine from which no Catholic in good standing can veer, even today.

CHAPTER 5

FROM MOTHER TO VIRGIN

"They say miracles are past; and we have our philosophical persons, to make modern and familiar, things supernatural and causeless."

William Shakespeare, *All's Well That Ends Well*

For skeptics who still had reservations about a virgin mother, the fourth-century monk St. Basil the Great of Caesarea had a ready answer: look at the animal world. Vultures, he wrote in his tract *On True Virginity*, become mothers from a blast of wind; weasels conceive through their ears. For spontaneous generation, Origen pointed to bees emerging from the bodies of oxen or worms crawling out of corpses of men. Certain mystics also believed that a true virgin's body is like a delicate veil that can receive a spiritual husband. Thus did Jesus's embryonic spirit pass through Mary's intact body with no difficulty at all.[1]

Nonetheless, the construction of Mary as perpetual virgin presented a thorny problem. How could it be reconciled with the fact that Jesus's humanity rested upon his being born of a real woman in a real way? What about the very real brothers and sisters of Jesus alluded to in the New Testament? Was Mary's virginity a temporary state that allowed Jesus to become human through birth yet remain untainted by original sin? Or was it perpetual virginity, a condition that would make Mary singular among all women, a new Eve completely free of any blemish of original sin?

Eventually those issues would be decided by official Church councils. Even so, as Christianity grew, ordinary folk wrestled with those nagging contradictions. Most were converts far removed from Christianity's origins who had formed Christian communities or house churches. Each group clustered about a particular leader; each had its own recollection of Jesus's life and teachings, creating a cacophony of beliefs and hundreds of idiosyncratic Gospels drawn from folklore, their stories too fantastical to be included in the official, canonical Gospels. Eventually the Church tried to destroy them altogether, but some survived. Known today as the Apocryphal Gospels, they are worth reading, for they offer a window into the folkways and beliefs of early Christianity.

In their rich mixture of folk tale, mythology, and fable we encounter the everyday world of early Christianity—not the educated, upper-class men who wrote the Canonical Gospels but ordinary folk, many of whom were illiterate and, to some extent, gullible. Like the ancient Greeks, they understood their history, legends, and religion through an oral tradition that filtered remembered events through the imagination. They attest not only to the teeming diversity of thought and belief amongst the earliest Christians, but to their willingness to suspend disbelief in the interest of embellishing a story.

Some lay claim to certain strange and bizarre teachings. In one, the Apocryphal *Gospel of Thomas,* Jesus tells the disciples that to fully understand him they must take off their clothes, tread them into the dust, and stand naked before him, inspiring certain splinter sects in the Middle Ages to practice nudity. Others provided what was missing from the canonical gospels: colorful stories about Jesus's family and childhood that found their way into popular myth, folk tale, art, and "Lives of the Saints" from the Middle Ages to the present day. A few stories even found their way into the canonical Gospels, as in segments from the *Infancy Gospel of Thomas* that have parallels in Luke.

In this Gospel Jesus is a precocious child whose amazing powers all too often prove lethal. In one story at age five, while playing by a brook on a Sabbath day, the boy sculpts twelve sparrows out of mud.* Joseph scolds him for profaning the Sabbath, but Jesus claps his hands, and the mud forms become real sparrows that fly away, chirping. Seized by jealousy, two boys attack Jesus, who causes one to wither away.† The other is struck dead.

The townspeople are amazed, but the dead boys' parents demand that Joseph either curb his son or send him away. For that they are stricken blind, and when Joseph sharply tweaks his son's ear the unrepentant boy exclaims, "Do not vex me." A teacher, Zacchaeus, offers to teach the boy respect for elders, but Jesus confounds him with complex questions. Zacchaeus begs Joseph to take him away: "I cannot endure the severity of his look. . . . This child is not earth-born." Pleased by this recognition of who he is, Jesus rescinds his curses and the two boys are revived.

As the remarkable child performs even more wonders, his

---

*The biblical twelve tribes.

†Like the fig tree in the garden at Gethsemane, a "tree (that) shall bear neither leaves nor root nor fruit."

parents accept his supernatural powers. As in Luke, Mary "kissed him and kept within herself the mysteries which she had seen him do." Still, they worry, and with good reason , for when another teacher, irritated by Jesus's questions, boxes the boy's ears, he too is struck dead. Terrified, Joseph orders Mary to lock him in the house, for "all those who provoke him die." But another teacher persuades Joseph to send the boy to his school. On hearing that a great crowd has gathered there, Joseph runs to the school, expecting to find the teacher dead. Instead, Jesus is so pleased by the teacher's testimony that he again rescinds the curse, and the former teacher is restored to life. Later, he saves three more people from the brink of death, among them his brother James.

Interestingly, the only one of these stories about Jesus's childhood that appears in the canonical Gospels is the tale of the Passover trip to the Temple in Jerusalem, as told in Luke. So too Thomas's concluding passage which echoes Luke's famous tribute Mary: "Blessed are you among women, because the lord has blessed the fruit of your womb. For such glory and excellence and wisdom we have never seen or heard."[2]

What did not get into the canonical Gospels was an elaborate story about Mary's family in the *Protovangelium of James,* allegedly written by Jesus's brother. Here Mary gets not only a family, but a complex history of her own.

Her parents are Joachim and Anna, a deeply pious couple who are childless and miserable. Anna, especially, suffers bitter shame because of her sterility. Taunted by the jibes of the high priest and even her own servants about her barrenness, she cries out:

> Woe is me, to what am I likened?
> (Not to) the birds of the heavens
> the dumb animals . . . the beasts of the earth.
> They are all fruitful . . .

Suddenly an angel appears, saying that she will have a child, whom Anna promises to dedicate to the Lord. This story of Mary's virgin birth to her mother, Anna, would eventually become official Church doctrine.

True to her promise Anna keeps the infant in a holy sanctuary surrounded by virgins. At age three Mary goes to live in the Temple, where she is "nurtured like a dove" and fed by angels. But at age twelve, with the onset of menses imminent, Mary must leave so as not to pollute the Temple. An angel tells the high priest to assemble all the widowers of the community. When a dove settles on the head of a wealthy building contractor, Joseph, the priest recognizes him as the chosen one. Joseph protests that he is an old man with grown sons, and Mary only a girl, but the priest reminds him what happens to a recalcitrant: the earth opens and swallows him. Joseph takes Mary home but postpones the wedding, leaving instead to supervise some new buildings. The high priest assigns Mary, assisted by seven "pure virgins," the task of weaving a beautiful veil for the sacred tabernacle of the Temple.

When three angels appear announcing that Mary will bear a child, she protests that she is a virgin. But when they reveal that her pregnancy is due to the Lord's intervention, she cries out, "Behold I am handmaid of the Lord," as in Luke. Returning to find her six months pregnant, Joseph "smote his face, threw himself down on sackcloth, and wept bitterly." Seething with rage, he hurls terrible accusations at Mary, who protests that she is "pure, and know not a man." Joseph weighs his options—hide her pregnancy and break the law; expose her, in which case she will be stoned; or "put her away" and send her out into a hostile world.

Mary is saved when an angel appears, testifying to her innocence. Her son, he says, will be "called Jesus, he will save his people from sin." Joseph gives thanks to God. When the outraged high priest discovers Mary's pregnancy, he drags the couple before the Temple court, accusing them of consummating the marriage in secret. They are forced to drink the "bitter waters," a lethal poison if they are guilty. When they survive there is general rejoicing, but news of a Roman census-taking throws Joseph into a panic again. To enroll her as his wife will heap him with shame; if he enrolls her as his daughter, he will be castigated for lying. Instead, he takes Mary away on a donkey led by his son. Strangely, she weeps at one moment and laughs the next, haunted by a vision of what is to come—a people divided between lamenting and rejoicing.[3]

Mary's labor begins in the midst of the wilderness, and Joseph finds a cave "to hide your shame." He goes to search for a midwife, and for one suspended moment birds, sheep, shepherds, workmen, and the flowing river become motionless. When Joseph tells the midwife of Mary's miraculous conception, a supernatural light shines over the cave, but a second midwife, Salome, is skeptical. She attempts to examine Mary to see if she is still intact, but howls with pain as the offending hand, seared by a blast of heat, withers away. She prays that her hand may be restored so that she may continue to serve the poor. An angel tells her to pick up the baby, and the withered arm is healed. (The story of Salomé and her withered arm is familiar to most Christians who have attended Bible School today.)

As in Luke, James's narrative includes the three wise men, the star in the east, the worship at the cave, and Herod's massacre of the innocents. The tale turns fantastical, however, when Elizabeth goes into the mountains to hide her son John from Herod's vicious murderers. They are saved when the mountain opens to shelter them, but her husband, Zacharias, is killed for refusing to tell Herod's men where his son in hidden. In a foretelling of Jesus's execution, Zacharias's body disappears, and the people mourn for three days and nights.[4] Later versions of James add further incredible details, including a magic spring and a palm tree that provide Mary with food and drink on the trip to Bethlehem, fabulous creatures such as dragons and lions who worship the holy child, and pagan idols that spontaneously topple over and crumble into dust during the flight into Egypt.[5] Yet James is also rich in folkways and customs that give a whiff of plausibility to the portrait of Joseph as elderly widower and reluctant husband.

In late antiquity it was not uncommon for an older widower to marry a prepubescent girl, postponing consummation as did Augustine with his ten-year-old bride-to-be. Joseph's age could also explain his disappearance from the Gospel narratives, although if Mary was only eleven or twelve at her betrothal, Joseph may well have been in his thirties or forties rather than the elderly, white-haired man depicted in art. Most important, the idea that Mary's large brood were actually stepchildren resolves the sticky problem of Jesus's siblings.

Indeed, James resolves several problems in Mary's story: Joseph was an elderly widower, the marriage was never consummated, and Jesus's brothers and sisters were stepchildren from Joseph's first marriage. As to her embarrassing pregnancy, in ancient and even recent times the lines between betrothal and marriage were more blurred than they are today—sometimes it was a pregnancy that made the marriage official. Moreover, the Old Testament was rife with stories of women conceiving through divine intervention.

Ancient mythology also abounds with stories about virgins, widows, and women with elderly husbands impregnated by supernatural means — by demons, or by the salacious god Zeus, who impregnated mortal women in disguises as improbable as a shower of gold (Danae), an erotic swan (Leda and the swan), an amorous bull (Europa). Well into the nineteenth century European and American folk tales told stories of demons and mysterious night figures (the night mare) responsible for pregnancies of unmarried women, widows, or wives whose husbands were away at war or on long journeys.

Such folk beliefs, however, lost their relevance as Mary's

virginity became increasingly central to Christian theology and the Christian position on sexuality. Having moved ever further away from its Jewish roots, the notion of chastity grew ever more central to the evolving Church, thereby demanding a more elevated explanation for the mystery of Jesus's birth and a radically new conception of marriage. Whereas sexuality within marriage was encouraged and even idealized, not only amongst Jews but by ancient peoples in general, the equation of chastity and holiness within Christianity presented a thorny problem. For that, Gnosticism came up with a solution—the strange phenomenon known as the "spiritual marriage," a peculiar domestic arrangement in which couples abstained from sex in order to remain pure and undefiled, yet still enjoyed the companionship and comforts of marriage.

Actually, there were two versions of the spiritual marriage. In one, the husband was breadwinner, the wife cook and housekeeper, but both, theoretically, remained celibate. (Cynics claimed that many of these "marriages" were a fraud, merely a cover for men who would give their mistresses and bastard children legitimacy.) More realistic perhaps was another kind of spiritual marriage in which couples sought to purify sexual relations by dampening the initial fires of passion, abstaining from consummation until they could no longer resist. For them the bridal chamber was a battleground wherein they fought off the demons of lust who inhabit wanton women and lecherous men, and subject them to horrendous temptations. Only when those "evil powers" were thwarted, and the husband and wife had purged themselves of unbridled desire, could they become true spiritual partners, or "soul-mates." But the moment when they finally succumbed must be kept a secret, the great "mystery" of the bedchamber known only to themselves.

In the Apocryphal *Gospel of Philip* the Virgin Mary participates in just such a "mystery of the bedchamber." In one version she becomes bride of Christ and "partner of his soul" in a wholly spiritual union, "not fleshly but pure." As with worldly couples, the "mirrored bridal chamber is invaded by "evil powers" who use every trick of carnal temptation, but are inevitably vanquished. The bridal chamber, then, becomes a sacred place of purification and initiation, "the holy of the holies" wherein man and wife are washed clean of original sin and lose their separate genders as male and female become one. Here, too, Jesus is conceived in this holy of holies by "The father of everything united with the virgin . . . [for if] A horse sires a horse, a man begets a man, a god brings forth a god." Mary is thus virgin bride and mother, God is father, and Jesus is born without Original Sin. Their innocence stands in sharp contrast to the corruption of Adam and Eve by Original Sin, which by now has become a sexual sin. For that, Adam's offspring inherited God's curse, being

> begotten in adultery, for he was child of the serpent. So he [Cain] became a murderer just like his father [Adam] and he killed his brother. Indeed every act of sexual intercourse which has occurred between those unlike one another is adultery.[6] *

In other words, human sexuality is tainted for all time. Of course, the Church would eventually suppress such Gnostic 'heresies', yet the notion of Mary's purity and absolution from Original Sin would become ever more central to Christian theology. At the Council of Nicaea in 325, and again at Constantinople in 381, Mary's perpetual virginity became official Church dogma. Dissenters who continued to raise the sticky question of Jesus's siblings or to defend the idea of temporary virginity risked excommunication. In 383, when a layman named

---

*Once again we are in the realm of ancient mythologies, among them Olympias, mother of Alexander the Great, impregnated by a god, and an ancient creation myth in which Eve is impregnated by the snake; thus her son, Cain, "became a murderer."

Helvidius insisted that Jesus had bothers and sisters, Jerome bellowed blasphemy: "You have defiled the sanctuary of the Holy Spirit."[7] Worse still, when the errant monk Jovinian advocated marriage and motherhood as a consecrated way of life for Christian women, a number of virgins exchanged vows of celibacy for marriage vows. For that, Jovinian was sent into exile.

Jerome, in fact, would brook no dissent from the doctrine of Mary's virginity, for in the grim struggle to condition Christian women to virtue, it was the essential psychological tool. Christian girls who followed her example would be more likely to become fastidious Christian women. To that end Jerome wrote out a detailed program for his student, Paula, a wealthy Roman matron, who sought his advice on the education of her daughter, Eustochium. Jerome's lengthy response would become a manual for the moral training of well brought up Christian girls.

Eustochium must always keep her eye on the ultimate prize—lifelong virginity, the highest perfection to which a women can strive. To that end she must be strictly segregated from the company of boys, dress plainly, never wear jewelry or makeup, never dye or artificially wave her hair, and avoid rich foods, sticking to a sparse diet of porridge and fruit. Avoiding the company of girls of her own age, she should make her sole companion "some aged virgin of approved faith, character and chastity." Furthermore, she should not attend a public bath where there might be eunuchs or married women, for "women big with child are a revolting sight."[8] Jerome's strategy was successful; Eustochium not only remained a virgin all her life, she outlived all her married sisters.

Today Jerome's manual might seem a program for abuse, but at the time virginity might seem a blessing to those who chafed under the tyranny of the Roman *paterfamilias*. In tightly knit Roman families the father wielded absolute authority; he decided whether newborn infants would live or die and whom his children would marry or, in some cases, be forced to divorce.

Cato the Elder held that a wife caught in adultery should be killed on the spot. For a widow, the *paterfamilias* might even be her own son who stepped into his father's shoes as guardian. For a serious offense against the state, a father was obligated to sentence his own children to death. David's famous painting *Lictors Bearing the Bodies of the Sons of Brutus* shows a stern-faced father watching impassively as the lifeless bodies of his sons, whom he condemned to death for treason, are carried into their home on a stretcher. In a corner, the women of the family weep and mourn, giving vent to their grief.

In manifold other ways virginity might seem an attractive option to what some women saw as the marital bed of woe. For one, there was the brutal 'sacrifice of the virgin' on the wedding night to an older, experienced husband whom she hardly knew. Afterward there was the trauma of being torn from the family's bosom, to live forever with strangers. Childbirth itself was at all times a brush with death. For most women their destiny was to "partake in the horrors of [the] shipwreck" of marriage. By contrast, "Every virgin is set above the . . . experience itself."[9]

Virginity, in fact, gave a woman the freedom to do as she wished with her body. The lore of the early Church is filled with tales of women of the Roman upper classes who defied family and civic authority in their determination to remain virgins, even after marriage. The fourth-century Saint Helia, purportedly the daughter of an important bishop, took a vow of virginity in defiance of her mother, who turned her over to the authorities to force her into marriage. At her trial Helia used arguments from Jerome: "Marriage is death; virginity salvation. Marriage is pain; virginity is benediction."[10] To no avail—the judge ordered her to marry, ruling that "No woman may be saved unless it is by bearing children."[11] But Helia desisted, arguing that, like the Virgin Mary, she would be made fertile by God with "spiritual fruits."[12] Some women even chose martyrdom rather than marriage. Thecla's adamant refusal to marry her betrothed,

Thamyris, allegedly led to Paul's imprisonment, and her own sentence was to be burned at the stake.

Widows, too, sometimes refused to remarry as expected, as was the case with Melania and Paula. Both were affluent Roman widows with children—Paula had five—who left their children, traveled to the east, gave away much of their inheritance to missionary and church causes, and founded monasteries.

Yet if virginity offered freedom from the despotism of marriage, by the end of the second century a new despotism arose as the Church became increasingly patriarchal. While Paul suggested that women should remain silent in mixed congregations for fear of compromising their modesty, an increasingly rigid male hierarchy declared prophecy, preaching, baptizing, and missionary work to be off-limits to women. Now only virginity offered them a chance to achieve holiness on a par with men. The fifth-century desert mother Sarah lived for sixty years in the desert, disproving the alleged handicap of her sex. When visited by some monks of Scetis in her desert retreat, she reportedly told them, "It is I who am a man, and you who are women."[13]

Even as women were barred from active participation in Church offices, they were targeted as a constant and dangerous temptation to men. In his tract *On the Dress of Women,* Tertullian echoed Jerome in his war against cosmetics—white powders, charcoal eyeliner, red lip paint, jewelry, and revealing or brightly colored clothing. Rather, he said, Christian women should dress in dark mourning clothes as perpetual penance for their responsibility in the Fall.[14] Even Clement, generally a moderate, advised women to wear long, loose, baggy dresses to the ankles at home, and a veil in public to avoid "inviting another to fall into sin by uncovering her face."[15]

Thus could Christian women avoid the pitfall of ensnaring men with their beauty, beneath which lurks "phlegm, blood, bile, rheum."[16] But the real problem, wrote Jerome, "is not the harlot or the adulteress . . . but woman's love in general [which] is . . . ever insatiable; put it out, it bursts into flame; give it plenty, it is again in need."[17] Or in plain speaking, women can never be satiated sexually; even after orgasm desire springs anew. But if the eternal Eve beckons men to sin, corruption and death, Mary, the New Eve, will lead them to grace and eternal paradise. Whereas the old Eve cast mankind into perdition, "the knot of Eve's disobedience was loosened through the obedience of Mary."[18] That compliance becomes the salvation for the whole human race.[19]

Thus did Mary become the sum total of perfect womanhood: mild, meek, obedient to her son, pure in thought and deed, the vessel by which both she and her son were absolved from Original Sin. In 451, and again in 649 in the First Lateran Council, Mary's *Aeiparthenos,* perpetual virginity, became an article of Christian faith almost equivalent to the resurrection.[20] Splinter groups who desisted such as the Docetists, Arians, and Nestorians were pronounced heretics and ruthlessly persecuted. Henceforth, the humble woman hardly mentioned in the Gospels (save for Luke) would occupy a throne next to her son as Queen of Heaven. Churches would be dedicated to her and Christians address their prayers directly to her, begging her to intercede with her son. In time to come the intoning of the Hail Mary would become a requirement for all good Catholics.

Today, despite or perhaps because of Mary's demise in the Protestant Church, the official position of the Catholic Church on Mary's virginity has solidified. In 1854 her own Immaculate Conception — Mary's virgin birth to her mother, Anne—became official dogma. In 1950 the Assumption, her entry into heaven to take her place beside her son, became an article of faith. Like her son, Mary now evoked the essential mystery, becoming a figure at once human yet untainted by the pollution of the flesh.

And so for all time the paradox remains—how to emulate Mary's absolute purity and still function as wives and mothers, how to be the all-loving, all-giving woman that husbands desire—yet remain immaculate in thought and action, like Mary, untouchable in her virginal sanctity.

CHAPTER 6

THE MANY FACES OF MARY

O Queen of all courtesy
To thee I come and kneel
My wounded heart to heal
To thee for succor I pray
He who drank from thy breast
Madonna, the price will pay.
. . .
Madonna pity my thirst
Grant me thy counsel meet!
Succor me, Lily most sweet!

Jacopone Da Todi, thirteenth-century poet

As Christianity moved inexorably westward, it embraced whole cultures within its fold in the so-called mass conversions of the fourth and fifth centuries. More accurately, after powerful tribal chieftains or rulers were converted, they brought their people with them into the new religion. For the masses of peasants, such conversions were only skin deep. Clinging to their folkways and beliefs, they slyly amended them to fit the new religion, retaining beliefs in ancient fertility deities deeply ingrained in agricultural peoples.

For droves of converts from pagan religions, the new Christian goddess was conflated with powerful mother/earth goddesses whom they had no intention of abandoning. It is no accident that Mary's elevation in 431 C.E. as Mother of God took place at Ephesus in Asia Minor (now Turkey), ancient center for the cult of the virgin goddess Artemis of Ephesus (in Rome, Diana the Huntress), sometimes depicted as a fertility goddess with multiple breasts.[1] There, ecstatic throngs transferred their veneration of the pagan goddess to the Blessed Virgin with great enthusiasm.

Other Near East goddesses contributed to Mary's composite form as well—the Canaanite Ashtoreth, called Queen of Heaven, and Ishtar of Babylonia, who could heal the sick and raise the dead. Most important was Isis of Egypt who founded civilization itself; giver of law, language, agriculture, navigation, and justice, mistress of wind, sea, and sun; overseer of fame and of war; at once wife and sister and consort of Osiris. [2] In ancient Egypt her priests were tonsured and celibate; in Rome her cult remained powerful, attracting women especially. Rather than expunging these ancient mother goddesses, Mary became their apotheosis—symbol of the awesome mystery of creation.*

---

*Others were Cybele, great earth mother of Asia Minor, and the Greek Athena. Athena, although a virgin, was an androgynous figure, and hardly maternal. Endowed with "masculine" wisdom, she dressed and fought like a man—in Homer she strides through the ranks of soldiers, wielding her spear and bellowing out fearsome war cries.

At the same time, as Christianity militantly stamped out all vestiges of paganism, Mary became her own person, especially in the Middle Ages as Christians took refuge from a violent world within those great citadels of celibacy, the monasteries and convents. For the monk in his lonely, bare cell, the Virgin Mary brought solace, amending the austere life of the cloister with her sweet compassion. For the nun she was a model of purity, uncontaminated by the "fleshly filthiness" of sex. In taking their final vows novitiates enacted a ceremony complete with wedding gown and ring, taking Christ as the spiritual bridegroom who would never use them as "indecent playlings," never pollute them with "all the foulnesses" of the "dreary deed", never force them to risk their lives in childbirth.[3]

For those too flawed for such a life, marriage at least saved them from the sin of fornication. Yet, wives could still emulate the Virgin's purity by maintaining modesty and restraint in the marriage bed. To that purpose guidebooks for marital sex called Penitentials became popular in the sixth and seventh centuries, itemizing sins to be avoided and methods for purging oneself of sexual pollution.

Pious couples who fell into sin by enjoying sex could submit to public confession before a priest, followed by fasting or whipping. But as confession and penance became a private matter, the Penitentials stressed the deportment of Christian wives. Above all they must avoid the "extraordinary voluptuousness" of women who delight in "... whorish pleasures . . . the flaming itch of carnal lust . . . that loathsome act, that beastly copulation, that shameless coition, that fullness of stinking ordure and uncomely deed."[4]

As descendants of Eve, wives corrupted their husbands as well. To avoid that disaster, the Penitentials offered various remedies. As in the "sacred bridal chamber," newlyweds might abstain from sex for thirty days. After consummation they must do forty days penance to cleanse themselves before coming to church. Thereafter they should abstain during menstruation and pregnancy, after childbirth, and while breastfeeding (the latter restriction being one reason why upper-class women gave their infants to wet-nurses). Sundays, spent in prayer, were off-limits; some Penitentials added Wednesdays, Fridays, and Saturdays as well as the three Lenten periods, the three weeks before Easter, Advent, and Pentecost. Add to that three to seven days before and after communion, and the proliferation of prostitution during the Middle Ages becomes understandable.

In addition the Penitentials laid out strict rules for bedroom behavior: no full nudity, sex only under the cloak of darkness, no anal or oral sex, and no experimental positions, especially the man entering from the rear which smacked of the ultimate sin, sodomy. Thus could wives remain pure in spirit, if not intact in body.

Even after the Penitentials went out of style, the sexual behavior they taught remained deeply ingrained in the Christian psyche. Yet human nature is not so easily amended. Indeed, the more men and women struggled to deny their sexuality, the more they became obsessed with it. Blatant infringement of vows of celibacy by nuns and monks were widely known, as well as the bizarre effects of sexual repression. At the Convent of Loudon in France, for example, nuns became 'possessed' by some strange malady that brought about involuntary convulsions. At such time they would writhe about the floor in obscene positions, screaming all manner of lewd phrases. Conveniently, when visitors came to observe, their convulsions began precisely at 'showtime'. Upon investigation the nuns blamed their condition on the sorcery of their father confessor, who was executed as a witch after horrible tortures.[5]

Boccaccio's tales are also full of bawdy stories about monks, priests, and nuns who hardly took their vows seriously. One tells of a young monk who regularly relieved his urges with a peasant girl in his cell. Aware that his abbot had discovered him, the monk left the girl alone in his room when the abbot came to confront them. Overcome by desire, the abbot himself succumbed to temptation. Being both old and fat, " ... he did not mount her; but had her mount him instead.", unaware that the monk was watching through a peephole. Confronted by the abbot with his crime, the monk slyly mentioned his ignorance of the rule that monks "... should humble themselves under women as in fasting and vigils." Knowing that he had been caught red-handed, the abbot dropped the charges.[6]

With their natural, earthy acceptance of sex, Boccacio's tales are, perhaps, a more accurate reflection of sexual mores of the time than the Penitentials. In peasant villages and hamlets Christianity merged with local beliefs and folkways, incorporating pagan holidays, myths, and superstitions into a hybrid religion far removed from the Christianity of synods and Church councils. In particular, agricultural peoples stubbornly held on to their reverence for the mother-goddess whose awesome power blessed them with rain and good crops and protected them against natural disasters—famine, insect plagues, drought, unseasonable cold or heat, lethal epidemic diseases. It is no accident that the Virgin's feast days coincide with ancient agricultural festivals marking periods of spring sowing in May, harvesting of wheat and vintage in mid-August, and the December winter solstice that marks the rebirth of the sun.

Thus Mary's duality became more pronounced; at once the gentle, pure Virgin of official doctrine, while at the same time the powerful earth-mother, source of energy and life itself. For the latter image we turn again to an apocryphal work, the fifth-century Gospel of Bartholomew, in which the narrator tells of how the Apostles cajole Mary to describe how God descended into her at Jesus's conception. At first she desists, for merely telling the story could unleash her awesome, creative energy. When the Apostles persist, they have to hold all her limbs to prevent her from flying apart, so great is the story's force. Fire shoots out of her mouth, and only Jesus's intervention averts the world's destruction in a fiery apocalypse.

At the same time, with the ascendancy of the Trinity—father, son, and holy ghost—who sternly judge mankind, Mary's loving and forgiving nature provided an antidote to terrifying stories of sin and the burning fires of hell. For St. Bernard of Clairvaux, the father of medieval monasticism, Mary not only assuaged those fears but brought, to the lonely monk in his desolate cell, solace and an unconditional mother's love.

Bernard's *Rules* for the monastic life amended the severe asceticism of Eastern monks and hermits who lived alone rather than in communities. Rather, Bernard understood too well the frightful deprivations on which the monk's vows constantly threatened to founder. Praying one day before a statue of the Virgin, he came to the passage, "Show thyself a mother." Suddenly, Mary appeared in a brilliant halo of light. Pressing her breast to his lips, she expressed three precious drops of mother's milk. From that moment on Bernard devoted himself to the Virgin. For him she was the loving mother who forgives even the most wayward of her children; her intercession with Christ's harsh judgments might save even the most hardened of sinners. For the rest of his life Bernard composed prayers to the Virgin filled with tender emotion and poetry.

For ordinary folk, countless folktales emerged telling of Mary's sweet sympathy, her power to save even the most depraved of sinners if they remained faithful to her. It was Mary who saved hardened criminals from the hangman's noose in a miraculous eleventh-hour pardon (or, more likely, the frequency with which the hangman botched the job). Her healing milk could also snatch the sick from the grave on their deathbed, as in the legend of a monk saved from a fatal illness by a few drops of milk from Mary's breast. Another story concerns Theophilus, who was just about to sell his soul to the devil when Mary flew down from heaven with the deed to his soul, saving him from everlasting perdition. At the Cathedral of Notre Dame, a statue of Mary shows her, sword in hand, about to deliver Satan the fatal blow.

Mary's miraculous ability to save sinners from Hell's everlasting torments was a favorite subject for artists, as in a painting showing Mary rescuing sinners about to be herded into the ghastly flames of hell by grotesque demons.* Another fifteenth-century painting shows Mary surrounded by sinners on their knees, pleading for a reprieve from the everlasting flames. The inscription reads, "Dearest son, because of the milk I gave you, have mercy on them."† Another panel announces a happy ending as God the Father reverses his stern judgment and the sinners are saved.[7]

Especially touching is the story of Our Lady's Tumbler, about a humble, illiterate minstrel who enters a monastery but falls into despair when he cannot join in the prayers and rituals of the more educated monks. In secret he pays homage to the Virgin with his one skill, his acrobatics: "Sweet Lady, Sweet Queen . . . I cannot read your Hours, nor chant your praise, . . . [but] at the least I can set before you what art I have. Now will I be as the lamb that plays and skips before his mother . . . Lady, I worship you with heart, body, feet, hands."[8] After years of practicing this novel form of worship, the Tumbler is discovered by the abbot, amazed by his performance. Suddenly Mary appears in a gown "heavy with gold and gleaming stones." Fanning the sweating tumbler with her napkin, she "Meekly . . . served him as a handmaid in his need."[9] Astonished, the abbot receives the Tumbler into the brotherhood and begs him to pray for his salvation.

Interestingly, the narrator in this story echoes the language of chivalry, or courtly love, in which Mary played a central role. For the knight engaged in brutal combat and warfare, devotion

---

*anonymous artist

†Now in the Cloisters in New York.

to an idealized woman deflected from the harsh reality of his life. In the elaborate code of courtly love, the knight chastely worshipped his lady from afar with a love purified of carnal passion, creating the ultimate woman on a pedestal. As the poet Shelley later put it, such a love was like "The desire of the moth for the star / of the night for the morrow / the devotion to something afar."[10]

That ambiguity stands at the heart of Dante's towering work, the *Divine Comedy*. Haunted all his life by the conflict between sensual and spiritual love, Dante was a boy of only nine when he became obsessed with a young girl of eight, Beatrice Portinari, whom he passed in the street one day. Struck as if by lightning, he heard a voice whisper, "Here is a deity stronger than I; who, coming, shall rule over me."[11]

Dante did not see Beatrice again until she was seventeen. Too shy to look at her directly, he averted his glances to her companions, which she took for rudeness. Eventually she married a Florentine banker and died when only in her twenties. Bereft, Dante took a lover who resembled Beatrice. But one day her memory abruptly overwhelmed him. Abandoning his lover, at twenty-six Dante married a woman chosen by his father. Although they had three, possibly four children, he never mentioned his wife in any of his writings, nor did she seem to have joined him in his exile. Rather, his obsession with Beatrice grew in intensity. Immortalized in his two greatest literary works, in the *Divine Comedy* Beatrice returns to him in her immortal form. By conflating her image with that of the Virgin, Dante created the ideal woman for whom he yearned, but could never attain in real life.

As such, the literary Beatrice, like a mother scolding a naughty child, sharply rebukes the poet for deserting her when "from flesh to spirit I had risen,", thus allowing the "false loveliness" of an earthly woman to turn him away from the true pathway.[12] She then guides the poet through the vital stages of remorse and confession of sin. Only when the flood-gate to bitter tears of penitence are opened can he complete his epic journey, culminating in a dazzling vision of the Virgin Mary as divine love.

Overcome, words fail him. Instead he quotes St. Bernard's lovely homage to the Virgin: "Hope, that forever springs in living stream, . . . Charity . . . in thy bounty's large excess, . . . In thee is pity, in thee is tenderness . . . thou to us art the full noonday beam of love revealed."[13] Having journeyed through purgatory and hell, Dante apprehends Paradise in an ecstatic vision of the Virgin as "The Love that moves the sun and other stars."[14]

All too soon, in the increasingly secular, commercial, and cosmopolitan society of the Renaissance, Dante's sublime vision would appear anachronistic. More and more, Christians concerned themselves with the here-and-now of life rather than with eternity, while humanist scholars looked at the Gospels anew. Inevitably, as the search for an authentic, human Jesus extended itself to a human mother as well, the Virgin began to descend from her pedestal, commuting the idealized Mary into a real flesh and blood woman.

Logically, the next step was to ask what the real Mary actually looked like. For that the Gospels were no help, nor were the earliest known portraits of Mary; fresco paintings found on the walls of the Christian catacombs in Rome. Generally, the early Christians depicted Mary as a figure resembling the Egyptian goddess, Isis, either holding her dead son / consort in her lap (as in Michelangelo's famous *Pieta*), or suckling her child. Later artists of the fifth and sixth centuries transformed her into a stiffly stylized, iconic figure. Swathed from head to toe in a flowing dark tunic, she holds a strangely mature child on her lap who, clutching a scroll or an orb, seems more an authority figure than a beloved infant.[15] Throughout the medieval period artists rarely veered from that stiff, stylized figure, her face somber and expressionless, her body non-existent beneath a nun's black habit.

With the Renaissance, however, the hotly debated question of what the biblical Mary might have looked like resumed. A Dominican Friar, Gabriel Barletta, asked, "Was the Virgin dark or fair"? Albertus Magnus felt certain that she could not have been either brunette, red, or fair-haired, for her perfect beauty demanded a blending of all complexions. Yet, says Albertus, "we must admit, she was a little on the dark side . . . since Jews tend to be dark and she was a Jewess."[16]

Ultimately, it would be a quest for beauty, not verisimilitude, that shaped Mary's image in Renaissance art. Like a butterfly emerging from its cocoon, the de-sexed, shapeless figure metamorphosed into a richly garbed, young and beautiful woman of the period. Beneath the folds of her gowns were hints at soft feminine curves, divested of her nun's cowl her hair tumbled about her shoulders in ambient waves, and in Florence artists gave her the blond hair so coveted in that city. Ambrogio Lorenzetti, a fourteenth-century Tuscan artist, turned out hundreds of portraits of Mary portraying her as a lovely young woman, fashionably dressed in brilliant colors, tenderly cradling her infant. So popular were these Virgin pinups called *Madonnieri,* some painters produced nothing else.

Increasingly, too, Madonna portraiture conveniently disguised a growing market for portraits of women of the upper classes, who posed as models. Consequently, the Madonna might appear as a worldly, richly dressed woman, her hair pulled tightly back to expose the broad forehead considered a mark of beauty. But in the hands of a master a Virgin and Child might become the apotheosis of the tender bond between mother and child, as in Dieric Bouts' *Madonna and Child* (1455-60). With wavy, red hair pulled sharply back from her forehead, fleshy chin, and coarse, work-hardened hands, Bouts' Mary is utterly real, as is her love for her infant, whose cheek and lips affectionately nestle against hers.*

Soon the quest for realism extended to portraits of Mary as a nursing mother, often revealing a shapely breast complete with rosy nipple. Actually, a nursing Madonna was hardly new. But medieval artists, in defiance of simple anatomy, might have the Virgin's breast jutting out of a shoulder blade or placed just below the neckline.[17] By contrast, the sixteenth-century Dutch artist Marinus Van Roymerswaele used a Jewish woman nursing her infant as model for an utterly real *Virgin and Child.*† Here the mother expertly positions the nipple in the mouth of her half-asleep, blissfully satiated infant.

So too the German artist Hans Baldung Grien. In his *Madonna and Child with Parrot* (1484-85),a rather mature infant contentedly suckles his mother's breast. This Madonna, however, is a striking beauty with long, crimped, red hair and red lips, her white neck encircled by a gold necklace. The scene includes two well-known symbols for erotic love—a parrot who nibbles at the Madonna's cheek, and a winged cupid who mischievously pulls back a gossamer veil to expose a lovely face that seems more courtesan than Holy Mother.

Soon it became a commonplace for wealthy patrons to portray their favorite mistresses as Madonnas. The Borgia pope, Alexander VI, used his favorite mistress, Guilietta Farnese, as model for a portrait of the Virgin that hung in the entryway to his private apartments. Similarly, Charles VII of France had his mistress Agnes Sorrel painted as the Holy Virgin holding her infant son on her lap, one fashionably firm and rounded breast exposed as if to nurse her child. In reality a woman of her class would have given her infant to a wet-nurse immediately after birth, for that lovely breast had to serve the pleasures of her lover, not her child.

In the hands of great masters such as Fra Filippo Lippi,

---

*Metropolitan Museum of Art, New York.

† The Prado, Madrid.

Raphael, and Sandro Boticelli, the Madonna became a symbol for the humanist's cherished notion of ideal beauty. Freed of original sin, her beauty is never marred by the burdens of motherhood or the decrepitude of aging. Yet in Leonardo da Vinci's great masterpiece *Virgin of the Rocks,* the line between real and ideal is tenuous. Set in a mysterious but naturalistic grotto, it depicts a lovely young mother tenderly embracing her infant son. If there is something otherworldly about her, a spirituality that places her in the realm of angels, she seems at once mundane and heavenly. Both earthly mother and virgin, she is the timeless image of pure, unblemished womanhood.

In lesser hands—artists who catered to popular taste—Madonna portraiture could be brazenly profane, even sensual, provoking the wrath of Protestant reformers. In their zeal to stamp out greed gone wild, lechery, hypocrisy, and phony indulgences—purchased tickets out of purgatory and hell—Protestants not only attacked those great citadels of celibacy, monasteries and convents, but Christianity's principal symbol for celibacy, the Virgin herself;

Having become a female deity rivaling her son in popular piety, she would not be spared the fate of the pantheon of saints, along with their relics, processions, saint days, and miracles. In their fervor, reformers rampaged through churches, smashing statues of the male and female saints to smithereens in an orgy of cleansing. But dethroning the Queen of Heaven would be no easy matter.

No force, it seems, could entirely deprive her of her unsullied innocence, or dislodge her from her place in the Christian psyche. Especially when the elimination of confession internalized the profound dynamic of sin and repentance, Mary would become more powerful than ever, though in a wholly new way. Migrating from her marble pedestal to the innermost psyche of Protestant women, she would remain the model whom they would continue to emulate in thought and deed.

CHAPTER 7

OUR LADY OF PERPETUAL INVIOLABILITY

When I find myself in times of trouble
Mother Mary comes to me
Speaking words of wisdom,
Let it be.

The Beatles

Darkness was falling as the young man strode quickly through the tall grasses in the field, anxious to reach home before night obscured the path. With his eyes on the setting sun, Martin never saw the jagged rock until it collided with the tip if his boot. The fall was swift, and even before he felt the sharp pain in his thigh he saw the blood spurting out of an artery, lanced by his unsheathed sword. Pressing his hand tightly against the wound, he stumbled home where his mother bathed and bound the laceration.

By the next day a red ring around the wound announced the onset of infection. Soon Martin was burning with fever, his body shaking with chills, his lips parched with thirst. As his mind clouded over, certain that death was imminent, Martin cried out to the Blessed Virgin, "O Mary, help!" Years later, on recalling the episode, Martin Luther remarked: "Had I died then I should have died calling on Mary."[1]

The irony of that instinctive reflex was not lost on the man responsible for the great schism with the Catholic Church. In many ways Mary symbolized what Protestants saw as the abuses of original Christianity: the superstitions associated with saints, the power accrued by Mary to whom supplicants often addressed their prayers, the hated ethic of celibacy, of which Mary's virginity was an essential factor.

If Protestants rejected her cult, they also understood that Mary was far more than a saint. As the apotheosis of womanly love, tenderness, and compassion, she reached out to sinners mired in the muck of their transgressions. Luther himself, a convinced Augustinian obsessed with original sin in his youth, cherished her all his life. Yet reverence for the Virgin did not mean that Christian men and women had to endure the strait-jacket of celibacy to live a holy life, or to find favor in the eyes of God.

Like Augustine, Luther felt that sexuality was a force of nature too powerful to be denied, marriage being "necessary as a remedy for lust."[2] Unlike Augustine, Luther came to believe that since God created man and woman for the purpose of reproducing, marriage "covers the sin."[3] As to celibacy, Luther drew on common sense and his own experience as a monk. In his opinion the monk's denial of sexuality only led to sickness and misery, for "Nature must and will compel him to produce seed and to multiply."[4] Deprivation only causes the body to turn against itself, producing a foul poison that makes the flesh "unhealthy, enervated, sweaty and foul-smelling."[5] Luther also saw celibacy as the root cause of a depravity amongst the clergy that he detested. God, then, had ordained marriage as a "plaster for that sore."[6]

Luther also genuinely liked women and enjoyed their company, although he never entirely rid himself of the notion of women as daughters of Eve. Only through subservience to their husbands and in motherhood can women be redeemed: "You will be saved if you have subjected yourselves and bear your children with pain."[7] But after his marriage Luther became an enthusiast, writing , "he who recognizes the estate of marriage will find therein delight, love, and joy without end; as Solomon says, "He who finds a wife finds a good thing."[8] For Luther, the "estate of marriage" was a mindset, a way of life that rises above humdrum drudgery and the inevitable grief of parents in an age of high infant mortality. Luther, then, countered the argument used by the Church against a married clergy—the contrast between the endless demands of infants, their constant crying, their "rashes and sores," the stench of dirty diapers and sleepless nights, and the "peaceful, carefree life" of the priest or nun.[9]

On the contrary, Luther held that marriage brings peace of mind, a resolution of worldly trials and tribulations, and saves men from the "secret sin" of masturbation. Above all, marriage and fatherhood is divinely ordained—"O God, . . . I am certain that thou hast created me a man and hast from my body begotten this child."[10]

Yet Luther could never rid himself of a certain ambivalence about sexuality, the mechanics of which seemed to him rather awkward. Despite an exuberantly earthy nature and his own happy marriage, in his writings he avoided its sensual aspect. In private, however, amongst family and friends, he freely joked about the physical delights experienced by newly-weds, humorously referring to woman's natural craving for sex.* If he thought of himself as a somewhat clumsy lover, he was an unfailingly warm and affectionate husband to Catherine von Bora, an ex-nun with whom he had six children .

In fact, Luther's tract, *The Estate of Marriage,* is a paean to the joys of parenting. At a time when housework of any kind was considered demeaning to a man, Luther was an extraordinary parent, and admonished other fathers to follow his example. For him no task was too mean or too low—rocking the infant to sleep, bathing them, even washing diapers: "Oh how gladly will I do so, though the duties should be even more insignificant and despised. Neither frost nor heat, drudgery nor labor, will distress or dissuade me." In this a man must be impervious to the sneers of other men who will "ridicule him as an effeminate fool," for these menial tasks are done in the highest spirit of "Christian faith."[11]

But if a man can have two vocations, women have only one; motherhood. For her there is no higher calling. If she dies in childbirth, as many women did in that day, she will "depart happily, for [she] will die in a noble deed." Even harlots and unwed mothers are "pleasing in God's sight" when they are mothers.[12] Luther also advised wives to follow the Virgin's example of obedience, despite his genial admission that in his own household his wife, Catherine, held the real power. A strong, capable, generous woman, Catherine managed both the household and their family farm, accepting with open arms eleven orphaned nephews and nieces whom they adopted, and a constant stream of guests at their hospitable table.

All this did not come easily to Luther. Only after intense anguish and self-doubt did he arrive at that ecstatic moment when the harsh, judgmental God of his childhood and the

---

*Recorded in "Table Talk, a collection of informal, often earthy and scatological sayings around the dinner table.

monastery gave way to a tolerant, loving, forgiving God. Not so John Calvin, the twin architect of Protestantism, for whom the Augustinian obsession with Original Sin was sealed into his deepest soul.

Calvin, too, supported marriage as ordained by God, and considered celibacy an impiety. For him, Jerome's rantings against marriage as "hateful and infamous . . . wicked suggestions of Satan" were sheer apostasy.[13] But Calvin's position derives from an arid, logical reasoning devoid of the experience of marriage. Despite his belief that man is a "social animal," he himself was cold and reclusive, a life-long bachelor. Solitary and spartan in all his habits, he ate only plain foods, fasted often, slept only six hours a night, and took no holidays. Somewhere, buried deeply inside his psyche, lived an ascetic monk.

A deep-seated misogyny also constantly intrudes itself into Calvin's conception of woman, darkening his view of marriage. Calvin conceded that woman was intended by God to be "companion and an associate to the man, to assist him to live well." Unfortunately, Eve ruined it all; in punishment for the Fall, marriage will always be marred by "strifes, troubles, sorrows, dissensions, and a boundless sea of evils."[14] For all its "residue" of good, marriage is woman's punishment for "bringing the serpent forward." In his anger God decreed two great punishments: woman must bear her children in pain, and for all time be humbled by servitude—"Thou shalt desire nothing but what thy husband wishes."[15] Little wonder that the nuns of the Convent of St. Claire in Geneva rebelled when ordered to leave its sanctuary by Protestant city officials, their worse fear being to be forced to marry.[16]

Nor did Calvin ever rid himself of an aversion for the corrupt body. Rather, his driving obsession with mankind's essential depravity deposited a considerable residue of guilt within the Protestant psyche. Ironically, Calvin's theocracy in Geneva seemed nothing less than a secularized monasticism, his ideal state being a "community of saints." Under his governance Geneva inflicted severe punishments for even the slightest moral infractions: gambling, cursing, blasphemy, disobedience to parents, laziness, working on the Sabbath day. The injunction against idolatry forbade frivolities such as church bells, "showy songs," pictures, statues, or sumptuous robes for the clergy. Fornication was punishable by exile or drowning, adultery was punishable by death. On one occasion a child was beheaded for having struck its parents.[17]

Inevitably, Calvin's theology became deeply imbedded in the Puritan psyche. To this very day laws in various American states derived from our Puritans forefathers remain on the books. Several states forbid the selling of alcohol on Sunday; in many states sodomy and oral sex are criminal acts. Less obvious, but more intrusive into the American character is the legacy of Puritanism that drives the American work ethic, and a tendency to throws a cloak of depravity over sex , nudity, and too much frivolity that only forces such things underground.

So, too, Calvin's attitude toward women. As one sixteenth-century Protestant pastor put it: "Women are still Eve, they hold the apple in their hand."[18] Consequently, if Luther's idealization of motherhood kept the Virgin Mary teetering on her pedestal, Calvin's stern Puritanism points the finger at women as descendants of Eve forever after. Thus, the ancient duality was made manifest: woman as temptress juxtaposed against Mary's example of modesty, chastity, and obedience. The latter underscored the authority of the Protestant husband who now gave Bible readings at home. But the former—modesty and chastity--kept the model of Mary sacrosanct and firmly embedded in the psyche of Protestant wives, if not in the sanctuary of the Church.

In the absence of convent schools, mothers could no longer rely on the nuns to set their daughters on the right track. Instead they turned to a popular literature known as the conduct book or chapbook—some of them strangely reminiscent of Jerome's essay on the upbringing of Eustochium. A good example would be *The Ladies Calling*, a chapbook published in 1673 to help mothers inculcate "modesty and obedience" and teach their daughters proper female decorum.

Accordingly, she should refrain from any kind of bold or assertive behavior, instead manifesting "a humble distrust of herself; she is to look on herself but as a novice, a probationer in the world . . . rather to learn and observe, than to dictate and prescribe." In speech she must be restrained, gentle, reserved, her "tongue . . . like the imaginary music of the spheres, sweet and charming, but not to be heard at a distance," for excessive talkativeness is the mark of a bold woman. She should also refrain from reading romantic novels—a dangerous incentive to emulate the wanton behavior and stormy passions of their protagonists—or anger, which puts a woman's calm equilibrium in peril. Should she find herself helplessly in its grip, the best course is to "Seal up [her] lips . . . [for] humility is the most natural cure for anger."

Ironically, having freed women from the prison of the cloister, having given them dignity as wives and mothers, the Protestant ethic exhorted them to emulate the gentle, nurturing, self-denying aspect of the Holy Mother. More than ever, bourgeois standards of feminine propriety robbed women of their essential vitality, independence, and natural sexuality. Indeed, despite the enlightenment's rebellion against the repressive sexual mores of the traditional Church, the emerging middle-class woman was anything but sexually liberated.

Rather, she was to function as a bulwark against the casual promiscuity of the upper classes, its root cause being the arranged, loveless marriage. But whereas the new "companionate marriage" stressed mutual compatibility, it skirted the issue of sex altogether. For at its heart the companionate marriage was not new at all, but a secularization of the module set up by the Church Fathers—faithful monogamy based on solid friendship, companionship, and parenthood.

Concealed beneath the surface of the new bourgeois code of feminine Virtue were those embodied by the Virgin Mary—female modesty, chastity, and humility—virtues propagated not only from the pulpit, but in art, literature, and fashion. Catering to the tastes of a gentrified merchant class, artists painted homey scenes, replete with modest housewives and mothers, rather than the voluptuous nude goddesses of rococo art. Fashion too reflected the modesty, thrift and industrious life style of the bourgeois housewife. No longer did women spend hours at their toilette, painting their faces with powder and rouge, squeezing their bodies into tightly drawn waist cinchers that exposed a generous bosom above the plunging necklines of high fashion.

A pair of paintings by Etienne Jeaurat done in 1734 illustrates the deepening feminine polarity. *La Coquette* (The Flirt) shows a woman, possibly a courtesan, at a dressing table loaded with mirrors, perfumes, jewelry—all the implements of her art. The accompanying verse reads: "The coquettish spirit is not a vice, when taken in moderation, it is only an artifice, to make love the more enjoyable."[19] Conversely, its pendant, *L'Econome,* shows a plain woman, without makeup, wearing a simple dress and modest cap and completely absorbed in her needlework. The caption announces: "The thrifty, modest wife, consulting only her common sense, devotes herself to her household, with no dancing in the home."[20] The message is clear—one woman is for pleasure, the other for domestic tranquility.

Of them all, the great French painter Chardin immortalized the virtuous, self-effacing wives, mothers, and daughters of the bourgeoisie. In *Grace before Meals,* a modestly attired young mother instructs her young daughter—dressed exactly like her—in the obligatory prayer before a meal. In *The Lesson,* a mother wearing a clean white apron and cap instructs her child in writing. Many of Greuze's most important paintings, in fact, were meant to be read as moral allegories—stark warnings against the ever present danger of seduction that robbed innocent young women of their virtue.

To dramatize the point, Greuze sometimes borrowed from the theater. Such was the case with *The Neapolitan Gesture,* based on a popular Burletta, or melodrama, in which a handsome nobleman disguises himself as a peddler in order to seduce a charming young woman of the common class. As the enamored girl eagerly reaches out to accept the enticing bauble offered by the peddler, an elderly servant pushes him away with one hand, while restraining the girl with the other. Not accidentally, her hand falls between the girl's legs, a protective gesture meant to keep her mistress' virtue intact at all costs.

In another work, *The Broken Eggs,* it is too late. A dejected young woman sits next to a basket of eggs, one of which lies broken on the ground—a metaphor for the girl's loss of virginity—while an elderly servant furiously berates her and her lover for their transgression. In *La Mere Courroux,* however, a mother, having discovered a love letter hidden by her daughter in a chest, savagely attacks her terrified daughter whose face is a mask of fear and remorse. Greuze's ardent admirer, the philosoph, Denis Diderot, pronounced these works to be "moral painting. And why not, hasn't the artist's brush been devoted to debauchery and vice for long enough?"[21]

Diderot's favorite novelist was the English writer, Samuel Richardson, whose heroines embraced Virtue so zealously as to call up the image of the Virgin Mary herself. Richardson's most popular novel, *Pamela, Or Virtue Rewarded,* is the story of a beautiful servant girl who ferociously resists the sexual advances of her young master, an experienced libertine accustomed to having his way with servants. Fending off Mr. B's sometimes brutal forays against her virginity, Pamela is a veritable tiger. And she is proud as well. No servant to be abused, she declares that as a Christian, she is inferior to no one: "My soul is of equal importance with the soul of a princess."[22]

Yet she is no saint either, for Mr. B's awkward gropings sometimes bring an involuntary but knowing blush to her cheeks. In the end Mr. B will have his way, but only on her terms. When Pamela proves unassailable, Mr. B., driven to the extremity, marries her; but only after a radical transformation from jaded libertine typical of his class, to solid, bourgeois husband and family man. Pamela, too, is reformed. As fiery defiance becomes docile, wifely obedience, she addresses her husband only as "Sir."

Not coincidentally, the novel recalls the Renaissance legend of the Unicorn and the Virgin in which the wild unicorn can only be captured by a virgin—the only one who can transform the untamed beast into a docile, gentle creature. On one level, the unicorn symbolizes Christ, and the virgin the Madonna. On another, he is the noble man who must abandon his dissolute sexual habits when he marries, but only a pure and spotless virgin is capable of domesticating him.

In *Clarissa,* the sequel to *Pamela,* Richardson went even further in creating a militantly virtuous heroine whose angelic perfection is inevitably too good for this world. Pursued by the despicable Lovelace, whose sole passion in life is the seduction and conquest of innocent women, Clarissa's fierce resistance forces him to resort to desperate measures. When her greedy family tries to force her into an arranged marriage, Clarissa runs away. Homeless and alone, she falls into the clutches of Loveless, who offers shelter. Relentless in his pursuit of the maidenhead, he abducts her to a brothel in London, drugs her, and rapes the unconscious woman. Awakening to the awful truth, Clarissa cries out to heaven for divine grace to save both her seducer and herself. Her wish will be granted, but both her violation and Lovelace's jaded, dissolute character demand the ultimate price: their respective deaths.

Her death, in fact, is the stuff of saints and martyrs. As she expires with "a sweet smile beaming over her countenance," her weeping family invokes the Virgin, specifically "the divine lady's last blessing." Pamela's breathless final speech also evokes the spirit of Saint Theresa of Avilla, whose visions of Christ were strongly tinged with sexual overtones:

> She spoke faltering and inwardly: Bless—bless—bless—you all—and now —holding up her almost lifeless hands for the last time . . . come—o come—blessed lord—Jesus.[23]

Seized in the end by a transforming rapture, Clarissa dies in an ecstasy worthy of the great Spanish mystic.

Richardson's fellow novelist Henry Fielding was both disgusted and amused by *Clarissa*'s religious overtones, its apotheosis of the Christian ethic of chastity. Yet in many ways Clarissa's angelic purity was a forecast of the age to come. For as society moved into the new industrial age of the nineteenth century, the mythology of the Virgin Mary would exert an influence far beyond the religious realm. Precisely as the Cult of the Virgin became obscured within the shadows of a secularized society, it burrowed its way deeply into the psyche of that army of womanly virtue—Victorian wives, mothers and daughters.

CHAPTER 8

THIS HEART OF STONE

What would I give for a heart of flesh to warm me through
Instead of this heart of stone ice-cold whatever I do.
Hard and cold and small, of all hearts the worst of all.
Christina Rossetti

The church father Jerome would surely have approved of the proper Victorian wife—a saintly creature who put the needs of family above her own, kept an orderly home, disciplined her children without raising her voice, looked up to and revered her husband, as Mary did her son. Modest and pure in thought, deed and action, motherhood was her highest calling. Trapped by the age old duality, if nature had allowed her to emulate the Virgin Mother, she would have. At the very least, she could try to follow her example. The Victorian poet Coventry Pattmore dubbed her "The Angel in the House": "a woman deck'd / With saintly honours, chaste and good / Whose thoughts celestial things affect / Whose eyes express her heavenly mood."[1]

Pattmore's poem was a eulogy to his adored wife who died of tuberculosis at an early age. Such an "Angel" wife would have suited the famous art critic, John Ruskin, perfectly, were it not for certain expectations about marriage held by his real wife, the lovely Effie Gray. In his book, *Sesame and Lilies,* Ruskin described the ideal Victorian husband as a modernized, chivalrous knight who goes out to do battle in the competitive world of business and affairs, while sheltering his wife from "all danger and temptation . . . [and] anxieties of the outer world." She in turn guards the home, making it "a sacred place, a vestal temple" in which the husband/knight finds refuge from the tense world of the marketplace.[2]

Ruskin deliberately employed the language of courtly love to describe the ideal wife who, like the noble lady of old, was incorruptibly good, infallibly wise, a seeker of knowledge, not for self-development, but for self-renunciation. Like the Virgin, she wears a starry crown reflecting her innocence, the "majestic peace" that will never age.[3] So seriously did Ruskin take this equation of wife and Virgin that in almost seven years of marriage to a woman widely admired for her beauty, the marriage was never consummated. Both partners entered the marriage as virgins and departed in exactly the same way. Whenever Effie brought the matter up for discussion Ruskin cited the Christian invocation to chastity, and the holy men and women who had honored that sacred ethic.

For six years Effie lived in hope that that her husband would honor his promise to become a sexual partner in time, repressing the fact that there was something bizarre in the relationship. Perhaps it was when Ruskin's colleague, the painter John Stuart Millais, came to stay with them one summer, and fell in love with her, that Effie woke up. At any rate, when, finally, Ruskin reneged, Effie's anger erupted. After years of neglect and psychological abuse, she sued for divorce—almost unheard of at the time, particularly when initiated by a wife. In the sensational trial that followed, Ruskin put the full blame on Effie, even implying that she was insane.

Above all, he based his defense on his repulsion for her body, saying that the sight of her nude body on their wedding night shocked and sickened him. Having been assiduously shielded by his parents from any notion of what a mature woman looked like, her body was entirely different than what he had imagined—the body of a child without breasts or pubic hair. In later life Ruskin was drawn to pre-adolescent girls, and fell in love with a ten-year-old. Effie herself married Millais, had a long and happy marriage, and eight children.[4]

Ironically, Millais belonged to a group of painters dubbed the Pre-Raphaelites for whom Ruskin had a particular fondness. Like Ruskin and the romantics, the Pre-Raphaelites looked back to the Middle Ages, to courtly love, chivalry, chaste maidens, and the cult of the Virgin Mary for subject matter, costume, historic time and place. Yet the original seven of the Pre-Raphaelite Brotherhood, as they were called, were very much a product of their own time—ambitious young men molded by the self-same Victorian society they both idealized and subtly attacked in their art.

To a man they came from respectable, if not particularly affluent, well-educated families. Thus on one level their paintings reflected the moral proprieties of the Victorian middle classes—chaste maidens in innocuous, pastoral settings, pure virgins sometimes depicted as saints, knights and their courtly ladies, narratives taken from romances of the Middle Ages, beautiful damsels in prayer. Whatever sexual innuendo might creep into that genre of their work (as opposed to their portraits of fallen women), remained cloaked beneath outward proprieties. Even on the rare occasion of nudity, as in Edward Burne-Jones series of paintings, *Pygmalion and the Image,* vulgar realism is circumvented. Like Ruskin's ideal woman, Burne-Jones's nude has no pubic hair.

Indeed, like all his colleagues in the Brotherhood, Burne—Jones was typically Victorian in his polarization of women as either saints or sinners. The former they married, the latter they obsessed over. Portraying them as half angel, half seductress, they highlighted their long, slender necks, brilliant, large eyes, full sensuous mouth, deep scarlet lips, thick, wavy hair reaching down to the waist. Conversely the opposite of these haunting beauties were their portraits of innocent, spotless virgins, schooled in a chastity strongly reminiscent of Jerome. The Pre-Raphaelites, in fact, helped to reinstate a Cult of the Virgin in predominantly Protestant England, despite a militant campaign to rid England of Popery and all it residual trappings.[5]

Of them all, perhaps it was Dante Gabriel Rossetti who dramatized the virgin/whore split most vividly. In Rossetti's portraits of chaste women he explored the contradictions and psychological effects of the cult of virtue on the Victorian wife and daughter. For his painting *The Girlhood of Mary Virgin* (1849), Rossetti even used his own mother and his sister Christina as models. The latter, as Mary, wears a drab, gray dress, with her straight, reddish hair hanging below her waist and her pinched, passive expression conveying meekness and modesty. Wearing a nun's cowl, Mary's mother, Anne, helps in her embroidery of a lily, symbol of purity, onto a stole. A thin, gold halo hovers over their respective heads; through a window we see Joseph outside, tending grape vines that symbolize the coming of Christ. Next to the women, a boy-angel with wings rests his hand on a mound of books inscribed with the womanly virtues: charity, faith, hope, fortitude—precisely as Jerome described it centuries earlier. Atop the books a tall, white lily signifies virginity.

In real life Rossetti's mother (and her mother as well), were ardent Evangelical Christians, while Christina was a brilliant poet—possibly the finest woman poet of her day. Both mother and grandmother had strayed from their Church by marrying Italian, Catholic men. Nonetheless, the Rossetti women clung more doggedly than ever to their evangelical Anglican faith, while the Rossetti men rebelled against religion altogether. Rossetti's grandmother, especially, had a reputation for "severe virtue," and inculcated both daughter and granddaughters into the more puritanical doctrines of the Anglican faith. Significantly, neither one of Rossetti's sisters ever married.

Maria, the elder sister, became an Anglican nun, while Christina poured into her poetry her personal torment—a yearning for physical love thwarted by sexual frigidity, an oppressive and excruciating sense of sin and guilt. Gradually, this gifted woman slipped into the bleak, emotionally starved world of Victorian spinsterhood so poignantly described in her poem "What Would I Give?"

> What would I give for a heart of flesh to warm me through,
> Instead of this heart of stone, ice-cold whatever I do:
> Hard and cold and small, of all hearts the worst of all.

To the outside world Christina seemed to lead a rather liberated life, being beautiful, high-spirited, and surrounded by her brother's circle of artists and poets. Two of them formally proposed marriage to her, but she found one too lethargic, the other too pedantic, and she loved neither one. Possibly, the frigidity alluded to in the poem just quoted precluded marriage. Yet the case is not simple, for in the poem "Look on This Picture and on This," Christina hints at some intense experience of love, either actual or imagined:

> The wine of love that warms me from this life's mortal chill:
> Drunk with love, I drink again, athirst I drink my fill
> lapped in love I care not doth it make alive or kill.[6]

Possibly the lover in these poems was a figment of the imagination, but biographer, Lona Packer, believes it was the poet and painter, William Bell Scott, with whom Christina had a conflicted relationship. Bell pursued her both before and after his marriage, knowing only too well the fatal split that made her at once "fearful as well as . . . lovable . . . Cold as that icy water . . . rather sacred and terrible is she without knowing it."[7] Christina herself understood the icy grip that held her psyche in thrall, writing:

> There's a leaden tester to my bed:
> Find you a warmer playfellow
> A warmer pillow for your head,
> A kinder love to love than mine.[8]

Apparently that is precisely what happened. Bell, who was extremely attractive to women, seems to have abandoned her on more than one occasion for more worldly women. Christina writes of a rival:

> You have seen her hazel eyes, her warm dark skin,
> Dark hair—but oh those hazel eyes a devil is dancing in:..
> You, my saint, lead up to heaven, she lures down to sin.[9]

Yet all her life Christina was haunted by remorse for some dark, hidden sin, real or imagined, possibly a scar inflicted by her own father, who may have sexually abused her (not an uncommon phenomenon in Victorian families). In her poem "Convent Threshold" she confesses:

> My lily feet are soiled with mud,
> With scarlet mud which tells a tale
> Of hope there was, of guilt that was,
> Of love that shall not yet avail.

There is, too, an oblique hint at a close encounter of some kind with Bell early in their relationship: "You sinned with me a pleasant sin:/ Repent with me, for I repent."[10] As a young girl, Christina's self-chastisement sometimes flared into acute self-hatred. Given to violent outbursts of temper, she once dug huge slashes into her arms with a scissors after a rebuke from her mother. But the deeper wound was clearly in Christina's psyche, in the painful pull between need, desire, and renunciation. In her religious poem "A Bruised Reed He Shall Not Break," she yields to her fate: "I will accept thy will to do and be,/Thy hatred and intolerance of sin." Yet in the aforementioned "Look on This Picture," written long after Bell rejected her, she poignantly alludes to the heartbreak of a lost love:

> For after all I loved you, loved you then, I love you yet:
> Listen, love, I love you: see the truth is set
> On my face, with tears—you cannot see? then feel the wet.[11]

The anguished ambivalence of Christina's poetry sheds some light on the sexual symbolism of another of her brother's paintings, *Ecce Ancilla Domini,* for which she was the model. Once again she is the Virgin Mary, but this time a mature woman with flowing, long red hair, brilliant eyes and red lips. Crouched on a narrow bed in a stark room suggestive of a convent cell (Christina herself often slept in such a room in the Anglican Sisterhood Convent), she wears a plain, white shift, and leans into the wall, her knees drawn up as in a defensive motion. Before her stands the archangel Gabriel, a handsome young man whose nude body shows through a slit in his white tunic. His feet are engulfed in brilliant flame, and he holds a long-stemmed lily pointed at her womb. On one level Rossetti depicts the annunciation, the lily symbolizing the immaculate conception. Psychologically, however, Mary appears as a conflicted young woman wrestling with her inner fear of the angel-man with feet of flame, who holds a lily with phallic connotations. Trapped in a vise of isolating piety, she evokes the desolation described in Christina's poem "The Heart Knows Its Own Bitterness":

> Weep, sick and lonely,

> Bow thy heart to tears,
> For none shall guess the secret
> Of thy grief and fears.[12]

Christina's sister, Maria, understood that grief as well. Loved by the Pre-Raphaelite painter Charles Collins, she was model for a painting based on Shelley's poem "The Sensitive Plant." It was originally intended as a sentimental scene of a young woman tending her garden, but after Maria took her vows Collins changed its title to *Convent Thoughts.* Located now in a convent, the garden is filled with red roses (representing passion) and white lilies (representing chastity). Maria, as young novice, gazes down at a passion-flower, symbol for the passion and the suffering of Christ. In the background white water-lilies and pale white goldfish also harp on the idea of female purity. In her hand she holds an illuminated manuscript with a painting of the annunciation of the Virgin Mary, whose example she will follow. Having renounced worldly marriage, she will become the virginal "bride of Christ" symbolized by the passion-flower.[13]

The case of the Rossetti sisters may been out of the ordinary, but Christina Rossetti's poetry reveals, in the most immediate way, the sharp split embedded in the psyche of so many Victorian women—the stifling repression not only of sexuality but of the vital self. Encased from head to toe in swathes of fabric, in corsets, bustles, and high collars that both hid and distorted her body, the respectable Victorian woman lived by codes similar to those laid out by the Church Fathers and the Penitentials: modest, chaste behavior even in bed, no experimental positions or nudity, no participation in or seeking after pleasure in marital sex. To behave with "vulgar abandon" in the marital bed risked being categorized as one of those "whorish women."

To condition their daughters to virtue, Victorian mothers adopted methods not unlike that of Jerome. Boys and girls both were raised in total ignorance of sex and strictly segregated from the opposite gender. Girls raised by mothers too embarrassed to mention the changes that occur at puberty were often terrified by the first appearance of menstrual blood. One such woman later wrote that when her periods began she became hysterical and went into a fainting fit, thinking that she had seriously wounded herself in some way. A pall of guilt and shame about nudity and the genitals became locked into women's psyches. Another Victorian matron claimed that she had never in her life looked on her own naked body. As to sex, Victorian children were kept strictly in the dark. The early feminist Annie Besant felt that her total ignorance of sex traumatized her indefinitely and destroyed her marriage.[14] Marie Stopes, the author of *Married Love,* one of the first sex education manuals, agreed. She herself was married for six months before she discovered that the problem in her marriage was that she was still a virgin![15]

An English wife interviewed for a survey of female sexuality in 1884 believed that most women of her class came to the wedding night "as innocent as the grave."[16] For that the American novelist Edith Wharton blamed her mother, who turned a deaf ear to her daughter's pleadings for information— "I'm afraid Mamma. . . . I want to know what will happen to me." The response was a stern admonishment:

> haven't you seen enough pictures and statues in your life? Haven't you noticed that men are . . . made differently than women? . . . Don't ask me any more silly questions. You can't be as stupid as you pretend.[17]

Wharton's marriage remained unconsummated for three weeks, and even after the fact her fears and repulsion were only confirmed. In her view, her abysmal ignorance about sex "did more than anything else to falsify and misdirect my whole life."[18] Only in her forties, living as an expatriate in France, did Wharton finally awaken to her sexual being—not with her husband, whom she divorced, but with her lover, Morton Fullerton.[19]

Edith Wharton was one of the lucky ones. For countless

wives, sex was an abhorrent duty to which they submitted with grim loathing. In England, mothers counseled their daughters to "Close your eyes, lay flat on your back, grit your teeth, and sing two verses of Hail Britannia." The respected English gynecologist William Acton confirmed the belief that women had an attenuated, if not nonexistent, sex drive:

> As a general rule, a modest woman seldom desires any sexual gratification for herself. She submits to her husband's embraces, but principally to gratify him; and were it not for the desire of maternity, would far rather be relieved from his attentions.[20]

As evidence, Acton cited the case of a couple unable to conceive because they were both completely in the dark as to what to do. Convinced of the normalcy of living as platonic friends, they also desperately wanted a family. The wife said that she had loved her husband since childhood, but "assured me that she felt no sexual passions whatever." Her one desire was to do whatever was needed to become a mother; nor was her husband perturbed by her frigidity. For Dr. Acton such a woman is the

> perfect ideal of an English wife and mother . . . so pure-hearted as to be utterly ignorant of and adverse to any sensual indulgence, but so unselfishly attached to the man she loves, as to be willing to give up her own wishes and feelings for his sake.[21]

The gynecologist Henry Baker Brown took more draconian steps to promote female purity by surgically removing the locus of excitement and pleasure, the clitoris. Clitirodectomy, he wrote, wrought a remarkable transformation in patients suffering from psychosomatic illnesses caused by "peripheral excitement" or masturbation. After surgery these women became, in his view, normal and capable of becoming "a happy and healthy wife and mother."[22] Despite his good intentions, Dr. Brown was subsequently expelled from the Obstetrical Society for neglecting to inform his patients or their families about the radical nature of the surgery until after it was done.[23]

Today, we find such a practice horrific, although it is still widely practiced by various Muslim sects and African tribes, while such antiquated notions about sexuality seem to us merely amusing. Yet thanks to our Puritan forefathers, certain antiquated laws regulating sexuality derived from church law of the twelfth and thirteenth centuries remain extent. In some states the archaic English law that prescribed the death penalty for sodomy is still on the books, while in Nebraska the law allows child molesters to be castrated.[24] In several states today oral sex is a crime. Recently, an angry wife who understood the law better than her husband submitted to his demand for oral sex, then called the police who saw to it that he did penance for the act in a jail cell.*

Indeed, beneath our much-touted modern sexual freedom lies a substantial residue of guilt and shame about sexuality and the body. Some years ago Demi Moore created a sensation when she appeared pregnant and nude on the cover of *Vogue.* The edition sold out immediately. Only recently, a woman reporter was apprehended by the police while nursing her baby in a park in a suburban area of New York and threatened with arrest. The charge: indecent exposure in a public place.

In deeper and more hidden ways, American culture and mores continue to submit to the legacy of "Victorian" morality. Recent scientific studies of sexual practices in America suggest that prior to the "sexual revolution" of the sixties, women were conditioned to squelch their sexuality from childhood on in the most devastating way—shame about body parts, no touching of certain off-limits organs, the idea that orgasm was for husbands, not wives. It would seem that, deep within the psyche of men and women both, the ancient dichotomy still pertained—nice girl or bad girl, prude or whore. For women who remained trapped in it, the effect might be the failure to achieve full intimacy as

---

*As of July 2003 the Supreme Court has declared the sodomy laws unconstitutional.

sexual partners. Conversely, for men the price to be paid could be the guilt-ridden dishonesty of a "secret life."

Writer Marina Warner holds that even today the Virgin Mary remains the quintessential paradigm of woman for Catholic girls and women: "in thought, word and deed; her chastity, her humility, her gentleness."[25] Journalist Stephen Dunbar, a convert to Judaism raised as a Catholic, agrees. For his oldest sister, Mary, conversion was more difficult since she had been conditioned to emulate the Virgin "in every way when she was a girl."[26] Significantly, as soon as she got to college, Mary changed her name to Mona. For many women, however, the Virgin's image remains deeply buried in the psyche—not merely in respect to sexuality, but in a compulsion to live up to standards of perfection impossible to achieve; the "perfect" mother who never complains, never experiences fatigue or frustration, and always puts the needs of husband and children first.

That compulsion for perfection manifests itself in various other ways—the obsession with a female body divested of mature femininity, with cellulite-free thighs, board-flat tummies, and slender, boyish hips. To get that look models have been known to resort to the ultimate self mutilation, a hysterectomy, while any number of women abuse their bodies by rigorous dieting and grueling exercise programs. Ironically, the eating disorders that have become endemic among young women today have their parallel in the spiritual perfection sought by nuns of the Middle Ages, some of whom starved themselves to death on diets of lettuce and water.

Saint Catherine of Sienna, who periodically practiced austerities such as vows of silence and whipping herself with an iron chain, gave up meat and wine at an early age. From the age of sixteen on, she ate only bread, water, and raw vegetables. Eventually she gave up even bread, and finally water for almost a month. Needless to say, her death followed shortly thereafter.[27] St. Veronica, who adulated the Virgin Mary from earliest childhood, was a classic anorexic who could hold down nothing but bread and water (unless her food was mixed with the most disgusting ingredients; cat vomit, bits of rodents, hair). St. Clare of Assisi was reported to have fasted completely on Mondays, Wednesdays and Fridays. On other days she ate so little that her health declined. Eventually, her beloved friend, St. Francis, ordered that she eat a minimum of an ounce and a half of bread a day.[28]

Such extremes may seem irrelevant to today's woman. Yet in Jungian theory, the archetypes, like genes, are passed down from one generation to the next: "They are and have always been timeless . . . not contained within one man's personal life. We do not create them; they create us."[29] Buried deep within the collective unconscious, they shape our behavior, our psyche, our attitudes and actions. In that respect, to dismiss the myth of the Virgin Mary as irrelevant to a secular society is to deny the myriad influences that define woman. Certainly, it factors into the conception of woman as loving, nurturing, compassionate, compliant, self-denying—an ideal as difficult to realize for today's woman struggling with the competing demands of marriage, motherhood, work and competitive professional lives, as it has ever been .

As to those who have chosen another, more independent pathway, we have another archetype: Mary Magdalen.

CHAPTER 9

MARY MAGDALEN

> Jesus loved me, this I know
> Why on earth did I ever let him go?
> He was always faithful, he was always kind
> But he walked off with this heart of mine
> Richard Shindell, "The Ballad of Mary Magdalene"

One of the most compelling moments of Andrew Lloyd Webber's rock musical *Jesus Christ Superstar* is Mary Magdalen's singing of the lovely "I Don't Know How to Love Him." A seductive woman with a compromised past, she finds herself painfully aware of a wholly new experience. Musing on Jesus's strange effect on her, she struggles to redefine the meaning of love and the word lover. In that Webber draws from long-standing tradition of the Magdalen as the sinner who achieves redemption through her love for Jesus. In the popular mind, however, she remains the quintessential fallen woman—in vulgar terms, the whore.

In actual fact the Mary of Magdala of the Gospels was a highly respected figure, perhaps even the most important of Jesus's women followers, for she played a central role at the most crucial juncture of his brief ministry—his death and resurrection. Both the Gospels of Mark and John make it clear that she is the first to whom the risen Christ appears. Of itself an extraordinary honor, in John the scene is emotionally laden, dramatic and mysterious.

Later, as the Jesus movement began to define itself as separate from its Jewish roots, Mary Magdalen once again appears as a central figure in the strange and enigmatic Apocryphal Gospels. Fantastical as their stories may be, they have much to tell us about what early Christians thought of Mary Magdalen, thus putting some flesh on the bare bones of the Magdalen of the synoptic Gospels. Here Mary Magdalen is portrayed as gifted teacher and visionary, Jesus's closest female companion, closer even than his mother. Jesus's special love for her provokes the jealousy of the male disciples. Indeed, she is referred to as a female disciple, a proposition that would become anathema to an increasingly patriarchal Church.

From that seed as well springs the legend that the Magdalen was Jesus's lover, or even his wife, while later legend embroidered her story even further. In one tradition she becomes a hermit; a holy woman fed by angels. In another she is a gifted missionary/preacher who travels to southern France, converts its rulers to Christianity, and with her companion, Maximus, founds the city of Aix. By the twelfth century her cult in the south of France was so famous that pilgrims came from far and wide to venerate her in the magnificent Church of the Magdalene in Vezelay. Even today her connection to the grail legend stands at the center of the sensational mystery novel *The Da Vinci Code,* provoking a storm of controversy.

Oddly enough, while Brown's novel has catapulted Mary Magdalen into fame as the obligatory wife for a human Jesus, it tells us nothing at all about her actual persona. Nor has her transition from whore to wife entirely dislodged her from her traditional role as Christianity's primary symbol for sin and redemption; the archetypal fallen woman who repents of her wayward life, abandons her life of luxury and dissipation, and is forgiven.

Actually, as with Mary, Jesus's mother, we know very little of the New Testament Mary of Magdala, otherwise known as Tarichaea, a prosperous fishing village located on the western side of the Sea of Galilee. In all four Gospels she appears as one of the women who were healed by Jesus and became his followers. In Mark and Luke, however, she is singled out as having been exorcised of not one but "seven devils," on the basis of which some have assumed that she must have been mad. As the historian William Klingaman puts it, the Magdalen "had never been married; she was far too emotionally and psychologically disturbed for that."[1] More sympathetic scholars have suggested that the "seven devils" passage was merely an interpolation intended to demean her because she had become too influential in the early Church. Like other women with too much power, the problem was resolved by dismissing her as a madwoman.

As one of the few women cited by name and place in the Gospels, Mary of Magdala was undoubtedly a figure of some importance. The fact that she traveled with Jesus and his followers suggests that she was a mature woman—in ancient times any one past their teens. More than likely she was a widow who came from the wealthier classes, since she must have had resources of her own—property or wealth of some kind inherited from a deceased husband. As to age, we are in the dark. However, at a time when women married at puberty, about age twelve to fourteen, widows were often young women, possibly even in their twenties or thirties. Most important, a widow had a rare thing for a woman: independence. Indeed, unlike other women followers of Jesus, in her case neither husband nor son is mentioned, compounding her mystery. Yet widowhood would have allowed her to travel about the countryside without drawing the ire of the community as a disreputable woman.

As to her affliction, her "seven devils," in ancient times any illness, physical or mental, was commonly regarded as caused by demonic possession. However, the Magdalen's seven devils might have signified something positive, for the number seven had mystical connotations, and in the Apocryphal Gospels she is a woman who has visions. Above all, her encounter with the risen Christ, as described in *John,* stresses a powerful and instinctive faith and a close bond to Jesus. Whatever the case, any of the aforementioned attributes might have posed a threat to the male disciples, especially in the confusion following the loss of their leader, and later in the ensuing debate about the role of women as the Church began to move back to the traditional patriarchalism of antiquity.

Close reading of the dark events leading to Jesus's arrest and trial raise some thorny questions about how Jesus's close followers reacted to his foreboding, his morose state of mind as they approached Jerusalem. As told in Mark's *Gospel,* the time is the Passover, the place just outside the city proper. Jesus knows very well the danger at hand, for powerful Jewish authorities have been smarting under his criticism, while the Roman authorities are always especially wary of any sign of Jewish resistance during Passover. After sharing a ritual meal with his disciples, Jesus tells them that on this night one of them will betray him, all of them will lose faith, and Peter will "disown" him three times before the cock crows. Shocked at the very idea, Peter protests, "Even if I have to die with you, I will never disown you." The rest of the disciples echo that promise.

Later that night they arrive at Gethsemane, and Jesus says, "My heart is ready to break with grief; stop here and stay awake." Three times he asks the disciples to keep vigil with him, three times he finds them sleeping. When an armed crowd sent by priests, scribes and elders comes to arrest him, only one of his followers resists, cutting off the ear of the high priest's servant. The rest scatter in panic: "then the disciples all deserted him and ran away." All in all, the scene is a melee of fear, confusion, desertion (Mark 14:26-72).

Later, Peter lurks about the courtyard outside the Council Chamber hoping to find out something about its proceedings. The crowd becomes suspicious, and accuses him of being one of Jesus's followers. Three times he denies it, and when the cock crows he bursts into tears, overcome by remorse. Judas Iscariot, too, fulfills Jesus's prophesy by accepting a bribe for providing the court with the evidence they need to bring charges.

Peter's faintness of heart becomes understandable in light of the Roman's well-known penchant for cruelty. Crucifixion, a punishment already inflicted on thousands of rebels, was a brutal, drawn out method of execution. Prior to the execution itself, condemned prisoners were brutally tortured and scourged with metal studded whips that flayed their bodies. After being nailed to the cross, death came from slow, agonizing suffocation due to the collapse of the rib cage. Often, birds of prey swooped down upon the limp, mangled bodies while they still clung to life by a fragile thread.

In Jesus's case, the suffering was prolonged, since he was not granted the privilege of having his legs broken, thereby throwing the unsupported body forward to hasten the collapse of the lungs. Nor would he allow himself to be drugged by taking wine laced with myrrh. And through the waves of wrenching pain and dreadful thirst came the jeers and taunts of an ugly crowd. Perhaps, too, Peter's oath echoed in Jesus's waning consciousness: "Even if I must die with you, I will never disown you."

In the end they all did, except for three of his women followers: Mary, the mother of James the younger and Joseph; Salomé; and Mary of Magdala. Choking back the great wail of grief for fear that the crowd would turn on them, they silently "watched from a distance." For seven hours Jesus's courage held out. At nine in the morning the soldiers drove the huge nails through his palms and feet, at mid-day, the sky turned black -a metaphor for the tenebrous pain enveloping his body. Finally, at three o'clock Jesus gave a great cry of despair: *"Eli, Eli, lema sabachtani?"* ("My God, my God, why hast thou forsaken me?") The echo of that disconsolate cry would resonate throughout time—stark symbol of suffering mankind, alone in a silent universe. And only Jesus's women followers were there to hear it (Mark 15: 33-41).*

In the ancient world the real horror of crucifixion was the dread of a body left on the cross for ravenous, flesh-eating crows and wild dogs.[2] Denied proper burial, the deceased's soul would never find rest. In this case Joseph of Arimathaea, an important council-member, persuaded Pilate to let him have the body, despite Pilate's astonishment that Jesus had expired so soon. Wrapping it in a linen shroud, Joseph interred the body in a hollowed out rock sealed with a huge stone, since Jewish law forbade the burial of those executed as criminals in common burial places.

Meanwhile, the three women watch silently, noting the burial site, for anointing the body and mourning was "women's work." Immediately after the Sabbath they purchase the necessary sweet-smelling oils, arriving at the tomb just after sunrise on Sunday. To their amazement, the huge rock is rolled back. Inside the tomb is a young man dressed in a white robe who tells them, "Jesus of Nazareth who was crucified . . . has been raised again; he is not here." He instructs them to tell the

---

disciples and Peter that Jesus has gone ahead to Galilee and will meet them there.

Terrified by what they take for a ghostly apparition, the women nevertheless relay the message to "Peter and his companions." But only later, when Jesus himself appears to them, do the men begin their mission.

Quite abruptly, Mark's narrative shifts back to the tomb where, on Sunday morning, Jesus "appeared *first* to Mary of Magdala from whom he had driven out seven devils." Now it is she alone who reports the miracle to the men who refuse to believe her. Later, Jesus appears as a stranger to two of the male followers, but again "no one believed them." For the third time, Jesus appears to the disciples while at table, "and reproached them for their incredulity and dullness." Only then do they mobilize themselves to go out and proclaim the gospel, the great news, to the world (Mark 15:42, 16:1-20).

In this spare but remarkable passage Mark accords Mary of Magdala an extraordinary honor. She is the first not only to *see* but to *believe in* the risen Christ and to announce the 'good news' to the disciples. In that respect her importance is immeasurable, for the resurrection is the key article of faith on which Christianity rests, the singular event that transformed an essentially localized Messianic movement within Judaism into a vigorously assertive religion that would transcend its Palestinian origins. It is here that Christianity begins to veer away from its Jewish roots, for without the Resurrection Jesus would have been merely another great Hebrew prophet.

In Matthew's *Gospel* the story of the tomb is slightly altered. Here only Mary mother of James and Joseph and Mary Magdalen arrive at the tomb where Pilate, at the instigation of the Jewish priests, has posted guards to insure that Jesus's followers do not steal the body, then claim that he had risen. Suddenly, the earth trembles as in a violent earthquake, and an angel descends from heaven to role away the stone. The guards collapse, quaking in fear, and the angel tells the women: "Jesus is raised from the dead and is going ahead of you into Galilee."

Abruptly, Jesus appears to them directly. Dropping to their knees, they embrace his feet, then hurry off to carry their message to the disciples. The guards, too, rush to relate the supernatural event to the chief priest, who bribes them to say that Jesus's disciples came and stole the body during the night. That story, Matthew says, "became widely known, and is current in Jewish circles to this day." Later, Jesus appears to the Disciples at the appointed place in Galilee and tells them to go forth and teach, knowing that "I am with you always, to the end of time" (Matt. 27:62-28:20).

Matthew may have been concerned to dispel rumors that have survived to the present day that Jesus either survived his ordeal, or that his followers took the body, thereby disproving the resurrection. Possibly, too, Matthew reflects a more conservative Jewish faction who may have felt uncomfortable in awarding a woman the honor of first to witness the resurrection. Indeed, in the ensuing scramble to fill the vacuum created by Jesus's execution, the Magdalen's influence may have become increasingly problematic, as did Jesus's somewhat radical inclusion of women in the work at hand.

Once again, in Luke's *Gospel* we have a somewhat altered version of the final events. Here two criminals are crucified alongside Jesus, while many in the crowd openly express their grief: "they went home beating their breasts." Watching from a distance are the women from Galilee: Mary of Magdala, Joanna, and Mary, mother of James. All three go to the tomb on Sunday morning where "two men in dazzling garments" appear to announce that Jesus has risen. They rush to tell the disciples, who declare the story "to be nonsense. . . . (They) would not believe them." Even when Jesus appears to the disciples in various forms they remain skeptical, and he admonishes them: "How dull you are!" When some of them declare that the apparition is a ghost,

Jesus invites them to touch him, and eats a piece of fish to prove his corporeality (Luke 23:48-24:43).

Most striking, in Luke's *Gospel* principal blame for Jesus's execution is shifted from Pilate and his Jewish puppet Herod to the Jewish Council, who trump up charges of nonpayment of taxes, subversion, and fomenting unrest "among the people all over Judea"—the latter two incurring the death penalty.* Strangely, both Pilate and Herod, two of the most notoriously brutal and sadistic governors of the period, are made to appear sympathetic to Jesus. They propose reducing the sentence to flogging, but the chief priests insist on the death penalty. When Pilate declares Jesus innocent of insurrection, the mob shouts, "Crucify him, crucify him" (Luke 23:5-25).

That Luke, a Gentile Christian writing in 90 C.E., white-washes Pilate and his Jewish puppet Herod might well have something to do with a highly charged political climate. That either Herod or Pilate would concern themselves with the fate of a powerless Jewish prophet flies in the face of historical reality. More likely is the fact that by that time many Christians were converted Romans with ample reason for placating the authorities: the horrors attendant on revolt against Rome were still fresh in their memories.

Some might remember that in 4 B.C.E., after a Jewish revolt following the death of the hated Herod the elder, some two thousand suspected rebels were crucified as reported by the Jewish historian, Josephus. More recently, in the wake of the Roman-Jewish war of 66 C.E., some "three thousand six hundred" Jews were crucified, including "peaceable citizens," and women and children. Finally, after the ultimate calamity, the destruction of the Temple in 70 C.E., Roman soldiers indulged in an orgy of wrath. Upwards of five hundred captives a day were

---

*Earlier in this text Jesus does speak an inflammatory language of revolution: "Be ready for action, with belts fastened and lamps alight. . . . I have come to set fire to the earth," etc. (see Luke 12:35-53).

crucified "in different postures; and so great was their number, that space could not be found for the crosses nor crosses for the bodies."[3]

Little wonder that some Christians sought to disassociate themselves from the Jews. To incite the Romans further would be suicidal. Tragically, by assigning blame for the crucifixion to the mobs and the Jewish authorities, they effectively branded a homeless, defenseless people with a crime that would haunt them throughout centuries of hapless wanderings.[4]*

By contrast, in John's *Gospel* the narrative concerns itself with issues of authority and leadership, as in Matthew, rather than political issues. Yet, it is here that the tomb scene becomes the stuff of great literature, and the bedrock for the legend of the Magdalen as Jesus's lover. Indeed, *John*'s dramatic rendering of that seminal moment when the risen Christ appears to the Magdalen seems strangely out of keeping with an otherwise pragmatic concern—who was first to comprehend the great miracle; either Peter, or the "beloved disciple" (John himself in the view of some scholars), or Mary Magdalen.

John also smoothes over certain troubling aspects of the passion story. Here the disciples are not at all skeptical, no one sleeps while Jesus prays, and there is none of the tumult, confusion and panic at Gethsemane.† *John*'s account of the crucifixion is also strangely lacking in drama. There are no supernatural events—no earthquakes or darkening of the sky. Jesus's suffering is down-played, his last words being, "I thirst," in fulfillment of scripture. After receiving a sponge soaked with wine to his parched lips, he murmurs "It is accomplished," bows his head, and dies.

---

*Of course, this can hardly be taken as an indictment of Jews per se, but of a faction that many regarded as corrupt, self-seeking, and indifferent to the growing plight of the poor and dispossessed.

†John does, however, whitewash Pilate by having him offer to hand Jesus over to the Jewish court, who refuse, saying, "We have no king but Caesar" (John 19:15).

Gathered at the foot of the cross are four Marys: Mary the wife of Cleopas, Jesus's mother, her sister (also Mary), and Mary of Magdala, as well as a male follower—the enigmatic "beloved disciple." Here Joseph of Arimathaea and Nicodemus claim the body, place it in a tomb located in a garden, and perform the embalming themselves. On Sunday morning Mary Magdalen goes alone to the tomb to mourn, only to find it empty. She rushes back to tell the "beloved disciple" and Simon Peter, both of whom race to the tomb, "side by side." The former arrives first, but both men acknowledge the great miracle, making them the first to *believe* in the resurrection. However, it is Mary Magdalen who first *sees* the risen Christ, for after the men leave she remains at the tomb, weeping.

Venturing inside, she sees two angels in white who ask why she weeps. She answers that she doesn't know where the body is. Turning to leave, she sees a figure, standing outside in the muted, shadowy light of sunrise whom she takes to be the gardener. He too asks why she weeps, and she implores him to tell her where the body is. But when he calls her by name, Mary, she instantly recognizes him, exclaiming "*Rabbuni,*" the intimate word for teacher or master. Instinctively she stretches out her arms to embrace him, but he draws back, warning," Do not cling to me, for I have not yet ascended to the father. But go to my brothers and tell them I am now ascending to my father and your father, to my God and your God." Ecstatic, she rushes to tell the disciples, "I have seen the Lord!" (John 20:17-18)

Writer Reynolds Price has called this compelling episode "an extraordinary moment in world history and literature."[5] With deceptive simplicity John has suggested an experience of rapture that supersedes the theological meaning of the resurrection. Rather, he describes a deeply human phenomenon—the pain and grief in facing a world in which a loved one no longer moves, talks, listens, touches with tender love. Yet that person's spirit may be so deeply imprinted upon the consciousness as to materialize, called up by memory, longing, imagination.

In that respect that jubilant encounter in the garden adds a powerful emotional dimension to the idea of resurrection, or of a spirit life beyond death. Biblical scholar and writer Elaine Pagels said in an interview with Teri Gross on NPR's *Fresh Air* that after her husband's death she often felt his spirit in the house, in a familiar room or place accessible only to her. Others have testified that after the death of a spouse they sensed his or her spirit in their home, and talked to them as though they were there. Clearly we are not dealing with the supernatural here, but with a presence etched in the mind and soul—a laugh, a glance, a familiar voice that materializes out of a deep residue of memory.

Indeed, John's powerful rendition of the Magdalen's encounter with the risen Christ is as much a matter of love as of faith. She alone returns to the tomb to locate the body and anoint it as an act of compassion and tender care. Denied this final rite of devotion, she remains in the darkened tomb, weeping. And in the soft light and playing shadows of dawn, she alone sees a figure visible only to the eye that so longingly seeks it.

The passages that follow have neither the drama nor the poetry of her encounter with the risen Christ. Jesus appears to the disciples, still huddled behind locked doors. When he displays his wounds they believe him except for the "doubting" Thomas. A week later, Jesus materializes through the locked door of their house and invites Thomas to put his hand into the wound on his side, saying, "Because you have seen me you have found faith. Happy are they who find faith without seeing me" (John 20:29).

That faith would become the essence of Christianity, the belief in a miracle seen by only a few of Jesus's closest followers, the belief that the risen Christ was not merely a spirit, a ghost walking through solid wood doors, but a man of solid flesh. Yet, the Thomas story lacks the intimacy of the Magdalen's encounter. For her, faith is mixed with a heightened spirituality, the intimation of a supernatural vision granted her because of unique gifts which we will consider shortly.

By contrast, *John*'s treatment of the risen Christ's appearance to his male followers seems more political than spiritual. After further appearances and miracles, the narrative concludes with Jesus conferring leadership on Peter who, Jesus predicts, will die a martyr's death much like his own. Scholars today believe that Peter had assumed leadership of the Jerusalem Church by the time John was written, making the conferring of legitimacy no accident here. Yet, it is John's telling of that compelling moment of recognition in the garden that would inspire countless artists in future. For those who would search for a human Jesus capable of loving a woman, his account would confirm it.

As attractive as that legend may be, in the long run it has done the Magdalen an injustice. Not only does it detract from her true role in the original Jesus Movement, it has fed the legend casting her as "lost" or sexual woman, thereby demeaning both her person and that compelling moment of exaltation and hope at the tomb. Yet the recent discovery of the Apocryphal Gospels suggests that certain sects within early Christianity regarded the Magdalen as a key disciple (possibly even the mysterious "beloved disciple"), a gifted and respected teacher, and the embodiment of the ancient principle of feminine wisdom in which knowledge and love meld into one.

CHAPTER 10

"SOME CALL HER LOVE"

"She spoke as a woman who knew the All."
Dialogue of the Savior

There is, as we have seen, much mystery about the great mystery central to Christianity, the resurrection. To make matters even worse, within twenty years after the crucifixion hundreds of gospels with conflicting and often fantastical accounts of the passion story were circulated, further compounding the enigma. For the second-century bishop Papias of Hierapolis, their quirky, fantastical stories were closer to the beating heart of Christianity than the official Canonical Gospels: "I suppose that materials derived from "the books" did not help me as much as those from a living and continuous voice."[1]

Even today there is something compelling in their eccentric tales. Bizarre as they may seem to the modern reader, they tell us what common folk believed before the Church hammered out an official dogma. In particular, they suggest that in the early Church Mary of Magdala was regarded by many as a woman of exceptional wisdom, a gifted teacher, and in one of the earliest of these texts, the *Gospel of Peter*, as "a woman disciple of the Lord."[2]

In *Peter's* highly embellished version of the resurrection story two figures descend from heaven, enter the tomb and emerge supporting a third man. A huge cross follows their ascent back to the heavens, and a booming voice responds "Yea." When Pilate hears what happened from the terrified guards, he believes the rumors that Jesus is Son of God, and shifts the blame for his death to the Jewish authorities. Fearful that they will be stoned by their own people, they convince Pilate to keep the fulfillment of the prophecy a secret at all costs.[3]

Meanwhile Mary Magdalen and her companions are shocked to find an empty tomb, but they have no one to tell. Disheartened by the loss of their leader, the male disciples have scattered and are either in hiding or returned to their homes and farms, or in the case of Peter and his brother Andrew, to their fishing nets at sea. Unfortunately, *Peter* ends here in mid-sentence, leaving us dangling as to further events.

In various other Gnostic Gospels *Peter*'s identification of Mary Magdalen as disciple is not only echoed, her singularity is underscored. Most striking, in the *Gospel of Thomas* she is accorded what for the Gnostics is the highest honor for a woman—she becomes a man. Thus, when Jesus tells the disciples that they can enter the Kingdom only "when you make the male and the female one and the same," Peter seizes this opportunity to exclude Mary Magdalen: "Let Mary leave us, for women are not worthy of Life." But Jesus says,

> I myself will lead her in order to make her male, so that she too may become a living spirit resembling you males. For every woman who will make herself male will enter the kingdom of heaven.[4]

In so doing Jesus confers upon her the highest distinction, for as the Zostrianos put it, "Flee from the madness and bondage of femaleness, and choose for yourself the salvation of maleness." Philo of Alexandria too held that in becoming male a woman sheds her female passivity and slavishness to her body. To become a man is to become "active, rational, incorporeal and more akin to mind and thought."[5] Indeed, the natural and inborn superiority of men was accepted throughout the ancient world by the most distinguished minds, including Plato and Aristotle.

Yet in the Gnostic *Dialogue of the Savior,* Mary Magdalen not only remains female, she epitomizes the ancient Hebrew tradition of the *Shekinah,* or in Greek the *Sophia*—a specifically feminine, intuitive wisdom that has privileged access to divine revelation, not unlike the female sibyls who received oracles from the Greek gods.* Thus, in one dialogue three disciples, Mariam (the Magdalen), Judas, and Matthew, ask Jesus to tell them about the two worlds of good and evil; heaven and earth. When Matthew begs to see heaven where "there is no evil," Jesus replies, "you cannot see it, as long as you wear the flesh." But when Mariam asks about the beginnings of evil, Jesus promises to reveal the essential mystery to her in a "great vision."

Here the Magdalen has the special gift of a mystic or a visionary, something that was especially valued in the early Church. In the case of Paul, his validity as an Apostle rested on his vision of Jesus on the road to Damascus, since he had never encountered him in person. As to the Magdalen, perhaps her alleged "seven devils" was related to her gift, for prior to their seizures epileptics commonly experience intense flashes of light and visual distortions. Moreover, the tradition of women as mystics was deeply rooted in the ancient Jewish belief in wisdom as tripartite. Both *Hokhma,* abstract knowledge, and *Da,* applied knowledge, were considered masculine, while *Bina,* the intuitive knowledge essential to mystical revelation, was feminine

---

*A composite figure drawn from ancient Goddesses who are at once consort, mother, and principle of wisdom, the *Shekinah* can also be androgynous.

The *Dialogue of the Savior* harps on this very notion. When Mary Magdalen asks Jesus, "Tell me lord, why I have come to this place, to benefit or suffer loss?" he answers that her purpose is to teach and convey privileged knowledge "Because you reveal the greatness of the revealer." At the same time, in her various dialogues with Jesus she is "a woman who had understood completely", or as she puts it in her own words, "I want to understand all things, just as they are." When she does, indeed, astound the disciples by explaining the meaning of certain obtuse parables, they too concur. With one voice they declare: "she spoke as a woman who knew the All."[6]

This notion is expanded in one of the most complete of these texts, *The Gospel of Philip*. Here the Magdalen is one of a triad of Marys, including Jesus's mother and her sister who "always used to walk with the Lord." Only Mary Magdalen, however, "was called his companion," only she possesses the special "Wisdom . . . called 'the barren.' " Not only that, Jesus "often . . . kissed her on her [mouth]," provoking the jealousy of the disciples.* Petulantly they ask, "Why do you love her more than all of us?" Jesus answers with a parable. In the dark, two men, one blind and one sighted, are exactly alike. But in the light only the sighted man can see, while the blind man remains in darkness.[7]

Clearly, the parable refers to the Magdalen's special wisdom. Yet those who would see her as Jesus's lover have focused on the kiss, injecting an erotic element into passages that must be understood in light of the peculiarities of Gnostic thought. For one thing, in antiquity kissing was a common manner of greeting, even between men as it still is in parts of Europe, the Middle-East, and Latin America today. In the *Second Apocalypse of James,* Jesus "greets his brother James with a kiss on the mouth.," and in Gethsemane Judas betrays Jesus to the captors with a kiss. Paul regularly greeted and took leave of fellow Christians with a

---

*Caps indicate words obscured from original text.

kiss, instructing them to "Greet one another with the kiss of peace" no less than four times in his letters.[8]

That kissing was between men and women we know from the "kiss of peace," exchanged in church after mass well into the Middle Ages, sometimes a bit too enthusiastically. Eventually it was banned as being too erotic; today most churches encourage parishioners to hug or shake hands after mass or service.

More important is the Gnostic's insistent habit of spiritualizing all things, even sexuality. For them the principle function of the mouth is neither erotic, nor as a vessel to receive food that nourishes the body. Rather, the mouth is the organ of speech which conveys wisdom via the word—nourishment for the soul. A kiss, then, is a sacred thing, a means by which two people exchange "grace [from] one another."[9] In so doing, knowledge and love become one.

Perhaps, then, it is this extraordinary equivalence of love and wisdom that holds the key to Jesus's exceptional love for the Magdalen, the "woman who knows the All." That very notion - wisdom seasoned by love - runs throughout *The Sophia of Jesus Christ,* a text concerned with the essential nature of wisdom and truth. Here Jesus teaches that pure intellect must merge with love in order to attain the higher world. Thus, when the "First man, the Begetter" unites with his consort, the "Great Sophia", in the mystical Bridal Chamber, their androgynous offspring's female name is "Sophia, Mother of the Universe". As such, "Some call her Love."[10]

As we know from the diaries of the famous mystic, St. Theresa of Avilla, that ecstatic moment of revelation often comes as an overwhelming sensation of love—at once sensuous and spiritual, but not carnal. Rather, in *Philip's* Bridal Chamber love transcends the sexual to become wholly spiritual; "Spiritual love is wine and fragrance. All those who anoint themselves with it take pleasure in it."[11] Taken in this context, Jesus's love for Mary Magdalen has everything to do with wisdom, and nothing to do with eroticism.

In her own Gospel, the *Gospel of Mary,* this notion is emphasized. Once again, Jesus loves her more and transmits special knowledge through her, hence her reputation as teacher. In one passage, for example, she explicates Jesus's position on sin and evil. Both are man-made: "There is no sin, but it is you who make sin." As in traditional Jewish thinking, sin is an illness, an asymmetry with nature to be overcome by "restoring [one's nature] to its proper root"; in other words, to health and wholeness.

Here, too, she assuages the doubts and fears of the disciples, spurring them on to the work of evangelizing. After Jesus blesses them, he tells them to go out and preach, but they are bound by fear: "If they did not spare him, how will they spare us?" At this Mary Magdalen takes charge: "Do not weep, and do not grieve nor be irresolute . . . [for] he has prepared *us* and made *us* into men."(my italics). As they continue to flounder, this double entendre provokes Peter. Again he demands to know why "the Savior loved you more than the rest of the women." Jesus himself gives the answer—the Magdalen was the first to see him in his resurrected form, and "did not waver at the sight of me. For where the mind is, there is the treasure." But the Magdalen insists that her visions are not transmitted through the mind alone, but through soul and spirit as well. This is too much for Peter, who angrily accuses her of lying. Andrew, too, denounces her unorthodoxy: "these teachings are certainly strange ideas." *

---

*Gnosticism was eventually condemned as heretical, yet its ideas were never suppressed altogether, as witness the "seven deadly sins" of medieval Christianity, Michelangelo's, The Bound Slave, metaphor for soul's ongoing struggle to escape the "prison" of the body, seventeenth century English Evangelism, with its belief in the ongoing battle between the powers of good and evil, God and Satan. In eighteenth century America there was the transcendentalist belief in a dual world, the real and the ideal world of goodness and beauty. In our own time we encounter Gnostic ideas in the cult film *Star Wars* with its battle between the "forces" of good against Darth Vader and the "forces"

Surely, Peter says, Jesus would not have spoken so intimately to a woman, or preferred her to his male disciples. Bursting into tears, Mary asks if "My brother Peter [thinks] I am lying about the Savior?" At this point Levi intervenes:

> Peter, you have always been hot-tempered. . . . [I]f the Savior made her worthy, who are you to reject her? Surely the Savior knows her very well. That is why he loved her more than us. . . . [D]o as he commanded us, and preach the gospel.

Reminded of their ultimate purpose, the disciples reconcile the divisive breach. Together they set out to "proclaim and to preach."[12]

Interestingly, other anecdotal material also refers to Peter's hot temper. In one story, Peter's wrath was so deadly that a messenger who delivered a lie to him was struck dead on the spot.[13] More important, however, is the suggestion here of a tension between those who accepted Jesus's unorthodoxies about women, and traditionalists who would keep them in their place. As leader of the Jerusalem Church and the Hebraic party, Peter might well have taken issue with the various roles—teacher, visionary, evangelist—assigned Mary Magdalen in the Gospel of Mary. By contrast, the acknowledgement of the Magdalen's special gifts in the Gospel of Philip may reflect the fact that Philip, a 'Hellenist', had four daughters known for their gift of prophecy.

Taken in toto, these remarkable passages suggest that the Magdalen's assertiveness and special status was problematic for those who shared the common view of women. Yet they imply that some of the disciples, at least, were willing to accept her not only as equal, but as a gifted visionary who can tap into the supernatural. Most important, they describe a unique spirituality that bound her to Jesus, a man for whom the Kingdom of God was vivid; more real, perhaps, than a cruel and corrupt world. If

---

of evil.

for the disciples the Kingdom was a mystery, for Jesus it was immediate, the only true home he knew. And constantly we are told that Mary Magdalen understood this man with one foot in this world, and one foot already in his father's Kingdom. If it was to her that he revealed himself in his reincarnated form, perhaps it was the impulse of like spirits seeking one another.

The notion of the Magdalen as a mystic was also an idea very much in keeping with a long-standing Jewish tradition of women as mystics. Such temperaments have always been labeled as dangerous, even mad. In her case, however, the threat was compounded by the fact that she had had far too much power for a woman. Throughout history, and even today, society deals with such hussies by labeling them as whores.

Mary Magdalen's reputation also suffered from her association with the Gnostics, their fantastical stories and extreme beliefs, and the calumnies heaped upon them. In time they were cast out of main stream Christianity, especially those who lay claim to magical powers. Some Gnostic leaders, in fact, were exposed as downright charlatans.

One such person had a special appeal for wealthy matrons who turned over not only their worldly goods, but their bodies when he initiated them into the "bridal bedchamber." Some sects were rumored to engage in ritual intercourse, "holding their women in common." As rumors proliferated they became as fantastic as the texts themselves. It was said that certain sects mocked the Eucharist by offering up semen ejaculated during sex in prayer, others aborted infants, ground their remains with mortar and pestle, seasoned them with "honey, pepper, and other spices" on which they dined.[14]

Eventually the Gnostics would be brutally persecuted as heretics, slaughtered and burned, their writings suppressed and destroyed. Yet, certain of their beliefs, in particular the ongoing war between flesh and spirit, were incorporated into Christian theology, culminating in St. Augustine's doctrine of Original Sin.

Similarly, the idea of the Magdalen as Jesus's close companion would be incorporated into popular folklore. However, their peculiar notion of a spiritual love completely divested of sensuality eludes the modern mind, as does the notion of the *Sophia "whom some call love."*

Instead, that melding of wisdom and love has been suppressed along with the Gnostic "heresies." Indeed, as myth and legend proliferated, the radiant light exuded by the wise woman of the Gnostic Gospels would be extinguished by the dank misery of the primal whore.

CHAPTER 11

A Confusion of Marys

Mary, Mary, quite contrary, how does your garden grow?
Nursery rhyme

Clearly, the transformation of Mary Magdalen would be neither rapid nor wholly definitive. Legends concerning her special gifts continued to proliferate well into the Middle Ages and beyond. One claims that she traveled to the city of Ephesus (today in modern Turkey) where she lived for forty years with the Virgin and John, the beloved disciple, and was martyred. Supposedly, her severed head was placed in the famous Cave of the Seven Sleepers in which seven Christian men were buried alive, but awoke 200 years later. That Cave became an important shrine to the Magdalen, attracting pilgrims from all over Europe and Byzantium.

In the south of France, in Provence, her importance as preacher and evangelist remains even today. In the ninth century a splendid Abbey dedicated to the Magdalen at Vezelay became a powerful center of her cult. In 1265, the stunning news that her body was had been miraculously discovered there made the Abbey a major site for pilgrims who attested to miraculous healings. That reputation remains to this very day at Vezelay where the Magdalen is venerated as a saint almost equivalent to the Virgin.

How, then, did such a respected figure become a symbol for female degradation? The answer, of course, is complex, coming from several sources—mythology, confusion resulting from parallel stories and nameless women in the New Testament, the work of misogynists who needed a symbol for women's inborn corruption, hence the Magdalen as polar opposite of the Virgin's absolute purity.

There was, too, the turmoil that ensued when Jesus's followers found themselves adrift, deprived of their charismatic leader. If, as John tells us, Mary Magdalen stretched out her arms to the newly risen Christ in the murky light of sunrise, then she stood at the very crossroad of faith. If, as the Gnostics contend, she confounded the disciples with her wisdom, she was clearly a figure to be reckoned with. Yet to be so honored is also to invite envy and resentment. What better way to bring her down than to make her a whore rather than a key player in the birth pangs of Christianity?

A radical proposition, perhaps. Yet Peter's special vexation with her may well reflect fractious arguments about leadership at a time of chaos and confusion. In Gnostic tradition she repeatedly crossed boundaries by appropriating male functions, infuriating the disciples, not to mention an occasional sex change. With her privileged knowledge, her irritating habit of "taking charge," her audacity in explaining the meaning of Jesus's teachings, such a woman might easily offend. Such things were surely an abomination for Jewish traditionalists who held that women should not read the Torah, teach, or engage in public disputations. As the first-century Rabbi Eliezer put it: "Rather should the words of the Torah be burned than entrusted to a woman."[1]

For Roman converts as well, a woman in a leadership position would be uncomfortable; in fact, most of the Roman *collegia,* some of which were religious, were exclusively male. Yet, in the early Church women did assume various leadership roles from Bishops, "ruler" or "mother of the synagogue," to elders, priests, preachers, even prophets. Clearly the Magdalen was not alone.[2] One of the great attractions of early Christianity was its notion of equality of the sexes in the eyes of God. Roman women, especially, felt themselves little better than menial slaves under the stern patriarchalism of Rome. It is surely no coincidence that many Roman women of the noble classes converted to Christianity in company with their female slaves, becoming fierce adherents to the outlaw religion. Some bravely, even eagerly embraced martyrdom.

As Christianity became more mainstream, the problem of women's roles became an ever more thorny issue, especially for Paul. A Roman citizen born in Tarsus, Paul was not one of Jesus's original followers, having encountered him only in a dazzling vision on the road to Damascus. However, he came from a strongly traditional Jewish family who sent him to Jerusalem to be educated in the rabbinical school of Gamaliel. Even after his dramatic conversion, Paul drew on his rabbinical training, preaching in Hebrew when necessary. Perhaps, too, in his deepest heart Paul's view of women was more traditional than that of Jesus.

A certain physical awkwardness and the fact that he never married have led some to conclude that Paul had a pronounced reticence about women. Actually, Paul was not at all the rabid misogynist some have made him out to be. Rather, he held that men and women were equal in the Lord. He himself enjoyed warm relationships with several women leaders of Christian communities for whom he had the highest respect, as he did for Thecla, his colleague in missionary work. But as a pragmatist Paul recognized the problems inherent in women transcending traditional roles.

By engaging in prophesizing, teaching, preaching, evangelizing, they left themselves open to censure; to engage in such activities was to risk losing both modesty and reputation. Paul's famous dictum that "women were to keep silence in the church" was meant as much to protect them as to shield men from temptation.* Such activities also threatened the very fabric of marriage, which rested on a wife's subordination to her husband, inviting chaos and social instability. If women seek knowledge, said Paul, "Let them ask their husbands at home."

Equally powerful in eroding the position of women in the evolving Church was the growing hysteria about chastity. In that battle woman was the prime enemy, in Tertullian's words the "devil's gateway." As in every propaganda war, a lucid, immediately recognizable symbol was needed. Yet only by a strange and circuitous reasoning did Mary Magdalen come to fill that slot—the seductress polluted by primordial sin, a scapegoat for men's loathing of their own sexuality.

For that, she would have to undergo a radical transformation, a task made easier by the fact that the masses were illiterate. Unable to read the Gospels for themselves, confusion about her person was inevitable. To begin, with so many Marys and unnamed women in the Gospel stories, there were bound to be mistaken identities. The old nursery rhyme, "Mary, Mary, quite contrary," might well have been written with the New Testament in mind, with its seemingly endless profusion of Marys.†

---

*In *The Gnostic Gospels* Elaine Pagels notes that this passage might have been inserted by someone else.

†The Hebrew Mariam, or Mariamne, was a name common to several important eastern goddesses—the Persian Mariham, the Chaldean Marratu, the Syrian

Moreover, several of the stories featuring women as sinners, weepers, mourners, anointers bore striking similarities, as did various women forgiven by Jesus. In Luke there is the dramatic story of the long haired "sinner" who wept, anointed, embraced and kissed Jesus's feet at Simon the Pharisee's home.[3] In John, that woman is Mary of Bethany—another woman close to Jesus who is often confused with Mary of Magdala. In medieval legend the two figures even become merged—in one story, when Jesus raises Lazarus from the dead it is out of love for the latter.[4] In the Gnostic tradition the Magdalen is also associated with the ritual of chrism, or anointing with oil, for them as important as baptism for initiation into Christianity. Again, merging the anointing Magdalen with the long haired sinner/anointer in Simon's house was hard to avoid.

Equally important in her evolution is the phenomenon of converted pagans clinging to powerful fertility goddesses with their attendant myths. In ancient Persia, the "Great Mother," Jahi, allegedly introduced sex into the world when she seduced the first man in the garden. Hence the saying, "all women are whores because they descended from Jahi."[5] Several other goddess/whores wept and anointed. In the Mesopotamian epic, Gilgamesh, it is a harlot who civilizes the wild man, Enkidu, by seducing him. When he dies, she weeps and anoints him with oil. The Babylonian "Great Whore," Mari-Ishtar, "christens" and anoints her lover Tammuz, the vegetation deity, when he descends into the underworld in winter. Joining with her priestesses in a great cry of lament, she "made him a Christ," restoring him to life in the spring.[6]

Various other goddesses also weep and lament the death of consorts or lovers—Isis for Osiris, Venus for Adonis, Inanna, "Lady of Heaven," for her husband, Dumuzi. The second-

---

Meri, the Christian Marian, Miriam, Mariamne, Myrrhine, Myrtea. Some Jewish and early Christian sects also called Jesus' mother Mari-Yamm or Mariam.

century Montanists, a Gnostic Christian sect founded by a former priest of Cybele, maintained a reverence for the Roman goddess who wept for her consort Attis, called the Chrisus. Interestingly, the Montanists allowed women to preach and prophesy.[7]

From the ancient Hebrews comes the story of Na-amah, meaning "pleasing" or "lovely"—a Cainnite woman so strikingly beautiful that she seduced the Angels. In Gnostic mythology, Na-amah becomes Norea, beautiful, virgin daughter of Eve, for the Manicheans a seductress who drives the male archons mad with passion. In other Gnostic writings the Norea heroically fights off the evil archon's attempts to rape her. Rescued by the Illuminator, Eleleth, he grants her "salvation . . . in the form of—revelation." Thus, she symbolizes one aspect of the *Sophia*—redemption through revealed wisdom.[8]

Ancient myths also associate the Magdalen's trademark, her long hair, with magical powers. Isis, for one, used the warmth and powers of her hair to restore Osiris to life. Cybele and Kali could summon great storms by loosening their hair.[9] In ancient Greece, during the Dionysian festivals women loosened their hair from buns and nets, letting it fly wildly about during their frenzied dances. In ancient Rome prostitutes dyed their long hair in bright colors. In Jesus's time, for a wife to appear in public with her hair loose—the mark of a prostitute—was grounds for divorce.[10] During the Talmudic period (and in Hasidic circles today), married women were required to shave their heads to avoid tempting men other than their husbands.

The question of women's hair was a thorny issue for Paul who regarded long hair as a disgrace to a man, but "a woman's glory" (1 Cor. 11:15). Paul advised men to pray with uncovered head, for "every man has Christ for his head," but women must wear a veil for prayer or prophecy, since "a woman's head is man" (1 Cor. 11:2). Undoubtedly Paul was concerned to distinguish Christian women from pagans, who prayed bare-headed. Yet Paul also wrote that women must cover their hair "out of regard for the angels," that is, those lustful angels in Genesis who fell prey to the beauty of the "daughters of men," had intercourse with them, and produced the Nephalim, a race of giants (Gen. 6:1-4). Paul also advised married woman to crop their hair or shave it altogether (1 Cor. 11). Well into the eighteenth century, in European villages and towns women were required by law to keep their hair tucked into their white caps whenever they appeared in public.

Clearly, we are dealing with syncretism or cross-cultural fertilization here, as Christianity took whole populations of pagan peoples under its wing. Like the Virgin Mary, the Magdalen absorbed various aspects of ancient goddesses into her persona, in effect exchanging the Gnostic's divine light of wisdom for the reddish light of the brothel. As "holy harlot" she would serve a new purpose in a Christianity obsessed with sins of the flesh. Confused with both Luke's sinner/prostitute and the woman taken in adultery, she would become a dramatic reminder of the wages of sin and a model for redemption through remorse and repentance.

And so the Magdalen took on her composite form; in the popular mind the sinner who weeps and anoints. Identified by her copious mane of long, flowing hair, artists would depict her at the crucifixion with her spice jar, weeping and tenderly embracing the dead Christ's feet, sometimes in startlingly erotic fashion. In one fourteenth-century *Crucifixion* by an anonymous artist, the Magdalen literally wraps herself around the dead Christ's legs, in another from Bohemia, she fervidly embraces the cross to which the suffering Jesus is still nailed. In Boticelli's *Pieta* of 1495, the image is doubled as two women with long, flowing red hair and closed eyes tenderly embrace both the head and feet of a swooning, still life-like Christ

Thus, the wise woman and leader becomes the "sinning saint," her person ultimately ravaged by the untoward effect of untamed lusts. In her duality as seductive beauty and abject penitent she would symbolize the timeless ambivalence toward women. Indeed, as Christianity wrestled with the harsh struggle between body and soul, the Magdalen would come to embody the temptations of the flesh and their inevitably destructive effects.

CHAPTER 12

MARY MAGDALEN: REPENTANT WHORE

In a world in which time is measured by the birth of Christ, it is astonishing to recall how little we know of the historical Jesus. We know only his first name, nothing at all of his physical appearance, only the approximate date of his birth. His teachings come down to us by virtue of an oral tradition and the memory of followers who wrote them down some sixty to one hundred ten years after his death. We know very little about his family, his work-a-day world, his friends, nothing of his intimate life—whether he had a sweetheart, a wife, a family.

Given this dearth of information today, we can hardly imagine the dilemma for Christians during the Middle Ages—a time of virtually universal illiteracy. Of course, the concept of an historical Jesus would have been absurd at the time. Jesus was, plain and simply, God briefly made man. Not so the saints; flesh and blood human beings whose incredible faith, sufferings, martyrdom became the stuff of folk tale, art, literature, the theater, all of which pandered to the need of common folk for figures with human qualities and failings like themselves. In that company of saints, Mary Magdalen, still confused with Luke's sinner, would take a central role.

No Christian figure fit the ethos of the age better, being both sinner and saint. For medieval society abounded in contrast and contradiction—on the one hand it's general striving for spirituality, its imposition of the harsh triad of poverty, chastity, and obedience on the religious orders, on the other hand the overweening and oppressive sense of guilt, especially about sins of the flesh, when human needs clash with such self-denying ideals.

Traditionally, historians have given us a portrait of the Middle Ages as a world populated primarily by monks, nuns, would-be saints and ascetics, fasting and scourging the flesh as the price of a ticket to paradise. Yet, in truth, the bulk of medieval society were crude and lusty peasant folk who understood and celebrated life at its most basic level. Beneath the veneer of a Christianity often super-imposed on them by their rulers, they surreptitiously clung to pagan ways and beliefs. Drenched in the immediacy of nature and its cycles, they persisted in all manner of earthy and ancient ways, immune to the church's determined campaign to root out such abominations. Indeed, our medieval ancestors were far less suppressed than their polite and refined modern descendants today.

For that very reason, the more the peasantry resisted the iron grip of Christian guilt, following instead the dictates of nature, the more the Church redoubled its campaign against the seven deadly sins. And in that contest for the Christian soul, Mary Magdalen became a powerful propaganda tool, a vivid emblem for the wages of sin, striking a wholly sympathetic chord in the impressionable minds of the masses. Of course, since most Christians had not the slightest inkling of the Magdalen of the

Gospels, a new persona was necessary: a mirror of themselves, one who would be familiar in appearance, dress, speech, behavior, a composite figure who reflected the extremes of the age itself.

In part that figure looked back to the asceticism of the fifth and sixth centuries; the solitary, undernourished hermit who lived out the last thirty years of her life in the desert. Still extant, too, was Luke's "sinner," a figure who evoked a widely held view of women as shallow, vain, lusty, born liars, fickle, deceitful, whining, and devious. In that portrait of women the definitive medieval handbook on witchcraft, *Malleus Maleficarum,* fully agreed, describing them as creatures who

> for the sake of fulfilling their lusts . . . consort even with devils. . . . [B]eautiful to look upon, [they are] contaminating to the touch, and deadly to keep.[1]

As the Magdalen's popularity increased, however, she underwent a transformation, her life story taking on a whole new series of twists and turns. She now acquired a noble family, wealth, a splendid castle, rich clothing, and the worldly manners of a fine lady, with an insatiable hunger to be admired and pampered. In popular theater she would be portrayed as a shameless wench, singing bawdy songs and dancing in lascivious fashion. In all of these stories she would undergo a radical conversion after encountering Jesus, reverting back to gifted preacher and missionary. Eventually, however, she would retreat to the wilderness where, donning the rough, homespun garment of the penitent, her radiant beauty gave way to the emaciated body and sunken cheeks of the ascetic. Shriven of her sins, she would ascend to heaven and achieve sainthood. Perhaps more so than any great Christian figure of the period, the Magdalen epitomized its curious tension, being at once saint and sinner.

For the most part, the common people came to know her through the Lives, biographies of the saints in the form of colorful tales told by humble priests to inform and entertain their rural parishioners. Since most serfs or peasants would never in their lives venture beyond a ten-mile radius of their rural manors or villages, the magnificent paintings, sculpture, stained glass windows of the great cathedrals were totally unknown to them. Instead, they learned about Christianity in their rude, parish churches, eagerly imbibing the vivid; heroic, often gruesome tales about the lives of the saints. Later those stories were repeated around the family hearth, incorporated into folklore, and finally into plots of the popular mystery and passion plays.

Typically, a saint's day began with a *Contestatio,* a prayer summarizing the Saint's accomplishments, then mass, after which the priest, often barely more literate than his parishioners, would solemnly unfold the scroll containing the 'Life.' In histrionic fashion, he would then declaim its tale of travel, adventure, blood-curdling tortures inflicted by heathens, hair-raising skirmishes with death, fantastic miracles—the more violent, the more hushed the audience. Reciting from memory, he might add his own embellishments to keep their attention. Even in the great cathedrals the Bishops made the recitation of a Life as lively and entertaining as possible, resorting to dramatic license when necessary.

A good example would be the story of the martyred Saint Sophia and her three daughters, Faith, Hope and Charity, who scorned the Emperor Hadrian's offer to adopt them. For that they endured horrible tortures. Faith was brutally beaten, her breasts amputated, then flung onto a red-hot gridiron, and finally cast into a huge frying pan. Hope was put into a cauldron containing pitch, wax and resin so red-hot that drops of it cremated bystanders instantly. Charity had her bones broken on the rack. Beaten and scourged with whips, she was thrown into a white-hot furnace whose flames killed six thousand idolaters, and finally stabbed all over by white-hot nails. Yet all three miraculously survived, dying finally by the sword.[2]

At the conclusion of such sensational stories of courage and faith, miraculous healings would occur on the spot, as on the feast day of St. Martins when two blind men regained their sight. Afterward everyone joined in a splendid procession, headed by a litter carrying a plaster statue of the saint, hopefully with a relic of some body part inside.[3]

One of those Lives, composed in the early seventh century by the patriarch of Jerusalem, told the amazing story of Saint Mary of Egypt, a prostitute who repented and became a hermit and ascetic. (Not incidentally, Egypt was a stronghold of traditional goddess worship, in the form of the Isis cult.) At twelve, the age of marriage, Mary ran away from her parents and became a prostitute in Alexandria. For seventeen years she heedlessly indulged herself in "laughter, ardor and friends . . . not to accumulate riches, but just to live a luxurious life." But at age twenty-eight she suddenly changed after meeting a group of Libyan Christian pilgrims bound for Jerusalem. Resolving to join them, she bartered her body in exchange for passage.

In Jerusalem, when she tried to enter the Church of the True Cross, "an invisible force" blocked her way. Certain that her former life of "dreadful crimes" impeded her, Mary beat her breast and "shed bitter tears" of repentance. Begging the Virgin Mary for forgiveness, she promised to give up her former life, and suddenly the way was opened. After worshipping the True Cross, she heard a voice telling her to cross the Jordan to find salvation. To help her, a pious man gave her three loaves of bread, which, on reaching the desert "turned hard as stone." After shedding copious tears of penance, Mary lived utterly alone for forty-seven years, her clothes dissolving into pieces. With only roots, berries, and the unpalatable loaves for nourishment, she survived, thanks to angels who regularly came to feed her.

Only once was her solitude interrupted when, forty years into her desert life, a monk named Zosimas discovered her.

Having come to the desert to fast and pray, he had wandered aimlessly for twenty days when he spied a strange apparition on the other side of the Jordan. Coming closer, he saw a nude woman, her skin blackened by the sun, covered only by long hair that looked like white wool (an allusion to her former life as prostitute). The phantom figure fled, but Zosimas caught up with her. Mary then begged him to cover her nudity with his cloak and bless her. But Zosimas, recognizing a holy ascetic, begged for her blessing first. Thus, Mary "made herself male" by wearing a monk's cloak and giving the first blessing.

Mary then told Zosimas about her first seventeen years in the desert—the tormenting memories of her former life and its "carnal delights." Only when "the word of God" came to her spontaneously did she conquer them, since she was illiterate. Overcome by her holiness, Zosimas knelt at her feet. One year later he returned to bring her communion, and Mary walked to him across the waters of the Jordan. But on his next visit, he found her dead. Without a shovel, Zosimas was unable to dig a grave in the hard desert ground. Suddenly he saw "a lion meekly coming toward him" who dug the grave with his paws and departed "like a gentle lamb."[4] From then on Zosimas's monastery celebrated Mary's death annually.

Mary of Egypt's story soon merged with the Magdalen legend. A mid-eighth-century Life, the *Vita Eremitica Beatae Mariae Magdalenae,* repeats the story almost verbatim. Here the Magdalen also retires to the desert, is discovered by a kindly priest who clothes her nakedness, and takes her to live in his church where she dies after receiving Christian burial.[5] In art as well the Magdalen was often portrayed as an emaciated, wrinkled, sunburned hermit set in front of a cave in the wilderness. A well-known painting attributed to the School of Giotto, shows her nude, covered only by her long hair. As she kneels in prayer, angels lift her to heaven.[6] In the early sixteenth century, the artist Quentin Metsys conceived the two figures as mirror images in a diptych (two separate panels). Both are hermits whose long, unkempt hair conceals their nude, emaciated bodies, as they kneel on the barren desert ground, hands clasped in prayer.[7] Next to Maria Egyptiaca are the three stone-like loaves, next to Mary Magdalene the tell-tale ointment jar.

If Metsys' hermetic figures look back to the harsh asceticism of an earlier period, they reflect a contemporary image as well, that of the outcast—the poor, the mad, the criminal whom society relegated to the dark, wild forests. There these forsaken creatures lived as wild men and women, their tousled, tangled hair evidence of their savage, unruly nature. So too the hermetic Magdalen, her long, unkempt tresses suggesting one of those poor, demented souls. In a striking fifteenth-century woodcut from Bavaria by an anonymous artist, the Magdalen seems almost bestial, her entire body covered by thick, heavy tresses resembling animal fur. Wearing the ecstatic expression of a saint with eyes focused on heaven, her ascension to heaven is assisted by putti, or cherubs, whose scaly skin, like hers, alludes to their former wild state.*

Such powerful images fit perfectly into an age gripped by fear of eternal damnation and bombarded with graphic images of the horrors of hell and its gruesome tortures. In paintings, stained glass windows, and illustrated missals, loathsome demons with pitchforks were depicted pushing sinners into cauldrons of boiling water, or into the sinuous, never-ending flames of hell. In Hieronomous Bosch's great landscape of hell, *The Garden of Earthly Delights*, dismembered sinners hang upside down, some are impaled by giant daggers or spears, others are partially swallowed by grotesque monster birds or rodents, while lurid flames bathe the gruesome landscape in a ghastly light. Compounding such imagined horrors was the reality of a world infested with disease and plague, one in which death could come

---

*Now in Munich's National Bavarian Museum.

at anytime to anyone.

In such a world the Church offered a formula for cleansing and for hope. First must come true contrition, "sorrow of our hert that we have synned"; second confession, "open shrift of our mouth how we haf synned"; and third penance, "ammendes . . . for that we haf synned."[8] At the Fourth Lateran Sacrament Council in 1215–16, private confession to a priest became obligatory, while the aforementioned Penitentials listed the seven deadly sins and what penance was required to eradicate them. At the top of the list was lust, engendered by *woman* whose beauty thinly shields the hidden rot and filth of her sex.

At the forefront of the battle against sin were the mendicant orders, Dominicans and Franciscans who left their cells to become wandering friars preaching "hell fire and brimstone" sermons to an impressionable peasantry. In their zeal to eradicate sin and open the path to heaven, the good friars bombarded the common folk with the need for true repentance, a task to which the Magdalen was perfectly suited, having shared the experience of ordinary people. Unlike Jesus and the Virgin Mary, both absolved of original sin, she, too, was a 'sinner', a prostitute deeply mired in the filth of the flesh.

Yet having descended to the lowest level of degradation, through her love for Jesus she repented and was saved. Casting off her rich clothing, cosmetics and jewelry, her lascivious ways, she sought atonement by living as the meanest, most wretched beggar, clothed in rags, hollow-cheeked, her once luxuriant tresses hanging in stringy, limp shreds. Finally, raised by angels to heaven, she proved that it is never too late to repent. More so than any other medieval figure, the Magdalen manifested the strange conjunction between humans and angels, sinners and saints.

For Jacobus de Voragine, a humble twelfth-century Dominican monk who became archbishop of Genoa, the Magdalen was all these things and more. A gifted story teller with no qualms about skewing the facts when necessary, Voragine's collection of Lives, the *Golden Legend,* was the medieval equivalent of a best-seller. Translated into every European language, it was second in importance only to the Bible, and its expanded version of the Magdalen legend became a source book for medieval artists, dramatists, and playwrights from the twelfth century on.

For his biography of the Magdalen Voragine plumbed every known source and then some. Liberally adding spurious material to fill out the story, he assigns various meanings to her name—*amarum mare,* the "bitter sea" or "repentant"; *Sophia,* the "wise woman" enlightened by "heavenly glory"; *manens rea,* the "sinner" who, for "every pleasure she had enjoyed . . . [devised] a way of immolating herself."[9] The daughter of a wealthy nobleman, Syrus, with vast estates in and around Jerusalem, Voragine's Magdalen is sister to Lazarus and Martha of Bethany. After Syrus's death the estate is divided between all three, but "the prudent Martha" manages the entire properties since Lazarus is off at the wars, and Mary totally obsessed with the pursuit of worldly pleasures.

Drawing on Luke's Gospel, sometimes word for word, Voragine's worldly Magdalen is transformed into the "sinner" who wept and anointed Jesus in Simon the leper's house. After that Jesus's devotion to her knows no bounds; he "showed so many marks of love." Jesus weeps with her, drives out her seven devils, lives in her house, defends her from the Pharisees' hostility, from Martha's irritation with her idleness, and from Judas' anger at her extravagance for anointing him with expensive oil. He cures her sister Martha of a seven-year "issue of blood" and brings her brother Lazarus back to life. At the crucifixion she is one of the mourners, and at the tomb she is first to witness the resurrection.

All that, however, is only prelude for Voragine. Leaping ahead fourteen years, he places the Magdalen on a ship, along with seventy-two other disciples, bound for Marseilles. They all nearly drown when "infidels" try to sabotage the ship, but divine intervention saves them, and they reach Marseilles safely. There, the Magdalen's eloquent words, coming directly from the "mouth which had pressed such pious and beautiful kisses on the Saviour's feet," convert the pagans. The Royal couple, however, are not so easily convinced, but the Magdalen persuades the queen that God will bring down his wrath if she allows her Christian subjects to die of cold and hunger. Yet, it is only after God answers the Magdalen's prayer to give the barren queen a son that the royal couple accept Christianity.

Still somewhat skeptical, the King travels to Jerusalem to learn from Saint Peter if the Magdalen's teachings are true. During a great storm at sea the Queen gives birth prematurely to a boy, and dies. Cursing Mary Magdalen, the grief-stricken king places the queen's body on a rocky cove with the wailing infant at the dead woman's breast, then continues on to Jerusalem. After two years of instruction with Peter, the king sets out for home, first stopping by the island. There he is astonished to find his son, kept alive by the Magdalen, playing on the beach and nursing at the breast of a miraculously preserved mother. When the king beseeches Mary Magdalen to restore her, the "dead" woman's eyes open, for, with "blessed Mary Magdalen as my guide," she had been an invisible presence during her husband's entire pilgrimage. Back in Marseilles the grateful couple are baptized by Mary Magdalen, their subjects replace their pagan temples with Churches, and Lazarus is elected bishop of Marseilles.

Her work done, Mary Magdalen leaves for Aix with her followers and her colleague Maximus; after many miracles she converts its people as well. From then on, Voragine closely follows the career of Mary of Egypt. Desiring the contemplative life, the Magdalen retires to a remote mountain cave where she exists without sustenance for thirty years, sustained by angels who every day "at the seven canonical hours," lift her to the heavens. Just before her death, a hermit priest dwelling nearby witnesses her ascension. On approaching her grove he is suddenly paralyzed, but after three prayers to Christ, the Magdalen speaks, saying that she is the "notorious sinner" who washed Jesus feet.

Describing her heavenly visitations and the glorious celestial music, she says she must now depart the earth.* The priest is to tell Bishop Maximus of Aix that she will be carried by angels to his oratory, and on the appointed day she appears as promised, borne by angels, her face radiant as the sun. After Maximus gives her communion she falls lifeless to the altar, and the oratory is filled with perfume for seven days. Maximus embalms and buries her where, after his own death, he too will lie.[10]

Voragine is not through here. In a postscript he tells of the miraculous recovery of the Magdalen's bones from Aix and their transfer to the monastery at Vezelay, whose patron, the Duke of Burgundy, is granted his prayer for a son. Other miracles resemble the Virgin's various interventions—a soldier killed during a pilgrimage to the Magdalen's tomb is restored to life long enough to be given last rites, a pregnant woman caught in a storm at sea is saved by a mysterious woman "lifesaver" who, holding her by the chin, brings her safely to shore, a blind pilgrim recovers his sight on arriving at the monastery of Vezelay.

Most Virgin-like is the story of a clerk named Stephen who led a dissolute life, but nonetheless maintained a steady devotion to Mary Magdalen. On visiting her tomb, the Magdalen surrounded by angels appeared to him. Stephen repents, is 'born

---

*The late-fifteenth-century painter Giovan Pietro Birago, in his monumental work *St. Mary Magdalene,* includes the ship arriving at Marseilles, the dead queen suckling her child on the island, the mountain retreat, and the old priest kneeling in wonder at the sight of the Magdalen borne aloft by four angels. At the epicenter of the painting the Magdalen, levitated in midair by angels, devoutly clasps her hands in prayer. Her saintly face is encircled by a halo and her entire body encased in long, wavy hair down to her ankles.

again', enters the monastery, and leads a life of perfection from then on.

Among common folk the Magdalen ranked second only to the Virgin in the litany of saints. She, too, could intercede with Christ at the moment of judgment for those who showed her proper reverence. For gardeners, perfumers, ointment-makers, apothecaries, pharmacists, leather makers, glove and shoemakers, drapers and water-sellers, she was protectress and patron saint.[11] Conversely, those who in any way abominated her feast day on July 22 might be visited with supernatural or man-made punishments.

Criminals prayed to her with special intensity before execution, for like them, she had been a sinner. During the virulent plague epidemic of the thirteenth century, those bizarre "fraternities" of penitents, the Flagellants, who wound their way through the streets whipping themselves raw, carried her image on their banners. In fourteenth-century Spain, the Flagellants of San Sepolcro marched with banners displaying her image as a stern-faced, heavily robed, haloed figure. Surrounded by angels, she holds the crucified Jesus on her lap. Hardly distinguishable from the Virgin, only the tell-tale ointment jar reveals her identity.[12]

Yet for monks and nuns, the sinful Magdalen, unlike the Virgin, made the bitter pill of human imperfection easier to swallow. Like them she had known the cravings of the flesh, and made amends by turning to the ascetic life. And having relinquished the delights of carnal love for the sake of her soul, she too might become the bride of Christ. Thus, for society's most despised category of women, prostitutes, she offered redemption. After all, she had been one of them, yet Christ forgave her abominations.

Regarding the oldest profession, the Church harbored a distinct ambivalence. Officially, fornication of any kind was condemned. Yet in practice the Church condoned prostitution, regarding it as a necessary evil—a hedge against worse sins such as rape and homosexuality, a relief for wives worn out with pregnancy and childbirth, and an outlet for the male need for variety. The onus of her customer's sins were heaped on the prostitute's head, however—a creature of unnatural lust and a carrier of venereal diseases.

Thus, despite the tenacity of the legend of the Magdalen as mourner and weeper at the tomb, she who reached out to embrace the newly risen Christ, it is the penitent Magdalen who set off the deepest chords of empathy and personal identification. Even today one cannot encounter that great masterpiece of the fifteenth century, Donatello's bronze sculpture of Mary Magdalen as penitent, without experiencing some pang of remorse for the darker side of human nature, the icy chill of reflexive guilt for nameless sins harbored deep within the subconscious mind. Gaunt and wrinkled, haggard and toothless, covered by animal skins and rag-like hair, her skin darkened and leathery from the sun, her hands in penitent prayer, Donatello's Magdalen captures, as perhaps nothing else, the essential paradox of the Renaissance.

Despite its obsession with wealth, beauty, luxury, sensuality, power, Donatello's Magdalen reminds us that, ultimately, all such things are ephemeral. Beauty and worldly joys must inevitably fade; only sincere contrition can lead to eternal joy. In the ongoing battle for the soul in an increasingly secularized world, Mary Magdalen as 'holy harlot' would become Christianity's most potent image for repentance. Unlike the Virgin, whose perfection emits the brilliant, white rays of a diamond, the Magdalen was a prism emitting a spectrum of colors. Whereas the Virgin was always shown as a young woman free of the blemishes of aging, seemingly hardly older than her son, the Magdalen might present a moving portrait of the ravages of aging. Whereas the Virgin's role was utterly conscripted—she was mother above all—the Magdalen had several different roles: loyal follower, companion to Jesus, disciple, teacher, mystic, preacher, missionary, vain, richly dressed noblewoman, sexual sinner, and quintessential penitent.

Given those various dimensions, it would be Mary Magdalen rather than the Virgin who took a starring role in a new form of entertainment that brought the message of Christianity to rural folk all over Europe and England: the popular theater.

CHAPTER 13

MARY MAGDALEN, SUPERSTAR

Donatello's *Mary Magdalene,* masterpiece though it may have been, hearkened back to an earlier period in Christianity, when ascetics retired to remote Syrian deserts to fast and exist on juniper berries and roots. During the Middle Ages, however, for the ordinary *villein,* hunger pangs were a way of life, not a pathway to spirituality. Nor, living out their lives on their rustic domains as they did, would they encounter Christianity through works of high art such as Donatello's penitent *Magdelene.*

Instead, the largely illiterate populace gleaned an understanding of their new religion, in part, from the popular theater. On rough back roads throughout Europe, actors traveled from town to town in crude wagons, which they converted to stages in the town square. There, they enacted poignant dramas about

Christ's final Passion or earthy comedies portraying the struggle between Evil, in the form of the seven deadly sins, and Good, heavenly angels sent to save Everyman's soul. As to the Magdalen, in these rude productions a new figure was born: a lusty wench, worldly, brazen, and vain, who survives to this very day.

The church may, in fact, be said to be the birthplace of modern theater. In its darkened space all eyes were riveted on the priest, who invested his sermon with as much drama as possible to hold the attention of a restless audience. In the great cathedrals, colorful paintings, sculptures, and stained glass windows served as sets, transforming light and space; often music and dance enhanced the "performance." Even today a tradition of religious dance survives in Spain in the form of a popular dance, the *baile,* performed by a company of specially trained young boys.[1]

So too itinerant troupes of actors who, being hardly one step above beggars, depended upon their audiences for their very bread. Hoping to be pelted with applause and coins rather than rotting garbage, they veered from their declared purpose of saving souls from perdition to become the ancestors of modern theater.[2] Even today, playwrights sometimes adapt the format of their Everyman plays to a contemporary purpose, while the great Passion Plays that tell the Easter story are given yearly. In smaller towns in France, Germany, and Belgium, virtually everyone lends a hand in making costumes, sets, directing or acting in productions which have become major tourist events.

As early as the thirteenth-century passion plays had become complex productions, with elaborate sets and composite characters who invested the familiar story with every possible dramatic twist. In one such production the crucifixion was re-enacted on a stage that included three crosses for Jesus and the two criminals who shared his fate. Huddled at the foot of Jesus's cross were his mother and Mary Magdalen—the former dressed in a black robe with a white cowl, the latter in stylish clothing of the period.[3]

Despite the pathos of the suffering men on the cross, all eyes were riveted on the two women whose heart rending lamentations were the emotional center of these dramas. Just as opera-goers today wait for the climactic moment of a deeply moving aria, medieval audiences anticipated their lamentations, the hammered cry of anguish as they watched the life ebb out of the dying man.

As the Passion Plays developed into sophisticated dramas, the Magdalen's role grew in importance. Thus, in a French play from the Tours region, the Magdalen weeps on finding an empty tomb on Sunday morning. When an angel announces that Jesus has already risen, she stretches her arms toward heaven. Imploring Jesus not to abandon her, to "take pity" and show himself, she collapses into the arms of the two other Marys. As they support her limp body, she delivers her poignant lamentation: "My heart is burning. I long to see my Lord; / I search and do not find where they have placed him."[4] *

Having drawn upon the secular language of courtly love, the Tours playwright also introduces comic relief in the form of a familiar figure taken from real life—a wily merchant who hoodwinks the three women when they come to his shop to purchase embalming oils. Shrewdly, he talks them into buying an expensive unguent which, he claims, can suspend the natural process of decay.[5] The audience is, of course, delighted by such everyday events. Soon, such earthy, comic scenes became a staple of plays which ingeniously melded sacred and secular, serious and comic, high and low styles.

---

*Typically, these lamentations were delivered in Latin, as in a twelfth-century play from the Tours region: "*Me misera! Me misera! Me misera! /Quid agam? Heu tristis, quid dicam*" ("Wretch though I am! Wretch that I am! Wretch that I am! What shall I do? Alas, sorrowful that I am, what shall I say?").* But increasingly, in deference to an expanding popular audience, they were given in the vernacular, as in an early English mystery play: "Alas! my Boote looke thou be, / thy mother that thee bare! / Think on my freut! I fostered thee, / and gaue the suck upon my knee; / ypon mu payne hast thou pitty / thee fayles no power."

Thus, in the prologue to a German Passion Play based on the parable of the woman taken in adultery, Jesus announces its serious theme: "Man for thi synne take repentaunce."[6] The play opens with a group of Pharisees who plot to expose Jesus for expropriating the right to forgive sin. Suddenly, a man aptly named Accusator rushes in to breathlessly announce that a client has just entered the nearby chamber of a harlot. If they hurry they can catch him in the act. Hastily, they rush to the place and break down the door. Out dashes the embarrassed customer, pants in hand, loudly cursing the untimely interruption of his pleasure.

The sight of a fornicator caught with his pants down evoked howls of laughter from the audience. Further hilarity follows when the Pharisees, in vulgar street talk, order the harlot to "come forth thou hore and stynkyngr bych / . . . come forth thou sloven come forth thou slutte."[7] Quite abruptly the play turns serious again as the harlot pleads, "For goddys love have mercy on me / . . . haave mercy on me for charyte."[8] When her accusers turn a deaf ear she becomes hysterical, begging to be killed on the spot rather than suffer the shame of a public stoning. Instead, they drag her across the stage to the place where Jesus silently writes on the ground.

Freely confessing her guilt, she acknowledges that she deserves "bodly deth and werldly shame," and begs Jesus to pray for her. Swearing her "grett repentaunce for synnys Abhomynable," her protestations increase in intensity, like a preacher whose repetitions build to a dramatic climax. As her contrition intensifies, so too the audience's empathy for a deeply flawed figure in whom they see their own image. All breathe a mutual sigh of relief when Jesus intones the familiar phrase, "Let he who is blameless", and the Pharisees flee in shame. Clearly sermon and play have become one.[9]

Ultimately, however, audiences wanted entertainment, not a sermon; for that playwrights began to expand both plot and characters. Thus a later version of a *Hegge Passion Play* introduces Lucifer urging his followers to sin boldly and enjoy "the tresour of lovys Alyawns," John the Baptist sternly admonishing them to "Do penance," and Jesus promising that "the time of mercy . . . is come now."[10]

Abruptly, the scene shifts to the Last Supper and Jesus's arrest. The Council urges the Roman governor, Cayphas, to execute Jesus medieval style, by tying his body to a wild horse. Cayphus calls for a traitor willing to deliver a false charge, and the audience anticipates Judas. Instead Mary Magdalen bursts onstage decrying her sordid life as "a cursyd creature . . . a wyckd wrecche all wrappyd in wo." Anointing Jesus's "holy fote," she begs for "mercy lord ffor my trespace."[11] Acknowledging her true contrition, Jesus casts out her seven devils, and she promises never again to trespass in "wurd nor dede."[12]

The Magdalen remains at Jesus's side until the soldiers come to tear him away, her love and loyalty in sharp relief against Judas' cold betrayal. The latter, deprived of the cleansing balm of confession, is crushed by guilt and commits suicide. Thus the playwright illustrates two profoundly psychological states—the self-loathing of one who cannot confront his guilt, the blessed relief of one who exorcises her guilt through confession. Through the Magdalen the twin motifs of the play are realized: contrition and hope of forgiveness.

The play ends with Mary Magdalen and Mary the mother alone on stage. The latter asks why her innocent son must suffer, answering rhetorically: "I suppose veryly it is for the tresspace of me."[13] But the audience knows that the Virgin cannot sin. Not so the Magdalen, in whose person the audience perceives a reflection of their own tainted nature, and the possibility of redemption and forgiveness. Again, through her humanity, the playwright accomplishes a moral purpose.

In lesser hands such dramas could easily become tedious. Not so the earthy morality plays modeled after the bawdy, improvisational comedies of ancient Rome. Using stock plots and characters, the moralities presented simple allegories about the on-going warfare between Good and Evil. In a sense they were the sitcoms of the Middle Ages, with Evil represented by the seven deadly sins—envy, pride, greed, laziness, gluttony, anger, and lust. Grotesque in form, their ribald songs and dances were full of folk melody and vibrant dance rhythms played on shawm, sackbut, viols, and a wind instrument aptly named the serpent, whose coiled body looked like that of a snake—precisely the music banned from the church for its incitement to frivolity. By contrast, when the good angels enter to pluck Everyman out of the jaws of temptation, the music turned celestial—sweet bells, harps, psaltery, and a small, portable organ—the music of the church.

Despite their declared purpose of saving souls from damnation, the moralities relied more on raw, earthy humor to keep a peasant audience attentive, than on the refined idioms of the church. Indeed, throughout the Middle Ages a sexually explicit art flourished right under the nose of the Church. Erotic, even bawdy scenes appeared in the most unlikely places—perhaps an exquisitely wrought illuminated manuscript in which the artist has depicted of a lusty peasant couple romping in a haystack, or a monk and nun furtively coupling. On misericords (the underside of folding chairs in the choir-stalls), or in carved gargoyles, medieval artisans gave vent to a rich erotic imagination—women exposing breasts, behinds, genitalia, monks fondling, even penetrating female partners, some of whom are nuns, indecent postures of all kinds, sexual acts such as masturbation and even bestiality. Even today, on the side door of the great Cathedral at Orleans in France, a gargoyle in the form of an ape copulates with a woman. In the companion piece, the woman gives birth to the fruit of this unnatural union: an infant half human, half monkey.[14] Clearly, the church never succeeded in suppressing the ribald humor of the peasantry, nor their natural, open acceptance of sexuality.

Similarly, the moralities often depended upon the sex-appeal of the Magdalen and her provocative songs and dances to keep a restive audience from pelting the actors with rotten vegetables. Thus, in a fifteenth-century French play she cavorts and brazenly sings:

> I am . . . carnal and vain, . . .
> I spend my time in laziness
> I fight and threaten
> I am happy when I hoard the riches of the world.[15]

In another play from Arras she minces no words, boasting of

> My proud little breasts
> My beautiful vermillion petticoat which shows off my body.
> My flesh is rosy and white as a fairy's
> . . . I am available to all.[16]

Some of those earthy songs made their way into the taverns as drinking songs, and can be heard even today in German beer halls. For example, in a thirteenth-century German *Benediktbeuren* passion play the Magdalen brazenly boasts about the pleasure she takes in her various lovers. The pleadings of the Good Angel to give up her licentious ways becomes the signal for her to launch into her show-stopper, "*Mundi delectatio,*" "Delicious World," a hymn of praise to sensual pleasure:

> In worldly joy, I shall end my life.
> I shall serve under the banner of temporal well-being
> Caring nothing for all else
> I shall take care of my body and with different colors . . .
> I shall adorn it.[17]

Only after no less than three reprises of *Mundi Delectatio,* not to mention the suggestive *Venus generosa* and the rollicky *Chramer, gip die varwe mier,* does the obligatory conversion takes place. The play ends in a sudden rush of remorse for the "filth of my vices." Flinging off her fine clothes and jewels, the Magdalen dons a plain, black cloak and vanquishes both Flesh and the

Devil. Quite alone, she begins a new life as holy penitent.[18]

Yet what endured of the *Benediktheuren* was not the Magdalen's repentance, but her songs, which became even more lewd when absorbed into popular culture. Translated into the vernacular, they were appropriated by roving troubadours and Galliards—students who relieved the drudgery of the medieval university by drinking, wenching, and general mischief—in their drinking and love songs. Today, their frank obscenity comes as a shock to modern audiences who can hear them, word for word, in Carl Orff's *Carmina Burana.* Few would guess that they were originally sung by Christianity's most famous sinner turned saint.

Crossing the channel to England, we find an entirely different Magdalen, product of a rich theatrical tradition. Rather than a caricature of woman at her worst—lewd, greedy, vain—the Magdalen emerges here as a multi-layered person with human weaknesses, vulnerable, yet capable of change. Especially in the plays known as the Digbys (school or playwright), we meet, once again, the gifted, spiritual woman of the Gnostic Gospels.

A fifteenth-century Digby play, *Mary Magdalene,* initially portrays the familiar vain creature who cares only for her "Valnetyns" and "dear darlings." But here the playwright probes beneath the hackneyed stereotype. It is grief at her father's death that renders her vulnerable to lechery and the Devil. Assisted by the seven deadly sins, they, like the seven demons of the biblical Magdalen, have insinuated themselves into her being. Despite their clownish absurdity, they understand feminine psychology only too well.

First Lady Lechery, wife of Flesh, distracts the Magdalen from her mourning by praising her radiant "beams of beauty."[19] Flattered, the Magdalen goes with Lady Lechery to a tavern in Jerusalem where Pride, in the guise of Curiosity, seduces her with his torrid declaration of love. They drink and dance together, and she promises to follow her "dere derlyng" to the ends of the earth. As they leave, a quartet made up of the Bad Angel, World, Flesh, and the Devil enters, the latter so certain of victory that he "trembles and trots with glee."[20]

To further entrap her, Lady Lechery and Curiosity promise several more lovers. In a wooded bower she falls asleep, dreaming of her "dere derlyngs" and their delightful embraces. Instead, the Good Angel awakens her, sternly warning that the delights of "fleshly lust" only lead to the eternal fires of hell.[21] Instantly the Magdalen laments her sins, vowing to devote herself only to Jesus. At Simon's house she anoints him and bathes his feet with tears of remorse. For her humility and sincere contrition Jesus exorcises her seven devils, and she becomes his beloved spiritual partner. Having forsworn delights of the flesh, she now reflects the Light of Lights—divine wisdom.

After Jesus's death she encounters the risen Christ, as in John's Gospel, but with a variation. Here, Jesus tells her that man's heart is a like a garden watered by tears in which virtue will grow only if the foul weeds of the vices are torn out. The play ends with the Magdalen as ecstatic mystic who sets out to carry that message to the world.

And so it would remain in time: the duality of sinner and saint. But those who prefer the spice of life to the harsh burden of penance would turn to the worldly Magdalen who lives for the moment. Indeed, in the increasingly secularized world of the Renaissance, the Magdalen would become mirror image for those worldly and glamorous, briefly powerful but transgressive women—the fabled courtesans.

CHAPTER 14

From Whore to Courtesan

Under dark, transparent veils
One sees here
Angels from heaven in the flesh.
O Titian, you perfect spirit,
paint their noble semblances,
let us feast our eyes on them.
Pietro Aretino

As European civilization marched in quick step toward the modern world, a fresh spirit prevailed. Life need not be a vale of tears, a constant battle against cravings of the flesh, an ongoing penance for inborn sins, a morbid obsession with the exquisite tortures of hell. Euphoric about startling discoveries in astronomy and physics, Renaissance humanists celebrated humanity's infinite capacity for achievement and joy, quite the opposite of ascetic self-denial.

The Church, too, shifted its gaze from heaven to this world. Glutted with wealth, great prelates lived like great princes in palaces furnished with luxurious fittings and magnificent works of art. Just as the rude, homespun robe of the friar gave way to fine silks, velvets and furs, clerical vows, too, were scandalously violated. From simple priests to the pope, some clergy lived openly with their mistresses and fathered children euphemistically called nieces and nephews.

Indeed, to understand the Renaissance mind is to accept its contradictions, the flagrant way in which sacred and profane, natural and supernatural, sensual and spiritual stood side by side, each a reflection of the other. In Renaissance paintings humans often look like angels and angels like humans, while saints stand next to richly dressed princes and wealthy patrons of art.

So, too, an overt sensuality that flourished within the sacred precincts of the church itself, as artists looked back to antiquity for inspiration. Only the Renaissance spirit could have produced Michelangelo's nudes framing his narratives of God and the creation, the nakedness of Old Testament patriarchs and even God himself on the ceiling of the Sistine Chapel, the Pope's most sacred domain.[1] Only in the Renaissance could an artist, Fra Bartolomeo di San Marco (himself a man of the Church), do a nude painting of St. Sebastian so glorious in its manhood that many women claimed to have succumbed to adulteries inspired by gazing at the painting too long during prayer.[2] And only the bold humanism of the Italian Renaissance could have allowed the full-frontal nudity of Boticelli's glorious *Birth of Venus,* her modesty conserved only by her lovely, golden, flowing hair, not unlike the artistic convention associated with the Magdalen.

Unfortunately, such glaring contradictions exacted a psychological price. When Boticelli fell under the influence of the radical reformist monk, Savanarola, he had a massive attack of

Christian guilt. A charismatic preacher, Savanarola thundered against the corruption of wealth, the lascivious nudes that led to eternal damnation. Sending out corps of children to gather up paintings, sculptures, fine furniture, clothing, and other snares of the devil, Savanarola incinerated them in his blazing 'bonfires of the vanities.' Boticelli, however, made his own bonfire, burning most of his nude paintings, and banishing all pagan influences from his art from then on. Michelangelo, too, suffered the torments of the damned well before judgment day. All his life he was torn by an interior battle between the spiritual imperatives of the soul and the artistic imperatives which led to his obstinate celebration of the human body.

Inevitably, Savanarola went too far in his crusade against worldly things. The Florentines smeared his pulpit with animal dung, tried him under torture and convicted him of heresy. In company with two other colleagues he was burned at the stake in the middle of the Piazza della Signoria, and his ashes dumped into the Arno River. Clearly, Savanarola could not roll back the clock. Nor, in an increasingly worldly climate, could the traditional icons of Christianity resist the imperatives of humanism. In story, legend, song and art, Jesus, his family, the entire panoply of saints would be portrayed as real, even ordinary people.

So too Mary Magdalen. And so another persona evolved; the very antithesis of the ragged, gaunt penitent ravaged by sin. Especially in Italy where a modern art evolved, and a culture of the senses thrived, she would appear as a thinly disguised portrait of those women so coveted by wealthy patrons of art—the beautiful and desirable courtesan. Shedding the decrepit rags of the penitent, she was now richly attired in gowns that often revealed a voluptuous body. Even when portrayed as desert saint, her full figure, barely concealed by her long, flowing hair, seemed to invite desire rather than contrition and penance.

Indeed, the more worldly she became, the more the courtesan/Magdalen reflected the inescapable feminine polarity. Admired and courted for her beauty and sexuality when it served men's purposes, the courtesan hovered on the brink of poverty and disgrace when those attributes faded. Especially in Italy where the Madonna/whore divergence was profoundly imbedded in the culture, such was the fate of women who lived outside the perimeters of marriage. The distance between a luxurious villa and the filth and shame of the streets was precariously small.

Originally the term courtesan was used for the mistresses or lovers of nobles at the great courts, not to be confused with the official royal mistress who was treated as a member of the king's extended family. Chosen for reasons of the heart rather than reasons of state, the royal mistress's children were often acknowledged and given noble title, although there could be no question of accession to the throne. A figure of considerable influence, the royal mistress not only had her own apartments, liveried servants, and carriages, but the power conferred by accessibility to the royal ear.

Courtesans occupied a more tenuous position. A woman of high fashion and cultivation, costly and often haughty, she was supported by one or more lovers. Neither official mistress nor common prostitute, she was at the whim of her protector who might discard her at any time. Eventually, the term embraced women outside the courts who exchanged sexual favors to men of wealth and power for a hefty fee. The most desirable lived a luxurious lifestyle, and while some regarded them as merely gorgeously disguised whores, they were far more than that. In an age that prized male virility, they set the vigor and potency of their lovers in relief. In the eyes of their wealthy and powerful lovers they embodied all that is desirable in woman: beauty, sensuality, high style, wit, even erudition. Fashion shaped them as they shaped fashion. One might even call the period the golden age of the courtesan.

A few came from distinguished families and might have married well, but chose freedom and excitement over prosaic, stultifying domesticity. Others came from good families who couldn't afford the dowry; some only feigned good breeding, having risen from the very dregs of society. The famous *Matrema non vole* (mother doesn't want me to), one of the most learned women of her age, claimed patrician roots, but actually came from a miserably poor family of thieves. The lovely Lorenzina was a baker's daughter, the high living Beatrice of Ferrara a humble laundress's daughter, and Giulia del Sole the offspring of a herdsman and a vegetable vendor.

Essentially the liberated working women of their day, the most successful were showered with gifts by their lovers—money, clothing, jewelry, sumptuous apartments. In Rome the great courtesans lived in the city's most exclusive districts, as did the famous Imperia who furnished her splendid *palazzo* with gold embroidered cloth, magnificent carpets and priceless antique vases. Scattered about her sitting room were her musical instruments, scores, and scholarly books in both Latin and Italian. The extravagant Beatrice of Ferrara had a *palazzo* filled with silver cabinets, exquisite tapestries, fine linens and velvet cushions. Her dresses were made of the finest silks and velvets, set off by precious jewels and pearls, her coach was made of inlaid gold, all tended to by a small army of servants. Beatrice's dinner parties were the talk of Rome, featuring beautifully dressed pheasant, quail, or partridge and ornate marzipan desserts, a feast for the eyes as well as the stomach.

Unfortunately, such lavish living often ended in calamity. Beatrice wound up sleeping in the streets, horribly disfigured by syphilis—one step from the dreaded Hospital of San Giacomo, the last stop before the grave. As much as Italian society loved its courtesans, they also served as scapegoats for its moral lapses, especially during epidemics of syphilis and plague. In Venice courtesans and their procuresses were regularly rounded up and publicly humiliated in the Piazza San Marco by a mock crowning. In Rome they could be publicly whipped or branded on the forehead. When syphilis became epidemic, they would be rounded up, drawn through the streets in carts, and deposited at the grim Hospital for the Incurables.

Of all fates, the worst was to wind up on the infamous Ponte Sisto, reduced to street prostitution, satisfying customers in the open on rude straw mats where all could witness their shame. Courtesans also took enormous risks when they became too independent or insulted their wealthy patrons. Angela del Moro, a Venetian courtesan, one day closed her door to her powerful lover Lorenzo Venier at his prescribed hour. In retaliation she was subjected to the notorious "thirty-one"—a mass rape by thirty-one men of the lowest class. In her case it became a "royal thirty-one," eighty men altogether, a brutality from which she recovered only with medical help.[3]

Despite the risks involved, the courtesan might consider herself fortunate to have avoided the prison either of the nunnery, or of marriage and the dangers of childbearing. In Venice especially the family was a microcosm of the state, and wives living symbols of family honor. Zealously guarded, they were cloistered in their homes except for Church and festival days. When they did venture into the street, they could hardly walk, teetering on elevated clogs that lifted them several inches—some as much as twenty—off the ground to keep the filth of the street off their voluminous skirts. Supported on either side by servants, they resembled a giant balloon walking on stilts, a lack of mobility that made it unlikely, if not impossible, to engage in any affair that would compromise their husband's honor.

That same husband turned to the courtesan—not merely for sex, but for witty and polished conversation. Whereas wives were banned from Venice's great libraries for fear of what learning does to submissiveness, courtesans were admitted.

Admired as much for their intellect as for their beauty and erotic skills, some became the head of distinguished salons, some respected scholars, poets, and essayists. It was said that the courtesan might be a "scholar by day and lover by night."[4] As the Englishman Thomas Coryat put it, if the courtesan failed to captivate with her elegant clothes, jewels, and perfumes, "If she cannot move thee with all these foresaid delights, she will assay thy constancy with her rhetoricall tongue."[5]

The very best vied with and even surpassed their lovers in their many accomplishments. The learned Matrema could recite works of Petrach, Boccaccio, Virgil, Horace, and Ovid by heart. Rullia d'Aragona's salon in Florence rivaled the Academy of the Medicis. The first published women writers were courtesans. Veronica Franco and Gaspara Stampa both poured the exaltation and pain of their lives into their poetry.* Gaspara and her sister Cassandra, also a courtesan, were superb musicians. Indeed, courtesan and musician were interchangeable, since the moment a woman stepped onto a stage she lost respectability. In Rome, the word for female singer and whore were one and the same.

Of all Italy, Venice was famous for its courtesans, not to mention a ready supply of women on every rung of the sex trade, from occasional worker to street prostitute. A bustling port city and gateway to the east, Venice was teeming with sailors, crusaders, and visitors seeking the exotic. Practical and worldly in its outlook, it maintained an independence from Rome. As Pope Gregory XIII put it, "I am Pope everywhere except in Venice."[6] In 1606 the exasperated pope placed Venice under an interdict, meaning that priests could not give the sacraments, but the Venetian Council simply ignored the ban. The great Corpus Domini procession in San Marco Piazza that year featured a float

---

*Gaspara Stampa wrote, "Love made me such that I live in fire / like a new salamander on earth / or like that other rare creature, the Phoenix, / who expires or rises at the same time. / All the joys are there and are mine, my game's / to live burning but not to feel the pain. "

with a model of a collapsing church supported by the Venetian Doge.[7]

In truth, Venice had never been infected with the ethic of poverty, humility, chastity that produced saints such as Francis of Assisi. Rather, beneath a Christian veneer it celebrated the sensual in all its myriad forms—in music, literature, art, and in its famous courtesans. Reputed to be virtuosi of amatory arts imported from Constantinople and the Muslim world, their clients came from all over the continent and England. By the end of the sixteenth century the total number of women engaged in the sex trade (including the brothels and street prostitutes) was said to be ten times the number of Venetian wives.[8]

As a result, if ever there was a culture inundated by the Madonna/whore dichotomy, it would be sixteenth-century Venice. While 'good' wives' absorbed the Madonna image into their deepest beings, their husbands hardly bothered to keep their mistresses a secret. While wives were conditioned to an excessive modesty that squelched all the fire of passion, the nobleman's sexual textbook was the collected pornographic engravings of Marcantonio Raimondi. The sixteen ingenious postures, or positions for lovemaking, left little to the imagination, although their athleticism limited them to the most fit and supple. Nor did it ignore the Venetian nobleman's taste for boys and adult male prostitutes, which courtesans often accommodated by dressing in men's clothing and allowing their lovers to penetrate from the rear, or 'the unnatural way.'

In such a climate the Magdalen became almost equal to the Virgin Mary in popularity, and absolutely necessary to a population of women denied respectability. As the saint who "looks after the women of the world," it was she who understood their reality.[9] She too had preened and adorned her person, lured men with her seductive skills into perdition. Ironically, the great poet Aretino, famous for his erotic poetry, also wrote a so called sacred work entitled *La Maddalena* in which she is described as having the "same bad habits of lasciviousness which imbue the actions of courtesans."[10]

Perhaps for that very reason the Magdalen occupied a central place in the great flowering of Venetian art, for she offered a convergence of beauty, desire, and eroticism with shame, transgression, and guilt. In stunning rebellion against medieval notions of shame about the body, Venetian masters reveled in portraits of female nudes, often shown reclining, with heads thrown back and eyes closed as in post-coital bliss. Their corpulent abdomen and thighs, their larger than life figures referred back to ancient goddesses of fecundity, as in Titian's gloriously sensual *Venus of Urbino.* With firm, full breasts, plump abdomen and thighs, uncannily real, glowing flesh, she gazes directly at the viewer, one hand cupped over the pudenda, entryway to pleasure. The effect is a physicality so immediate and tactile as to completely shatter the Renaissance ideal of balance between the corporeal and the spiritual.

Still, some cloaking of such frank eroticism was necessary. Although Venetian artists regularly used famous courtesans as their models, they were disguised as mythological goddesses, sylvan nymphs, or as a Magdalen far too voluptuous for a penitent or a hermit living on roots and berries. Frequently, her supine body was rather too suggestive of the boudoir, her upward gaze more orgasmic than repentant. The popular artist Palma Giovane specialized in portraits of the Magdalen placed in front of a hermit's cave. Despite the prominence of her emblems—book, skull, eyes rolled upward to heaven—barely concealed beneath her skimpy rags was a figure of Rubenesque proportions.

Yet in the hands of a great master the baroque Magdalen became psychologically complex, a poignant figure wracked by the clash between puissant eroticism and remorse, between vibrant sensuality and society's condemnation of its power. Venice's greatest painter of the female nude, Titian, was fascinated by the Magdalen, painting her in various poses throughout his life. Most famously, his monumental *Noli Me Tangere* of 1512 draws on the familiar tomb scene from John's Gospel, as a fully clothed Magdalen on bent knees reaches out to embrace a strikingly human risen Christ, who draws away, for his soul has not yet ascended to heaven.

Less famous, but more moving and psychologically astute, is his stunning *Magdalene* of 1531. Here Titian focuses solely on the Magdalen set, as in a darkened theater, against the backdrop of a dark, thickly clouded, threatening sky. A small aperture in the storm clouds opens to allow a flash of light, illuminating the warm flesh tones of her nude torso. As in Boticelli's *Birth of Venus*, one arm modestly folds over her breasts, while a glorious mane of thick, reddish-gold hair drapes her chest and lower body. Yet, for all her sensuality she touches a sympathetic chord. Utterly alone and profoundly vulnerable, this Magdalen has a psychological depth totally missing from Boticelli's mythologized goddess.

If her full, shapely breasts, tipped by rosy, erect nipples, seem to invite an erotic response, there is tragedy and mystery here as well. A single tear rolls down her cheek, for she understands the penalty she must pay for her beauty and the life she has led—something Titian knew first hand given his close association with several famous Venetian courtesans. For the poet Francesco Maria Molza, the mixed message was clear:

> Your lovely features become humble and sad,
> Your wild sense disciplined,
> . . . Chaste, wise, pleasing, beautiful, lively,
> It must have been so
> this is no merely human Work:
> flesh here expresses both
> Chaste lasciviousness and lascivious chastity.* [11]

Vasari, too, regarded Titian's *Magdalene* as a woman who "moves not to lust, but to pity."[12] In her upward, imploring gaze, in the almost perceptible gasp of religious ecstasy, in the eyes brimming with tears, she suffers both remorse and a vision of a heavenly world. The moment is one of great pain and great joy intermixed, a dichotomy familiar to an age imbued with the conjunction between sacred and profane love. In such a climate Titian's *Magdalene* captures the blinding, ecstatic moment when heightened desire leads to realization of divine, rather than carnal love.

In Venice's humanist salons this *Magdalene* might be read as a parable on the *trattati d'amore,* the treatises of love describing the three rungs on the "ladder of love." The first rung, symbolizing erotic love with its "furious and burning thirst," inevitably disappoints when the fire of passion is dissipated.[13] On the second rung, symbolizing marital love, sexual love gives way to spiritual bonding. On the final rung the soul or reason masters the caprices of the body, and the bliss of divine love is realized.

Clearly, Titian's *Magdalene* has attained this third rung as, with tear filled eyes fixed on heaven, she anticipates the ecstasy of union with the divine. Indeed, Titian never again captured that poignant moment or the essential duality. Thirty years later, in 1560, he did another M*agdalene*—this one a figure of fashion rather than of penitence. Draped in a thin, delicate material that tantalizes rather than conceals, she wears an elegant striped shawl and carefully oiled, modish curls. Despite her emblems—book, skull, cave—there is no conflict here, only a stylish courtesan solely concerned with the delights of this world.

Indeed, many artists used the convention of a scantily clothed, hermetic Magdalen as an excuse for a study of female sensuality, as in *The Penitent Magdalen* (1619–20) of a Roman painter, Orazio Gentileschi. Despite her hermit's cave, book, and skull, her long hair barely conceals her nude, reclining body with ample breasts accented by a ray of strong light.* Such a figure

---

*Unlike his earlier *Mary Magdalene* (1605), which portrayed a fully draped, hermetic figure with long, stringy hair.

became the standard for paintings of the Magdalen by artists everywhere in Europe and England, with the notable exception of an artist closely associated with Gentileschi—his gifted daughter Artemesia. Her own *Penitent Magdalene,* done at virtually the same time (1617–20), presents, once again, the tragic, conflicted woman, a victim of an unrelentingly judgmental society.

Artemesia, in fact, knew firsthand the price to be paid for loss of honor in a society obsessed with it. One of the first women in Europe to have a major career as an artist—she was court painter to Charles I of England for four years—at age sixteen Artemesia suffered a trauma that haunted her for the rest of her life. Although cloistered by her father under the constant watch of a maid, Artemesia was raped in her own home by a colleague of her father's, the painter Agostino Tassi.

Despite Tassi's rough reputation, Orazio allowed Artemesia to work with him on a large ceiling mural for the Borgheses and engaged him to give her lessons in perspective, in which Tassi was an expert. To possess her became his obsession. One day Tassi bribed her maid to leave them alone, gagged Artemesia with a handkerchief, and brutally raped her. Although she fought like a wildcat, tearing some skin from his penis and attacking him with a knife afterward, he managed to sooth her with a promise of marriage.[14] What he didn't tell her was that he was already married, and had been briefly imprisoned for incest with his sister-in-law.

Eventually Orazio learned about the rape. When Tassi broke his promise of marriage, Orazio pressed charges against him for having ruined his daughter, a serious crime in seventeenth-century Italy. Once again Artemesia was victimized, for a public trial spelled shame and dishonor for her, regardless of the outcome.

After examination by midwives who testified that she was no longer a virgin, Artemesia voluntarily submitted to the thumb-screw torture as proof that she was telling the truth (a test administered only to the woman in such cases). Screaming with pain as the metal rings were progressively tightened, she stuck to her story. Tassi, however, swore that she had not been a virgin and that all the women in her family—including her mother and sisters—were notoriously licentious women. Although he was proven a serial liar, the outcome for him was negligible. The precise verdict in the case is not known, only that Tassi was exiled from Rome for a brief time. Artemesia, on the other hand, suffered a more lasting fate—that of the outcast woman. To save the family honor, a marriage was hastily arranged to a nonentity, a minor Florentine painter named Stiatesi. Although they lived together only briefly, he left her with a daughter and a marital status that banned her from ever marrying again.

Being illiterate at that point in her life, Artemesia could not leave a written testimony of the violence done her; only the court records reveal the trauma of an experience that left her with profound emotional scars. Yet she has left us a more potent testament in her art. Indeed, some of her most powerful paintings depict a graphic violence unusual for any artist, man or woman.

Her *Judith Slaying Holofernes* (1612–13) has a gruesome realism that stuns the viewer even today. Both Judith and her servant, their facial expressions contorted by fury, attend to their grisly task with focused energy. In the horrific moment when Judith's knife pierces Holofernes's throat, no curtain shields the expression of terror on his face, the eyes rolled back in panic, or the scream escaping the open mouth, while from his severed jugular artery spurts a small fountain of dark red blood.*

By comparison, Artemesia's *Penitent Magdalene* conveys the deep, searing pain of a disgraced woman whose stylish appearance suggests a courtesan. Shadows obscure her face; a

---

*Actually, there are two versions of this painting, this one in the Uffizi in Florence, the other slightly less graphic.

dark, hazy background stresses her isolation. Seated in a chair, she draws her legs up, almost in fetal position. One bare foot protrudes from under her gown, and one hand clutches her breast in a gesture of either pain, contrition, or self-defense. The other pushes away a small mirror—symbol of worldly vanity and things of this world.[15]

Typically, in Artemesia's work the latter gesture conveys a double meaning—perhaps an instinctive protective movement, a hand thrust against someone or something lurking in the darkness. Nor does this Magdalen gaze upward to heaven, but directly at the viewer with an imploring, pained expression that bears resemblance to another striking work—Artemesia's *Lucretia* of 1621. Coiled in precisely the same fetal position, Lucretia, herself a victim of rape, gathers her courage as she prepares to plunge a dagger into her breast.

Artemesia's *Penitent Magdalene,* however, is ambiguous, its meaning clouded in mystery. On the one hand it suggests the courtesan/Magdalen who must reap the awful consequences of her life. On the other hand, this woman seems more sinned against than sinner; a tragic figure far removed from the penitent racked by guilt. In that respect she is strangely modern—not the familiar sinner/saint, but something more human—the fallen woman who internalizes her guilt, a woman crushed by the sentence society imposes on its Magdalens.

Indeed, when syphilis arrived in Venice via its teeming ports to ravage the city, panicked officials placed the blame squarely on its prostitutes. To attack the source of this terrible blight on their city at its roots, reformers acknowledged that poverty, above all, drove women to prostitution. Thus was born the *Convertiti*—part shelter, part reformatory—where fallen women and prostitutes might take refuge and a find a new way of life.

The idea was simple—to provide food and shelter to save women from prostitution. Yet once released, too many women fell by the wayside, for their options remained unchanged—to eke out a miserable subsistence in the most menial of jobs, if they were lucky enough to get them, to starve if they couldn't. Something more was needed, nothing less than a radical moral reformation.

And so reformers turned to the Magdalen as their model, along with the tried-and-true formula of penitence and redemption. In one of the strictest of these reformatories, the Guidecca Convertite, inmates were constantly reminded that, like the Magdalen, they too might be "taken from the hands of the devil . . . and from the filth of the flesh." They too could repent and adopt "the chaste life of the spirit," living for the remainder of their lives in solitude and penitence.[16]

Courtesans too were targeted by reformers. Bombarded from the pulpit with terrifying sermons describing the tortures awaiting them in the after-life, they too were coerced into exchanging their luxurious apartments, clothes, jewels for the penitent's hair-shirt, the bare cell, hard work, and deprivation of the Convertiti.

In certain ways the Guidecca Convertite resembled a convent. Inmates endured a severe trial period at a separate house, just as nuns do as novitiates. Those who passed had their hair shorn off before taking up their austere life. But instead of the Virgin to console them, they might gaze instead at a painting on the ceiling of the chapel showing the Magdalen in ecstasy, as angels draw her upward to heaven.[17] Like her, their reward awaited them in heaven.

In the coming age the *Convertite* would be called Magdalen Houses, while all transgressive women—prostitutes, courtesans, mistresses, unwed mothers—were called Magdalens. Even as women gained a measure of independence through work as actresses, musicians, singers, milliners, maids, the category of outcast pertained, while the feminine dichotomy became more entrenched than ever. It would seem that the poet Aretino's blunt remark, "there are only three categories of women: nuns, wives and whores," applied as much to the coming age as to the sixteenth century.[18]

And in that very notion lies the cutting irony of John Ford's Restoration play *'Tis Pity She's a Whore.*

CHAPTER 15

"'Tis Pity She's a Whore"

One would think that Protestantism would spell the demise of Mary Magdalen in the Reformed Church. The Swiss reformer Zwingli rejected her out of hand. Calvin decried the false melding of Mary of Bethany and Luke's "sinner" with the true Mary of Magdala, thereby distorting the true biblical figure. Most important, Protestants rejected the elaborate Catholic formula of confession, contrition, and penance, maintaining that Protestants must look inward and search their own consciences. The penitent Magdalen, it would seem, had lost her function.

But the Magdalen's image, like that of the Virgin, was too deeply entrenched in Christian consciousness to be eradicated. Sinner/prostitute she would remain, symbol of the powerful lure of female sexuality. When society became too genteel to utter the word prostitute, the polite euphemism would be Magdalens. Nor would she be divested of her role as scapegoat for male lust. Amongst certain Protestants sects the notion of original sin became more pervasive than ever, while guilt became internalized into a ravaged conscience denied the balm of confession. Although divested of sainthood, the Magdalen remained, as ever, the temptress responsible for leading men into perdition.

Not that all Protestants agreed on matters of sexuality and sin. During one of the informal but heated debates held around Luther's dinner table, a guest made the startling proposition that Christ was not only a sexual man, but may have had sexual relations with several women, including the Samaritan woman, the woman taken in adultery, and the Magdalen.[1] Luther's response is not recorded. However, he made no secret of his fondness for feminine beauty, especially their long hair, for him

> the finest ornament women have. Of old, virgins used to wear it loose, except when they were in mourning. I like women to let their hair fall down their back; it's a most agreeable sight.

Luther also named his favorite daughter Magdalena, and when she died in his arms at age fourteen he exclaimed, "I have sent a saint to heaven."[2] *

As Luther grew older he also overcame his youthful conviction that he was the most miserable of sinners, and developed an aversion to pious souls wracked by guilt. Possessed of a healthy zest for life, Luther no longer cowered in fear before the glowering God of judgment. To the gloomy, unctuous Melanchthon he advised, "Sin powerfully; God can forgive only a hearty sinner."[3] He himself came to believe in a "loving God [who] wills that we eat drink and be merry," and he followed that example with good food and beer (in moderation).[4]

---

*At the gravesite he cried out, "My darling Lenichen, you will rise and shine like the stars and the sun," possibly a reference to the Virgin in respect to the young girl's innocence.

Luther also approved of card-playing and dancing, the latter being the best way for young men and women to court under supervision. Nor should

> Christians . . . shun plays because there are sometimes coarseness and adulteries therein; for such reasons they would have to give up the Bible too.[5]

Luther, in fact, held that it was sometimes necessary to "give the devil his due" by drinking, playing, or talking "bawdy . . . out of hate and contempt for the Devil."[6] Such occasional slips give a merciful God the chance to demonstrate His benevolence. Sin can even lead to a powerful intimacy with Christ, for it is faith, not penance, that evokes forgiveness. Christians should also remember that the only true penitent is Christ, not the Magdalen. Only Jesus died for the sins of mankind; hence, only he stands as intercessor between mankind and grace.

If Luther modified his obsession with original sin, Calvin only became more rigid in his dark view of mankind's depravity. Theoretically Calvin had no use for celibacy, believing that "Man was formed to be a social animal. . . . [S]olitude is not good." As to sexuality, nature itself demands it. Those who rail against marriage are in partnership with Satan, for God "ordains the conjugal life for man, not to his destruction, but to his salvation."[7] Yet we find no trace of Luther's earthy exuberance in Calvin's coldly logical, legalistic thinking. He himself never married, and beneath the rhetoric in support of sexuality lies a deep-seated repulsion, a virulent misogyny reminiscent of the early Church Fathers.

In particular, Calvin remained fixated on the Fall. In the beginning woman was created to be help-meet and "faithful assistant" to her husband, marriage being "a friendly and peaceful intercourse." Unfortunately, Eve ruined it all. Because of her woman must endure the agony of childbirth. Likewise, instead of "a liberal and gentle subjection" to her husband, "she is cast into servitude." A bad marriage is merely punishment for the Fall, which in its wake brought "strifes, troubles, sorrows, dissensions and a boundless sea of evils." Among the latter is sexuality, which Calvin regarded as a "depravity of appetite [that] requires a remedy."[8]

For Calvinists, then, the feminine polarity became more rigid than ever, an impassable chasm between chaste and fallen women. And despite a hue and cry about the misreading of the Gospels which confused Luke's 'sinner' with the Magdalen, Protestants in general not only adhered to the prostitute myth, they elaborated on it.

As to Catholics, to redeem the Magdalen would mean not only acknowledging a major doctrinal error but the loss of its most important symbol of penitence. However, a resurgence of mysticism throughout Europe brought with it a revival of the Gnostic Magdalen, whose blinding revelations tapped into the divine essence. Especially in Protestant England, where the High Anglican Church held on to many of the trappings of Catholicism, including the saints, the importation of a rich lode of mysticism from the continent resulted in a profusion of poems, sermons, and homilies dedicated to the Magdalen.[9] Seventeenth-century Protestant England saw the flourishing of a cult of the Magdalen, not as penitent sinner, but as inspired mystic who arrives at her visions via the self-same passions suppressed by the cold rationality of the Reform Church.

In a country still wracked by religious factionalism, England was a dangerous place for Catholics. Nonetheless, Robert Southwell, a renegade Englishman trained in Rome as a Jesuit, surreptitiously returned to England, bringing with him a penchant for mysticism and an obsession with the Magdalen. Southwell paid the price—he was eventually executed for his religious convictions—but his widely read *Mary Magdalen's Funerall Tears*, published in 1591, gave him an immortality of a kind.

In an overblown, highly emotional style, Southwell offers as "subject of this discourse" a Magdalen wholly consumed by a vehement love for Jesus. But Christians must take care not to emulate her excesses, for religion demands a balance: "neither too stormy nor too calm a mind . . . [but] a middle temper."[10] To illustrate the point, he draws from John's narrative, placing the Magdalen with Peter and John at the tomb where they discover the missing body.

The men flee in terror, but the Magdalen remains, almost prostrate in her grief. Weeping bitterly for "her master . . . the totall of her loves," she briefly considers suicide. But as sole witness to the resurrection, Jesus's living image would die with her. Putting aside self-pity, she is saved by her "most sincere and perfect love." Her destiny must be to live and endure "a death never ending," a "Love . . . as strong as Death." Here, then, is the Magdalen of the Gnostic Gospels 'whom some call Love'.

Blinded by her tears, she fails at first to recognize the resurrected Jesus in the garden, who sternly reprimands her for not discerning the one for whom "thy heart throbbeth . . . thy eye weepeth, thy whole body fainteth." Nonetheless, his merciful nature prevails. Her lapse will be used as an example to others:

> Learn sinfull man of this once sinfull woman
> that sinners may find Christ
> if their sinnes be ammended.

They, too, must "persevere in tears" in seeking Jesus, for only through a blinding veil of tears can the true penitent achieve an ecstasy akin to that of the Magdalen. The poem ends with the Magdalen proclaiming in a paroxysm of joy: "I have seen our Lord / and these things he said to me."[11]

Southwell's highly emotional style, his deliberate play on the passions, and his belief in the efficacy of weeping to release deeply felt emotions influenced not only future religious movements such as Wesley's Methodism, but writers and poets, among them John Donne and another renegade English Catholic poet, Richard Crashaw, also a devotee of the Magdalen.[12]

The son of a strict Puritan preacher, Crashaw saw his mother die when he was seven, followed by his stepmother fifteen months later. Perhaps those losses account for his passionate devotion to the Virgin, the Magdalen, and St. Teresa of Avila. Yet in his fervent *Hymn to Sainte Teresa,* there is something patently sexual in breathless phrases that virtually pant with physical desire: "Thou art love's victime; and must dy / . . . His is the Dart must make the Death / . . . A Dart thrice dip't in that richg flame."*[13] Clearly, like the Baroque sculptor Bernini (who crafted the *Ecstasy of St. Theresa*), Crashaw was familiar with the saint's diaries, which vividly describe the erotic fantasies that preceded her mystical visions.

Crashaw's hymn to the Magdalen, *The Weeper,* seems chaste by comparison. Yet its title page features a portrait of the Magdalen clutching a heart that weeps profuse tears, much like a human lover. Crashaw's overheated language reinforces the image:

> Thy fair eyes, sweet MAGDALENE!
> Heavens thy faire Eyes bee
> heavens of ever-falling stars
> Upwards thou dost weep
> . . .
> We are taught best by thy Teares
> . . .
> O wit of love! that thus could place
> Fountain and garden in one face.[14]

Like Southwell, Crashaw's fetish of tears anticipates the mania for weeping in the eighteenth century, when sentimentalism was at its height, and truly sensitive souls carried a handkerchief at all times to mop up their tears. In Crashaw's time, however, souls were more hardened, especially in the Jacobean theater with its penchant for gory tragedies that outdid even Shakespeare's darkest plays. For playwright, John Ford, the

---

*During the Renaissance die was also a code name for orgasm.

Magdalen's bitter tears took on a darker meaning. In his shocking play about an incestuous brother/sister passion, *Tis Pity She's a Whore,* Ford pulls out all the stops in his evocation of the ancient myth of woman as perpetrator of male lust.

Ostensibly a blood-and-guts "revenge play" typical of the early seventeenth century, Ford's play stretches the convention to its outer limits. In its intense scrutiny of sex, jealousy, and betrayal, it seems strikingly modern, yet even today its frank portrayal of incest makes audiences wince. And while Ford neither condemns nor denigrates the lovers, beneath his cutting irony lies the familiar duality. It is Anabella the sister, not Giovanni the brother, who must pay for their mutual crime, the great sin being her loss of virtue. Although Ford convinces us of the innocence of Anabella and the integrity of her passion, the audience must decide whether she is sinner or saint.

At first Anabella recoils in horror when Giovanni reveals his passion in a gloriously lyrical language reminiscent of Shakespeare's *Romeo and Juliet.* They are, he says, two souls who share a unique affinity, having shared the same womb, having been raised side by side in the same house. Their unsullied innocence sets them apart from the degeneracy and foolishness of the suitors whom Anabella's father thrusts upon her. True, such a love shatters powerful social and religious taboos. But the real villain here is the cold greed of an avaricious father who thinks only of his purse in making a match for his daughter.

As in *Romeo and Juliet,* they seek the advice of the family Friar who reacts cynically, oblivious to the sincerity of their love. Giovanni, he says, must take a mistress, Anabella must marry the sardonic, lecherous nobleman, Soranzo. But their passion is too strong, and they consummate their love in a scene of intense lovemaking. Despite the sublimity of her love, Giovanni convinces Anabella that it is her beauty that has brought them to this abyss of sin. Ultimately, it is she who must pay for their mutual crime.

Distraught, Anabella seeks out the Friar to make her confession and atone. In this remarkable scene the Friar uses a flickering candle to project shadows on the wall of a darkened room, creating a terrifying landscape of hell, that "black and hollow vault, where day is never seen." He urges her to "weep, weep on / these tears may do you good; weep faster yet, / Whiles I do read a lecture / Wretched creature!" Hysterical with fear and guilt, Anabella. drops to her knees. Weeping and wringing her hands, she vows to atone by marrying the despicable Soranzo.

Immediately the Friar abandons his diatribe on hell and damnation. Her marriage, he says, will restore her honor in society's eyes. But in so doing Anabella forfeits the balm of contrition and Christ's forgiveness. Hers will be a hell on earth when her husband discovers her pregnancy and his dishonor, despite his own infidelity with a married woman.

Ultimately, Anabella is cruelly martyred; first by her husband who brutally beats her, then by Giovanni. Driven mad by betrayal and his belief that the marriage is proof of her wanton nature,. he murders her. But even as he drives the knife into her breast, cleansing tears wash away his mad jealousy, restoring to him her true nature, the sacredness of her love. In a paroxysm of grief Giovanni forgives Annabella whispering, "Go thou white in thy soul, to fill a throne/ Of innocence and sanctity in Heaven. "

In the grisly culminating scene, Giovanni cuts out his sister's heart, displaying the bloody organ to husband and father whom he kills, then turns his dagger on himself. As epilogue, a cynical Cardinal, symbol of the Church, surveys the bloody carnage of bodies, proclaiming the moral behind this story of "incest and murder so strangely met." The fault, of course, lies not with the men, their lust, greed, and abuse, but with Anabella. The play ends with his cynical indictment of her: "Of one so young, so rich in nature's store,/Who could not say, *'Tis Pity She's a Whore*'?"[15]

The cutting irony of those final words is generally lost on

contemporary audiences, as is the allusion to the Magdalen legend in the repentance scene. Even in its own time Ford took care to make that obscure so as to avoid any taint of "popery." Soon, even the play itself would fall into obscurity when Cromwell's Puritan regime closed London's theaters in its campaign to imposed a stern Calvinist morality on "merry" England. With blasphemy, laziness, drunkenness, card-playing, gambling, adultery and fornication punishable crimes, the Magdalen now seemed superfluous.

Eventually, the pleasure loving English had their fill of Cromwell, returning to their "cakes and ales." Yet even after the restoration of the monarchy, a Calvinist morality remained deeply entrenched in English society. Although hard core Puritans went underground or emigrated to Holland or the New World, they left their mark on an emerging mercantile society. Gradually, the sexual permissiveness of the court and the aristocracy would give way to a bourgeois ethic of marriage and monogamy. Adultery would become the great sin even as prostitution swelled to unprecedented numbers, while the wealthy maintained expensive mistresses or courtesans. As always, the blame would fall squarely on the heads of the women in question, now commonly called Magdalens.

If anything, the equation of the Magdalen with prostitution became more entrenched than ever, absolving "respectable" men of responsibility for their own lustful impulses. This Magdalen, however, was neither weeper nor mystic, but an internalized, profoundly psychological idea about women and their sexuality. Women who violated the ever more rigid moral codes would be badgered into emulating her renunciation in the most rigorous, even fanatical way. Indeed, missionaries and reformers bent on saving fallen women from their cesspools of vice referred to them as Magdalens.

CHAPTER 16

MODERN MAGDALENS

The charming heroine of John Cleland's *Fanny Hill, Memoirs of a Woman of Pleasure,* one of the most notorious and widely read novels of the eighteenth century, was a prostitute who never at any time in her successful career repented her life.* Fanny's profession never gets the best of her, nor does she ever lose her near-religious belief in true love, experienced with her first lover, the beloved Charles. At the close of the novel she becomes his wife and a self-proclaimed woman of Virtue.

Initially, Fanny, a fresh and innocent young country girl, comes to London seeking work, only to be conscripted by a notorious bawd into her brothel. Fanny is saved from a deflowering by a rich but revolting old lecher by the handsome

*Published in London in 1749.

young Charles, who introduces her not merely to sex, but to love, and makes her his mistress. Even after Charles's uncle kidnaps him, forcing him to abandon her, Fanny cherishes that memory, despite her return to prostitution as her only option. After a series of incredible romps through every possible variation of sensual pleasure, graphically but elegantly described by Cleland, Charles returns. Once again Fanny knows the ecstasy of "love! that may be styled the Attic salt of enjoyment . . . Indeed, the joy, great as it is, is still a vulgar one, . . . for it is love alone that refines, ennobles and exalts it."[1]

Thus Fanny is redeemed by love, not penance. Rather than miseries and travails she becomes a respectable wife. Looking back on her former life, she proclaims her pity and disdain for "those who, immersed in gross sensuality, are insensible to the so delicate charms of VIRTUE, than which even pleasure has not a greater friend, nor than VICE a greater enemy."[2] In fact, Cleland's motivation for writing this eighteenth-century 'Joy of Sex' was to protest the Christian equation of sex with sin and shame, to advance the enlightenment belief in sex as natural and healthy, an essential ingredient in a monogamous marriage between compatible partners—one of the great ideals of eighteenth-century reformers.

To realize such an ideal, however, entailed a long and difficult struggle. For one thing, throughout Europe and England marital arrangements had been, and continued to be, loose and informal. In rural areas couples often pledged their troth by a clasp of hands, or a vow to marry at some future time. Some stood hand in hand amongst friends and family, some at the door of the church. Despite a concerted campaign by the Church to make marriage a sacrament performed by a priest, couples dodged church weddings for any number of reasons—lack of a dowry, disapproval of parents, social barriers against marrying out of one's class, the church's ban against divorce. Well into the nineteenth century the working poor lived together in "shameful concubinage," a church wedding being beyond their meager means.[3]

But the greatest impediment to monogamous marriage was the pervasiveness of the arranged marriage, essentially a business arrangement that solidified and expanded land, wealth, social status. Cutting across all classes, from affluent peasant to the bourgeoisie and the aristocracy, the idea of love and marriage was completely foreign, needs of the heart being met in extramarital relations—for men either courtesans, mistresses, concubines or prostitutes.

Although the English considered themselves to be higher moral beings than the French, such extramarital arrangements were thoroughly ingrained in English society from the court down. The Restoration monarch, Charles II, much admired for his sexual prowess, openly flaunted his numerous mistresses and a profusion of 'royal "bastards'. One of the most popular was the actress Nell Gwynn, who rose out of the dregs of society. However, a popular doggerel assured: "She hath got a trick / to handle his prick / But never lay hands on his scepter."[4] George I's principal mistress, Melusine Von Der Schulenberg, was declared by Walpole to be "in effect, as much Queen of England as any ever was." George II, a devoted husband, swore to Queen Caroline on her death bed never to marry again: "No, I will take only a mistress!," a promise he honored.[5] George IV openly paraded his various mistresses, but his great love was the lovely widow, Mrs. Fitzherbert. In defiance of the Royal marriage Act of 1772, he secretly married her. Although their union was technically illegal, in his will he declared her to be his only "true and real wife."[6]

His brother William IV lived in a 'common law' marriage for twenty years with the great comic actress, Dora Jordan, before acceding to the throne in 1830. Faithful and devoted to him and their ten children, it was she who supported him during the impoverished years of his dukedom. When duty forced him to put her aside to marry a young heiress with the correct pedigree to be Queen, Dora struggled valiantly to support herself and their children. For the rest of her life she suffering the degradation of fallen woman. In the end she died alone and impoverished in France.

For an affluent mercantile class bent on upward mobility, religion was only one factor in the rise of church sanctioned, monogamous marriages. Ashamed of the coarse behavior of ancestors who may have been peasants, farmers, or artisans, they worked assiduously to become genteel. Napkins came into use to keep clothing free of grease stains, handkerchiefs for blowing the nose. Coarse bathroom and bawdy talk, once commonly used by all classes including the highest aristocracy, was discouraged in company, especially when ladies were present. Breaking wind in public, spitting, and cleaning one's teeth at the dinner table were strictly prohibited. Above all, marriage became a requirement for respectability and status. Yet, if ever the double standard defined a society it would be the double-edged sword of Victorian respectability.

Ironically, an age built on a rigid belief in male superiority took its name from a woman—Queen Victoria—who was not the dour prude we have been led to believe. As a young girl Victoria's great passion was for dancing, as a woman for her beloved Albert. The Queen, in fact, could show herself to be surprisingly unvictorian, as when she caught sight of some nude drawings at an art exhibit, throwing her staff into a tizzy. At the time even the word nude was not mentioned in mixed company—rather the euphemism unclothed. Terrified of her reaction to such indecency, the Queen's staff tried desperately to conceal them. But when she accidentally spied them she was entranced, and purchased several for her private collection, which included portraits of robustly nude maidens that she had purchased as a birthday gift for "dear Albert."[7]

More typically Victorian was the attitude of the royal couple toward child-rearing. Haunted by the clouds of notoriety that hung over their forebears—the illicit relationships of Victoria's uncles, the dissolute court of Albert's father who divorced his mother when he was five—the royal couple went to extreme lengths to shelter their prodigious brood. Determined that Edward, heir to the throne, would not follow in the footsteps of his infamous ancestors, as a child he endured a fanatically rigid program of study, wholesome foods and activities that precluded even harmless indulgences such as an occasional sweet, sleeping late, or having a playmate. Of course, it merely produced the opposite effect. Edward became the quintessential raconteur, bon-vivant, and prodigious ladies' man. At his coronation the special pew reserved for Edward's close women friends was dubbed 'The King's Loose Box'.[8]

Immediately on escaping the watch-dog guardianship of his parents, Edward took up an endless string of affairs with women of every class—from notorious French courtesans, to the esteemed actress Lily Langtry, to the aristocratic Georgina, countess of Dudley, and, finally, to the devoted Alice Keppel, wife of an army officer. All this, in addition to his marriage to the lovely Alix, Princess Alexandra of Denmark, with whom he had six children in the first seven years of marriage. Like many another Victorian wife, worn out from constant pregnancies and her husband's prodigious sexual appetite, Alix turned a blind eye to her husband's affairs. Ultimately, she graciously acknowledged Mrs. Keppel, treating her as a friend and even inviting her into the family circle.[9]

Such open-minded tolerance was hardly characteristic of the archetypal Victorian wife, back bone of the Purity League or the White Cross, offended by the mere mention of certain body parts. In Victorian parlance a chicken had a bosom, not a breast, underwear became underclothes, and trousers were "inexpressibles."[10] But the worse affront to the delicacy of the Victorian wife was the spectacle of a fallen woman intruding herself into respectable society, a threat to daughters and other innocents who might be inspired to emulate them.

Never mind that some of these fallen women were themselves devoted mothers, or loving, monogamous partners to men barred by social codes from marrying them, or, like Mrs. Keppel, taking the pressure off marriages that might otherwise implode. Most dangerous of all, the fallen woman presented an example of independence, of liberation from domesticity and the snug security of the gilded cage. Moving outside her proper domain, she exposed herself to the indecent habits and loose language of men in violation of the proprieties demanded of women in polite society.

In its stern sobriety and hysterical dread of vice, Victorian society smacked of Calvin's community of saints. Yet beneath the ethic of self-denial lay a commercial rather than a religious motivation—a work ethic whose key words were duty, success, profit. For the famous art critic, John Ruskin, the two great sins were Idleness and Cruelty, the first being the worse since God commands us to "Work while you have light."[11] Worldly indulgences jeopardized work and duty more so than the soul. As the noted Dr. Arnold put it, life is "no pilgrimage of pleasure, but a scene of toil, of effort, of appointed work . . . of fearful evils to be uprooted or trampled down."[12] Calvin could not have said it more plainly.

That evil might be something as innocuous as the pleasure derived from a cigar. Stunned by the "delicious" sensation on smoking his first cigar, the Evangelical Sir James Stephen swore "never [to] smoke again."[13] As always, however, the greatest danger was the pleasures of the flesh, especially in maintaining class hegemony. In fact, modesty and chastity were the hallmark of a well-bred woman, even in marriage. Thus the resurrection of "chaste devotion", the archaic model for Christian marriage in which sex served only the purpose of procreation.[14]

For wives, chastity within marriage was no problem since it

was generally held that women had a feeble, attenuated sex drive. For her sex was a duty, not a pleasure. As to the husband's more vigorous natural drives, self-control was vital as well, since too much sex debilitated strength and the industry essential to commercial success. Periods of abstinence for seven, or better still, ten days were recommended, too much sex being the moral and financial ruin of many a. man. The famous doctor Acton, whose books were read religiously, warned that overindulgence in sex could spiral into bankruptcy, or even be fatal due to the physical ravages caused by masturbation and syphilis.[15] For full vigor of body, Acton recommended practicing mind over matter in "controlling all sexual excitement."[16] Most of all, unbridled sensuality smacked of the lower classes—the coarse, vulgar workers who manned the factories, then went to their hovels to breed like rabbits. Genteel men and women must take care not to degrade themselves with such animal sexuality.

The problem was that men, by nature competitive and aggressive, are as vigorous in their sexuality as in their minds and bodies, whereas women, timid, weak, more spiritual than sensual, need sex only for procreation. Scientists even found that women had a smaller cerebellum, the locus for sexual passion in the brain.[17] To display any sign of sexual pleasure was the mark of a lewd woman, the dead give-away being the emission of vaginal lubricants secreted "only by lascivious women."[18] A wife's duty was to gratify her husband's sensual needs, but not her own, on pain of losing his respect, or worse still, being suspected of having masculine tendencies.

Despite all that, we now know that many Victorians couples enjoyed mutually satisfactory sexual lives in which women were active partners.[19] Nonetheless, there is prodigious testimony attesting to a revulsion for sex by men and women both that justifies the term proper Victorian. Indeed, the Ruskin marriage, was hardly unique. William Rosetti broke his engagement to Henrietta Rintoul after she informed him that the marriage would be as celibate as their engagement. John Stuart Mill and Mrs. Harriet Taylor kept their extended liaison—no secret to Harriet's husband — platonic. When finally they married, they agreed that sex only denigrated real love. Whether the marriage was ever consummated remains a mystery, but in their writings the Mills expressed disdain for couples who "become a slave of . . . animal appetites."[20] Yet Mill had his doubts. In 1857 he told a friend that he had dreamed one night of a woman who could be both friend and Magdalen, that is, sexual. But she quickly vanished when a woman strongly resembling Harriet appeared to reprimand him sternly for his sensual fantasy.

Mill was not alone in his Magdalen fantasy. Almost compulsively, Victorian writers described the pull between the untouchable, virtuous woman, and the off-limits Magdalen of Mill's dream, a theme common to all the novels of the popular writer, Wilkie Collins, friend and. colleague of Charles Dickens. In particular, his novel, *Basil,* explores the quandary of an ingenuous young man torn between his sexual attraction to a woman from a vulgar, commercial class family, and the pure, untainted love of his chaste sister. If the concept of Madonna/whore was not yet in the common vocabulary, Wilkie's novel explores its psychological dynamic in full.

Central to the novel is Basil's bitter resentment of his distant, undemonstrative father, whose snobbish pride of caste and prudery have robbed him of all human warmth.[21] Totally innocent of the opposite sex except for his loving but prim sister, Clara, Basil is struck by the sensuous, dark beauty of a woman sitting opposite him on an omnibus one day. He later learns she is Margaret, a linen draper's daughter, and his dreams are haunted by the "voluptuous languor of black eyes . . . her full lips . . . that to other eyes might have looked too full."[22]

Soon Clara intrudes herself into his dreams as the antithesis of Margaret. In one dream Basil finds himself in a field bounded on one side by a dark wood, on the other by a hill reaching to the sky. From the woods emerges a tall woman with long, flowing black hair; on the hill sits a woman dressed in white who stretches out her arms, silently beseeching him to join her. The dark woman's "lustrous" eyes, her touch that "ran through me like fire," prove irresistible. As the woman in white ascends to the clouds, wringing her hands in grief, Basil enters the wood where the dark woman's kiss sets his "blood burning . . . my breath failing me."[23]

Freud would have had a field day with Collins's metaphors—the dark wood and swarthy woman symbolizing both female sexuality and evil, the woman in white symbolizing purity and goodness. Indeed, Margaret becomes Basil's undoing when he finally contrives to meet her. Beneath her feigned lady-like airs and finishing school education lurks the vulgarity of a father engaged in business, and the cheap, gaudy decor of her home. Delighted by the prospect of an alliance with Basil's genteel family, Margaret's father suggests that they marry at once, but delay consummation for one year until she reaches maturity.

Keeping the marriage a secret, Basil naively hopes that his father will eventually give his blessing. But on the eve of their honeymoon Basil discovers that Margaret has been having an affair with her tutor all along. The eleventh hour discovery saves Basil from polluting himself and his family with Margaret's vulgarity. Conveniently, she catches typhus from her lover and dies unrepentant, "her long black hair streaming over her face."[24] Gripped by guilt, Basil tells his father about the marriage. Disinherited and cast out of the family, he seeks refuge in a remote Cornwall village by the sea.

Desolate, on the verge of madness, Basil has visions of his good angel, Clara, "Her face so bright and calm! Her watchful, weeping eyes."[25] Clara's timely arrival plucks him from the jaws of death; from then on she shares Basil's humble cottage. Reflecting on past calamities, Basil devotes himself to good works among the poor. The novel ends with "Clara's voice . . . now the happy voice of the happy old times" calling him to sit beside her in the garden to watch the setting sun descend into the sea.[26]

In an interesting turnabout, the penitent here is Basil, the fallen man. Indeed, all too often the untoward effect of the double standard on men as well as women was ignored. The near-incestuous love between brother and sister described in Collins's *Basil* was a common phenomenon amongst writers and artists of the period, most notably Wordsworth and his sister Dorothy, who went mad after he married. John Ruskin's sexual pathology has already been noted, and in the next chapter we will explore the horrors of the sexual underlife of upper-class Victorian men.

Collins himself avoided marriage, living with Mrs. Caroline Graves and her daughter for almost thirty years. When Mrs. Graves married a second time, Collins took up with Martha Rudd, a shepherd's daughter and a barmaid in an inn. They had three children together, but when Caroline Graves became available once again, Collins resumed his life with her and her daughter as if nothing had ever intervened.

Ambivalence about marriage and class also marked the lives of the Pre-Raphaelite Brotherhood of painters, whose espousal of the Madonna cult we have already noted. See-sawing between respectability and a bohemian life style, they combed London's working-class districts and slums looking for models for another genre of their work—portraits of women whose bold sensuality recalls the courtesan portraits of the baroque masters. Some were working-class women—milliners or servants—others were prostitutes from London's cesspools of poverty and misery.

Some of the Brotherhood took their models as mistresses, educating them and teaching them proper manners. Dante Gabriel Rossetti, for one, fell in love with his model, Elizabeth Siddall, a milliner with delicate features, pale red hair, and considerable artistic talent. Under his tutelage, Lizzie, as she was known, became a competent painter, but by the time he married her she was already wasted by advanced tuberculosis. Addicted to laudanum, a widely used cough medicine and pain killer with an opium base, she was constantly weak, sickly, and irritable. As a consequence, the marriage deteriorated.

Just at that difficult juncture Rossetti met a prostitute, the striking, red-headed Fanny Cornforth, at one of London's Pleasure Gardens. With her glorious, thick mane of auburn hair, her full mouth and voluptuous body, Fanny soon became Rossetti's favorite model. The antithesis of his frail and sickly wife, Rossetti became obsessed with her "image of savage, active health." Tainted by her hard life on the streets, Fannie never metamorphosed into a lady, as did Lizzie. Rather, in Rossetti's words, she "remained for him the simplest, the most real of all ... women."[27] Undoubtedly he had her in mind when he composed the poem, *Jenny* in 1858, a reverie addressed to a Haymarket prostitute: "Lazy, laughing, languid Jenny / Fond of a kiss and fond of a guinea./ . . . as I watch you there / For all your wealth of loosened hair."[28]

Just as the poet allows Jenny a moral latitude, proximity to Fanny seems to have softened Rossetti's attitude toward prostitution. The year before they met, Rossetti painted a large canvas entitled *The Gate of Memory,* in which a prostitute, crouched in a dark alley, watches a happy, carefree group of dancing children, a reminder of her own lost innocence and joy. Clearly *Memory* was meant as a warning to women not to emulate its forlorn subject. In the sequel entitled *Found,* Fanny was the model for the prostitute. Discovered by her former sweetheart, a drover, on a deserted London street at dawn, her scarlet lips, powdered face, expensive dress and silken shawl plainly mark her profession.

In an agony of shame, she cowers against a brick wall, her eyes shut, desperately trying to avert her former lover's gaze. As in *Memory,* the sight of the plainly dressed, good, simple man reminds her of what she has lost. If Rossetti intended this painting too as a warning, his subject is more human and sympathetic, as if the artist understands what has driven her to such a fate. In twenty-seven years Rossetti could never bring himself to finish this painting, nor did Fanny suffer the miserable fate of its subject.

Instead, she served as model for a series of stunning, half-length portraits that Rossetti called his Venetian Figures, or "visions of carnal loveliness."[29] In particular, *Bocca Baciata,* or *Much Kissed Lips* (1859), celebrates Fanny's dazzling sensuality: the full, red mouth, long, sensuous throat and ample bosom, the splendid mane of thick, wavy auburn hair adorned with jewelry and flowers.* The title, taken from Boccaccio's story of a woman with several lovers whose "much kissed" lips remain fresh, implies an affectionate vindication of Fanny's easy promiscuity. Whether they were lovers is not known, although sex between an artist and his model was almost a given. All we know for certain is that Rossetti was obsessed with her, painting her portrait over and over again.

Although Rossetti's Venetian Figures bear a strong resemblance to the courtesans of the baroque period, there is no reference to shame or penitence. Rather they celebrate the sitter's natural, earthy sensuality. *Fazio's Mistress* of 1863 focuses on Fanny's beautiful, opulent hair, as she binds it into braids to create the sinuous, rippling waves so dearly loved by the pre—Raphaelites. The *Blue Bower,* another half-portrait, takes its title from Rosetti's own, frankly erotic poem, *Song of the Bower:* "What were my prize, could I enter thy bower / This day, tomorrow, at eve or at morn? / Large lovely arms and a neck like a tower /

---

*Interestingly, in his novel, *Madeleine Ferat,* Emile Zola describes his quintessential "fallen woman" as having a "magnificent mane of auburn hair, scarlet red lips, wide grey eyes, tall and lissom," a literary portrait with a striking resemblance to Rosetti's Fanny portraits.*

Bosom then heaving that now lies forlorn."[30] In none of these portraits is there any attempt at the Magdalen disguise, or any ambiguity about the sheer power of Fanny's sexuality. Rather, it seems a natural force that precludes guilt or remorse.

Not until a decade later, in 1857, did Rossetti turn to the Magdalen in a huge canvas entitled *Mary Magdalene Leaving the House Of Feasting.* This time the ravishingly beautiful Annie Miller was his model, her copious, flowing auburn hair hardly distinguishable from Rossetti's carnal women. One year later, using another model, Rossetti did another, *Mary Magdalene at the Door of Simon the Pharisee.* Surrounded by a gay crowd of comely young couples, musicians, dancers, even a topless servant, she has become the penitent Magdalen. Gazing fixedly at Jesus through a window, she flings off her jewelry in a dramatic gesture of renunciation. Seemingly, the moment of conversion has arrived, yet the scene is fraught with ambiguity, for her expression conveys more of a lover's passion than remorse. Similarly, two plants frame the entrance to the house—the white lily of chastity, and a brilliant, yellow sunflower, symbol of fecundity. And despite the expression of disdain on the faces of Simon and his servant, Jesus's handsome face radiates compassion.

In that very same year (1858) the Pre-Raphaelite Fred Sandys painted a melancholic *Mary Magdalene* with a strong resemblance to Rosetti's wife, Lizzie. Despite a richly patterned background suggestive of Rossetti's 'carnal women', this Magdalen's long, red-gold tresses hang limply, while her expression of remorse suggests the traditional penitent.[31] Bereft of the beauty, the exuberant sensuality of Rossetti's Magdalens, her joyless aspect suggests an outcast exiled from hearth, home, motherhood.

Indeed, it is Sandy's Magdalen, not Rossetti's, that more truly reflects the reality of a culture in which prostitution rose to staggering levels, even as society used them as scapegoats for its own criminal perversions. Thus it was that the term Magdalen became one of the most pejorative terms of Victorian society, code name for "fallen woman" of every stripe—from fashionable courtesan, to kept mistress, to lowly, common prostitute.

CHAPTER 17

"The Great Social Evil"

Prostitution is as inseparable from our present marriage customs as the shadow from the substance. They are two sides of the same shield.

Westminster Review, 1868

Precisely as Victorian society gripped its upper and middle classes in a tight vise of prudery, so too it fed the very plant it wished to stamp out. The underside of Victorian culture was a curious one, obsessed with precisely the thing it worked so hard to suppress. In a culture of concealment and camouflage, sex went underground as outwardly respectable men led double lives—upstanding family men at home, clients of brothels and streetwalkers, keepers of concubines and mistresses in their alternative lives.

Often they strove valiantly to reconcile competing affections and loyalties. When Victor Hugo vacationed with his family at his island retreat, he installed his mistress in an adjoining house with windows facing on his study. When Emile Zola fell in love with his wife's charming young seamstress, he installed his mistress and their children in a second home. All of Paris, including his wife, knew of Zola's double life, quietly sanctioning the masquerade.

Darker still was a proliferation of erotica and pornography that took on the hue of the age—the naughtiness of a child deprived of normal channels to satisfy a natural curiosity about sex, the voyeurism and perversity of adults bound by the shackles of propriety. Even the impeccable Coventry Patmore, author of *Angel In The House*, owned a collection of classic erotica, cleverly concealed behind the shelves of his impressive scholarly library.[1] More candidly, Edward Sellon, dean of English Victorian pornography, published twin autobiographical works, *The Ups and Downs of Life* and *The Adventures of a Schoolboy*, which purported to be authentic accounts of the 'upstairs, downstairs' of Victorian erotic life.*

Of them all, it is the eleven-volume *My Secret Life*, author unknown, that provides the clearest window into the bizarre sexual underworld of Victorian England. Fantastic as it may seem in the sheer depravity of its sexual adventures, scholars today consider it authentic. Nor is the compulsion of a British gentleman to keep a detailed record of his sexual life anything new. Samuel Pepys kept a similar diary in the seventeenth century, assiduously notating every sexual encounter with a broad spectrum of women from servants and household staff--dairy and servant maids, nurses and governesses--to married and single women of his own class.

---

*Officially entitled *The New Epicurian: The Delights of Sex, Facetiously and Philosophically Considered.*

In *My Secret Life,* however, class lines are rigid, its upper-class writer availing himself of a swollen population of desperate women from the impoverished underclass, as well as rubber condoms to safeguard against the venereal diseases that eventually destroyed Pepys's health. Notable, too, is an expanded class of shop-girls whom the author can seduce for a pretty bauble--a brooch, a necklace, a silk handkerchief—a windfall as compared to the one to five pounds charged by professionals.

Our author cites Cleland's *Fanny Hill* as his model. However, while Cleland fastidiously avoided even a single crude expression, *My Secret Life* is filled with "gutter talk" in order to convey "absolute truth . . . without any regard whatsoever for what the world calls decency. Decency and voluptuousness in its fullest acceptance cannot exist together, one would kill the other."[2] And therein lies the difference. Whereas Cleland's charming Fanny has a deep reverence for sex, especially when sanctified by love, the author of *My Secret Life* is completely callous and crippled emotionally. Even marriage to a woman he loves brings him no happiness due to his insatiable desire for cold, detached seduction.

As an only child raised by typically fastidious parents, he is denied even the friendship of other boys. Instead, fondlings by nannies and nurses, furtive sex play with household servants and male relatives leave him with a residue of anxiety, fear and guilt. Shy, traumatized by his experiences and a painful condition known as phymosis—an inelasticity of the foreskin of the penis—at age seven he is packed off to boarding school where his classmates initiate him into masturbation and voyeurism. Eventually he sinks into an abyss of adolescent sexual practices from which the grown man can never escape.

A favorite pastime of his schoolmates is to masturbate while observing women urinating in bushes or other sheltered spots, a common practice of all classes before the advent of public toilets.

When they locate a concealed grating used for such a purpose, the young voyeurs hide in the basement of a shop. There they can enjoy an unlimited spectacle of bare bottoms while masturbating, the great hope being that a fountain of ejaculated sperm spurting upward will leave its mark on the unsuspecting object of their desires.[3] These habits become so deeply ingrained that, even at age nineteen, they revert to group masturbation at a dinner party for five former schoolmates. A prize is awarded to the one that climaxes first.[4]

Worse is yet to come. Despite his professed love for women, our author compulsively seeks out girls as young as twelve and thirteen to whom he can offer a meager sum—the equivalent of a day's or week's wages—in exchange for fondling and petting. Increasingly callous to the cruelty of his actions, one day he pays the same paltry sum to the mother of a young girl who waits outside the family bedroom while they have sex. Lust finally drives him to violence. An attempted rape in a hackney cab is thwarted by the would-be victim. But one day in the country he manages to overpower a young farm worker whose "tears ran down. If I hadn't committed a rape, it looked uncommonly like one."

By now he is so brutalized that his wedding night seems more a rape than love making. As his relationship with his wife deteriorates into mutual hostility, he returns to the streets for sex. One night, unable to procure a prostitute in the streets, he turns to his wife in a paroxysm of lust mixed with rage: "I felt I could murder her with my prick."[5] When she does die he marries again, this time deeply and genuinely in love. For fifteen months he manages to stay faithful, yet despite all efforts, he falls into the old habits once again. Although tormented by fear of a discovery that would "sacrifice the happiness of one for whom I would sacrifice my life.," the pattern of stalking his prey, of aggressive, loveless encounters, is too entrenched.[6] Habit is too strong; he is doomed to live out his tawdry secret life.

Nor was our author entirely unique in his habits. By the turn of the century the extent of other such secret lives was becoming uncomfortably visible. The fiery reformer Josephine Butler declared that she had descended into the very "maws of hell" in her crusade to expose the evils of prostitution. In her writings and speeches Baker described the horrors of London's sordid sexual underground—children whipped and raped, sometimes in padded rooms where they were strapped down to make it easier for clients to act out their sadistic fantasies. Butler reported that one Harley Street physician had made a tidy profit by procuring up to one hundred young girls in one year to satiate the perverse tastes of his wealthy clients.[7]

Even as Victorians extolled domestic bliss as heaven on earth, the sex trades flourished as never before. While affluent wives wore the glorious crown of motherhood, their husbands fulfilled base needs with servant maids, mill-girls, laundresses, milliners, dress and hat makers, silk workers, shoe-binders, and the spiraling ranks of common prostitutes. As their numbers increased, so too their threat to the holy shrine of family. Hence, the obsession with the fallen woman or the whore, the great peril of the gilded age.

At the root of the problem lay the near-hysterical fear of sex that ruined so many marriages and made such women a reproach to wives and their thwarted sexuality. Their very existence was a nagging threat to the fairytale of home as heavenly bliss, the lure that drained their husbands economically and emotionally, even invading the sacrosanct home when husbands infected innocent wives and children with syphilis.* Rather than confronting its own responsibility for such disasters, Victorian society found its scapegoat in the fallen woman.

Indeed, a pervasive anxiety mixed with fear and repulsion for the trap of the fallen woman permeates nineteenth-century literature. Emile Zola vividly portrays that ambiguity in his

---

*The distinguished writer, Isaak Dineson, bitterly recounts in her *Memoir* that her sterility resulted from being infected by her husband with syphilis.

novel, *Nana,* a compelling portrait of Paris' demimonde: the actresses, dancers, prostitutes whose lovers came from the highest rungs of society, including even a thinly disguised portrait of Queen Victoria's son Edward, Prince of Wales.

At its epicenter is Nana, an actress whose luscious golden hair and magnificent body, rather than any real talent, makes her the star of a trashy musical, *The Blonde Venus.* In perhaps the novel's most erotically charged passage, Zola describes her affect on the men in the theater, whom she holds at her mercy:

> She was like an animal on heat whose ruttishness had permeated the whole theater. Her slightest movement aroused lust; a jerk of her little finger was sexy. Men were leaning forward with their backs twitching, as if their nerves were being vibrated by some invisible bow.[8]

But only in the show-stopping finale does Nana unleash the full force of the sexuality that proves the ruination of so many men:

> Beneath her thin, transparent, gauzy sheath, Nana was naked, naked and unashamed, serenely confident in the irresistible power of her young flesh, her well-rounded shoulders, her firm breasts with their hard, erect, pink nipples which seemed to be stabbing at the audience, her broad hips rolling and swaying voluptuously, her plump golden thighs . . . she could be a titan![9]

The sexual fervor that infects the men in the audience is visceral. Beneath their staid black suits and starched, white collars, bodies drip with sweat, muscles quiver with excitement. Nana's effect on this captive audience does not escape the cynical eye of a journalist, Fauchery, who perceives the inherent danger. He entitles an article for *Le Figaro* "The Golden Fly," a metaphor for Nana, who lives off wealthy men who are, themselves, predators living off the working classes from which she comes. Despite her "magnificently sensual body," she can never rise above generations of poverty and alcoholism that have made her "a plant flourishing on a dung-heap." Like a huge, gold-colored fly, she deposits the "deadly germs of the carrion" on her aristocratic lovers. Slipping through the windows of their palaces in her insect form, she infects all those in her path with rot and corruption.[10]

Fauchery's metaphor proves all too apt, for Nana's sexuality is like a blight of locusts that devours everything in its path. One after another her lovers pour their entire fortunes into her insatiable craving for luxury—expensive furniture, draperies, carriages drawn by the finest horses, servants dressed in livery. Even Count Muffat, a straight-laced Catholic nobleman, becomes her helpless victim. Sexually and emotionally alienated from his repressed wife, when desire for Nana breaks through his dam of restraint, he bursts the boundaries of his pious upbringing. His downfall is inevitable. Having squandered the family fortune to feed Nana's unquenchable greed, Muffat loses his privileged position at court. As a final degradation, Nana orders him to get down on all four limbs and bark like a dog. Meanwhile, Muffat's neglected wife takes a lover to avenge herself. But unable to break free of the chains of religion and respectability, she loses her lover as well as her husband.

If Muffat's wife is conditioned to act out the Madonna role, Nana is destined to play out the Magdalen scenario. Having fallen in love with another actor, she casts off her affluent lovers, determined now to live in monogamous domesticity. But her stubborn insistence on playing the role of a respectable woman in the theater spells her ruin. The audience finds the charade uproariously funny; she loses her place in the company, her meager income, and her domestic partner.

For a time Muffat maintains her, but eventually she sinks into common prostitution. In the end she dies of smallpox, its hideous pustules being an outward manifestation of the inner pollution camouflaged by her beauty. The novel ends with a close-up of the dead woman's face decomposed into a repulsive

> pile of blood and pus dumped on a pillow, a shovelful of rotten flesh ready for the boneyards. . . . And on this horrible and

grotesque death-mask, her hair, her lovely hair, still streamed like a glorious stream of sunlight.[11]

Zola's Nana sums up the conundrum of Victorian sexuality—the fetid decay, the moral and physical pollution that made its way from the slums, the brothels, the streets, to the highest rungs of society. In this London seemed to be the capital. Visitors from abroad, even Frenchmen, were amazed by the number and aggressiveness of prostitutes. Decent gentlemen grumbled about being harassed in the streets, the theaters, the Pleasure Gardens. The Morning Post dubbed the Haymarket "Hell's Corner," asking rhetorically, "Is there any capital in Europe where such undisguised profligacy is permitted?" More poetically, one commentator declared: "The stones [of London] were alive with lust."[12]

As to actual numbers, estimates varied. Dr. Acton counted some 3,325 brothels and 8,600 prostitutes in London alone in 1857. Another survey asserted that one house in every sixty in London was a brothel, and one woman in every sixteen a whore. The pioneering sociologist Henry Mayhew noted that these figures only included prostitutes known to the police, whereas the actual number would stagger the imagination.[13] The situation was such that any woman who ventured into the Haymarket, Pall Mall, or Regent Street might be accosted. A cartoon entitled "The Mistaken Rescue" shows a well-dressed woman taken for a prostitute by a genteel man in a top-hat. Drawing back in horror from his attempt to give her a booklet about reform, the woman exclaims, "Bless me, Sir, you're mistaken. I am not a social evil. I am only waiting for a bus."[14]

But the real "social evil" was the splintering of the invisible barrier between rich and poor, for venereal disease was no respecter of class or of family. Husbands infected innocent wives and newborn infants, they themselves might become hideously disfigured both mentally and physically, as was the central figure in Ibsen's morbid play, *Ghosts*. Desperate to contain the epidemic, officials followed the adage, *cherchez la femme*, find the woman—that is, prostitutes who, like Nana, spread their deadly contagion amongst the upper classes.

In 1864 the English Parliament passed the Contagious Diseases Act, requiring all prostitutes working in eleven designated garrison towns to register with the police and have regular medical examinations. As one doctor put it, "With speculum in hand . . . the medical man must be conjoined with the policeman in this dirty and degrading work . . . he must go from brothel to brothel . . . like a railway porter, with a hammer in hand, examining axle by axle in a newly arrived train, to see whether any be heated or no."[15]

The metaphor of hammer for speculum is apt. The brutality of these examinations provoked the ire of reformers for whom prostitutes were victims of vicious, dehumanizing poverty. For them, this was merely another cruelty practiced by men who professed to be Christians. Evangelical preachers thundered their outrage from their pulpits, writers twanged the Victorian heart and conscience with heart-rending portrayals of fallen women and prostitutes. Elizabeth Gaskel's pathetic and feverish *Esther* expires on the cold ground with "naught but skin and bone, with a cough to tear her in two." In Charles Dickens' *David Copperfield* his pathetic Martha gropes through the filth and slime of London streets to end her miserable life in the cold dark river Thames.[16] In America as well, Stephen Crane's *Maggie Girl of the Streets* is seduced, then abandoned by her brother's dandified friend. Turned out of her home by her mother, Maggie resorts to prostitution to stave off starvation. Inevitably, she becomes another anonymous body floating in the chill waters of the East River, the only haven open to her.

For reformers, the real criminal was a heartless industrial system, sadistic in its ravenous appetite for wealth. Especially in the thriving textile industries girls and women worked "seven days a week from five in the morning till midnight, sewing and buttonholing full-fronted shirts" for a paltry "1s. 3 and a half d"—barely a subsistence wage. Should they miss their quotas, prostitution was the only option for assuaging cruel hunger pangs. Florence Nightingale identified this "slop system" as the root cause of the "association between hunger and whoring."[17]

W. R. Greg, an early sociologist, agreed, stating categorically that prostitution arose from one thing only—desperate poverty and its concomitant "cold, hunger, disease, often absolute starvation."[18] In his essay "Prostitution," Greg cited society's "common guilt," the hypocrisy and heartlessness that projects its own sins onto those suffering creatures:

> forgetting our human frailty . . . our own heavy portion of guilt, we turn contemptuously aside from the kneeling and weeping Magdalen, coldly bidding her to despair. . . . Instead of helping her up, we thrust her down. . . . Every door is shut upon her. . . . She is driven to prostitution by the weight of all society pressing upon her.[19]

Less sinner than sinned against, Greg's Magdalen is also a reminder of Christ's compassion and forgiveness. Indeed, a powerful wave of commiseration for fallen women swept across London society, carrying even the wealthy in its powerful undertow. Jonas Hanway, a wealthy London merchant, decried the ensnaring of "poor, young, thoughtless females" by men endowed with "superior faculties," education and wealth.[20] Robert Bingley, a rich London silk-merchant, opened the first shelter, or Magdalen Home, with money collected through subscription. As preacher in its chapel he appointed a controversial clergyman, William Dodd, the author of *Sisters,* a novel that urged kind and humane treatment of prostitutes. Dodd warned, however, that shelter and food were not enough. Only powerful religious incentives would suffice if they were to truly alter the pattern of their lives.

Dodd's emotional sermons depicting prostitutes as victims of society drew huge crowds. Neatly dressed in simple but charming "uniforms," the young, often attractive inmates evoked compassion for "Their youthful Cheek . . . paled with early Care, / and sorrow dwells in their dejected Eye."[21] More important, Bingley's Magdalen Home trained inmates in practical skills to help them become seamstresses, milliners, flower makers—the surest way to keep them off the streets when they were on their own again.

So too was Urania Cottage, a shelter/reformatory founded by the wealthy heiress, Miss Burdett Coutts, who devoted her life and fortune to running it. Some of its inmates were barely twelve, having been sold into prostitution by their parents; often Mrs. Coutts plucked them out of prison, taking them in, lice and all. Silent partner in this worthy endeavor was the novelist, Charles Dickens, who took a personal interest in the inmates, learned their histories, and sometimes gave them a fresh start with money from his own pocket.

Such was the case with Caroline Maynard, whose intelligence, dignity and character profoundly impressed Dickens. Seduced by a businessman who eventually deserted her and their little daughter, she turned to prostitution out of desperation and a fierce love for her child. Dickens turned her life around by setting her up as a landlady, and later helped her emigrate to Canada.

Ironically, Urania Cottage closed down when Dickens fell in love with eighteen year old actress, Nelly Ternan, and lost interest in the project. Terrified by the scandal of divorce, Dickens began his own secret life, meeting Nelly in various locations to keep their relationship hidden from the world.[22] * However, Dickens was not alone in his compassion for fallen women. William Gladstone, the great Liberal prime minister, risked his reputation due to his habit of engaging in conversation with prostitutes while walking home alone at night. Gladstone

---

Even when she married after Dickens death, Nelly kept the bargain of secrecy. Neither her husband nor her children knew that she had been the mistress for years of England's most revered writer.

listened sympathetically to their plight; in dire cases he sometimes took a desperate prostitute into his own home for the night, with his wife's full approval.

At the center of the rescue movement were Evangelical Christians who believed that they emulated Jesus when they went into the streets to wrest fallen women from their degradation. Newly formed missionary societies such as the London by Moonlight Mission lured prostitutes to midnight meetings with tea and cakes, then bombarded them with melodramatic sermons about the Magdalen who was forgiven even though, like them, she had been sunk in the mire of sin. In one such sermon, the Reverend H. Drury assured his audience that no woman was so lost that she could not be redeemed:

> Who knows but if their sin shall drive them to some door of repentance? Some door that shall open wider as they approach it. . . . Having entered that door, they might emulate the Magdalen and . . . throw themselves at His feet; kiss His feet, and anoint them with the ointment? . . . and stand behind Him weeping, and weep, and weep until . . . he shall mercifully accept their repentance and bid them "go in peace."* [23]

The London by Moonlight Mission triumphantly reported that 4,000 women had come to their meetings, 600 of whom gave up their profession (undoubtedly an inflated figure). We do not know how many of these women actually changed their lives, for on returning to a cold, hard world hardly run by principles of Christian charity they often regressed. Not until a later age would real salvation be offered in the form of decent jobs for women. Moreover, the dismal road of penitence might seem less attractive in light of the extraordinary careers of certain women who followed the forbidden pathway to become rich and famous.

One such woman was the flamboyant Lola Montez. An Englishwoman who posed as a Spanish dancer of mysterious origins, she counted among her lovers Franz Liszt, Alexandre

---

*delivered to the Church Penitentiary Society in 1867

Dujarier, and King Ludwig of Bavaria. The latter was completely besotted with her, lavishly bestowing titles, estates, priceless art treasures, a magnificent mansion in which she received the highest dignitaries, becoming, in effect, the power behind the throne. When a political backlash overthrew the king and forced her expulsion, she escaped with a fortune in cash and jewels.

Despite her enormous wealth, on her return to England society closed its doors to her. Not even marriage to a naive young officer of good family could erase the blemish of her past life. The couple fled to Europe where the marriage fell apart. Montez emigrated to New York, but there, too, she was shunned. As she told a reporter for *The New York Tribune,* "The ladies of this city love to read about me, but they are afraid I will contaminate them if we should meet."[24]

Hoping to find a haven in the wide-open freedom of the frontier, Montez went west to San Francisco. At first she thrived in a city that tolerated a woman who smoked cigars and handled a whip with astonishing dexterity, inflicting deadly harm on her enemies. But now Montez was harassed by rude and crude men in the streets. Turning once again to domesticity she married Pat Hull, editor of *The San Francisco Whig*. When that also failed, she went off to Australia, then Paris, and finally back to New York.

Still branded as a pariah, at age thirty-eight Montez abruptly underwent conversion. Until then, openly contemptuous of religion, especially Catholicism, Montez now sought salvation in the example of the Magdalen. Moving into small, shabby rooms in a boarding house on East Ninth Street, she gave away her elegant wardrobe and furniture, smashed her costly perfume bottles, gave up alcohol, cigarettes, and her famous cigars. Binding the thick, auburn hair, once her crowning glory, into a severe bun, she scrubbed her face clean of cosmetics and wore loose, shapeless, wool dresses of drab brown or gray. Rumor had it that beneath her dress she wore a hair shirt.

Shorn of her beauty Montez became a missionary to fallen

women, declaring, "If I can assist just one woman in the avoidance of the pitfalls that made me so miserable, I shall be happy evermore."[25] Returning to London in 1858, she plunged into the reform movement, distributing bibles in London's seedy East End. At last society opened its doors to her. Christian women invited her into their homes, women's groups booked her lectures on famous fallen women of the past. Attended by overflow audiences, Lola Montez laced her talks with incentives to reform and warnings to avoid the misery that attended such a life.

Returning to New York in 1860, Montez continued her work, making daily visits to the Magdalen Asylum, New York's first rehabilitation center for prostitutes. But guilt and remorse overcame her. Sunk in apathy and depression she became a recluse indifferent even to eating, kept alive only by friends who forced her to eat at least enough to stave off starvation. When she died of a stroke at age forty-three Lola made a last, pathetic attempt at respectability. Her gravestone, she instructed, was to be marked Mrs. Eliza Gilbert, the original married name she had given up for the excitement, freedom, and marginality of the fallen woman.

Not all such women fell into Montez's pit of remorse. In 1858 *The Times* of London published a remarkable series of letters from prostitutes and 'kept women' who defended their way of life as neither immoral nor degrading. As one reporter put it, prostitution need not always be tarnished by

> the crudities with which the divines and philosophers, and romantic writers have surrounded it. . . . [T]he great bulk of London prostitutes are not Magdalens . . . nor specimens of humanity in agony . . . but are comfortably practicing their trade. . . . They have no remorse or misgivings about the nature of their pursuit. On the contrary they consider the calling an advantageous one, and they look upon their success in it with satisfaction. They have virtues, like others; they are good daughters, good sisters, and friends. [26]

Of course, the writer ignores the enormity of misery inherent in a life on the streets. On the other hand, several of the letters to *The Times* described the manner in which, when managed judiciously, such a career could wrest a woman out of the wretched existence of poverty. One writer, for example, had come from a whole "progeny of brothers and sisters," all of whom slept in the same room with their parents, both bricklayers who escaped their misery in chronic drink. Blessed with "good looks . . . and a good temper," she was rescued from penury by her first lover at age fifteen, not having "lost what I never had . . . my virtue."

At age eighteen she acquired a new "protector" who "treated me more kindly and considerately than I had ever before been treated," and gave her the education denied her by poverty. In her new life she was able to help her parents, apprentice her brother, and find generous "protectors" for her sisters. No less contemptuous of the Society of the Suppression of Vice than the society that spawned them, she writes:

> If I am a hideous cancer in society, are not the causes of the disease to be sought in the rottenness of the carcass. Am I not its legitimate child, no bastard, sir[?] . . . I earn my money and pay my way, and try to do good with it. . . . Why stand you, the pious, the moral, the respectable . . . mouthing with sleek face about morality? [27]

Other writers pointed out that prostitution supported society's hypocritical value system—the pressure cooker of marriages delayed until men were established financially, of wives frozen by the icy grip of chastity. An 1868 article in the *Westminster Review* put it bluntly: "Prostitution is as inseparable from our present marriage customs as the shadow from the substance. They are two sides of the same shield."[28] Even Dr. Acton admitted that for many women prostitution was only a temporary measure due to lack of work, or the meagerness of a shop-girl's wages. Nor did it exempt them from finding husbands of every class, "from the peerage to the stable."[29] In fact, they might even be preferable as a wife—stronger and healthier than their delicate counterparts hardly able to breathe in their tight-laced stays, worn out by child-bearing, suffocated mentally and spiritually by the stagnant air of her gilded cage.

Realistically, too, Christian compassion and mercy could not always suffice in the face of the hard reality of life at the bottom of the barrel of poverty. When Henry Mayhew went into London's worst slums, he found a veritable army of orphaned or abandoned children living in the dreadful Lodging Houses, dirt-cheap boardinghouses where three to a dozen boys and girls shared a single bed, usually infested with bedbugs and lice. A young prostitute told him that in those communal beds, "Whatever could take place in words or acts between boys and girls did take place."[30] On hot summer nights when they slept naked, these children who had never known childhood would often dance nude about the room, their shadows frolicking in the eerie candle-light. Illiterate and unskilled, their only option was the equally sordid life of petty thievery depicted in Dickens' *Oliver Twist*.

Similarly, in the majority of Magdalen houses, conditions were as harsh as the inmates' former lives. The Scottish Glasgow Magdalene Institution, a secular institution, hardly differed from a prison or work-house, its inmates being drawn from

> our rude, ill-mannered, and miserably educated street girls . . . bold, coarse women . . . not educated even to the extent that our poorest charity school children are.[31]

For such women the Magdalen House was merely the lesser of two evils, the alternative being the hazardous life of the streets. Often, contrition was only feigned in order to escape from a harsh, even sadistic regime.

Inmates were treated no differently than criminals. Dressed uniformly in drab garments of plain cloth, all contact with family or friends was strictly forbidden. Meals were bare subsistence—rice and barley porridge—punishments, especially for insolence or disobedience were severe—beatings, long, enforced periods of silence, bans on receiving packages from families. Of course, inmates hardened by life on the streets were hardly models of decorum. Habituated to stealing, lying, and fighting, they cursed one another in loud, raucous voices.[32] Even well-behaved inmates suffered from the cruel regime, while incorrigibles endured the worst punishments—solitary confinement, and/or having their heads completely shaved. The latter was the most dreaded punishment. Not even the most hardened could withstand the shame of going out into the world bald; even they refused release until their hair grew in.

The workday began between 5:30 and 7 a.m., a grinding monotony of cooking, cleaning, or for those skilled in knitting or sewing, piece work for which quotas were set. Some houses only took in laundry, grueling work that involved carrying heavy loads of laundry and huge buckets of water, enduring blistering temperatures from the fires that heated the great vats in which the laundry was "cooked," beating out by hand stubborn grease and dirt, raw, bleeding hands from constant soaking in lye and hot water. Such work could permanently ruin a woman's health, especially those already weakened from malnutrition and consumption. Yet it was considered especially appropriate—a cleansing function that helped inmates "purge themselves of their moral contagion."[33]

Often, as the laundries began to turn a good profit, all thoughts of rehabilitation were abandoned. In Ireland, especially, the so-called Magdalene Asylums run by nuns became prison - like forced labor camps. In time, as the problem of prostitution receded, they served as a repository for any woman who strayed from the path of virtue—from unwed mothers, to teenaged girls who were too flirtatious, disobedient, or otherwise brought dishonor on the family. As rationale for the misery inflicted upon them—beatings, having their heads sheared, sadistic humiliations, miserly meals, enforced silence that cut off all communication with each other—the mantra of penance and the Magdalen was evoked. Being abject sinners, only through degradation and suffering could they be spared the eternal fires of hell. One former inmate recalls that they were told that "Mary Magdalene was forgiven, and we would be forgiven in time."[34] Yet, in truth, society was not so forgiving. Those lucky enough to be released were labeled Maggies, a term of shame that would mark them as outcasts for life. Consequently, the Magdalene Asylums became Ireland's best kept secret, since former inmates maintained a code of silence; not even their families knew what they had endured.

Ironically, the demise of the Magdalene Asylums was brought about not by public outrage at the abuses inflicted on inmates, but by technology. Only when the washing machine made hand labor unprofitable did they became extinct, the very last closing in 1996.

So too, the euphemism Magdalen for prostitute. Today the notion of a Christian saint who was a prostitute has its own shock value, especially in America where the cult of the Magdalen seems quaintly outmoded. Yet the legend lives on, not in hell-fire sermons by moral reformers, or in archaic religious icons, but as an archetype for the sexually driven, dangerous and illicit temptress. In that respect, Mary Magdalen would undergo yet another transition. Casting off her ragged clothing, the suffering and remorse of the penitent, she would emerge as a new archetype—the beautiful, bold, and seductive femme fatale.

CHAPTER 18

THE MADONNA/WHORE SYNDROME

If God, a fat bank account and respectability were the watchwords of Victorian society, freedom would be the great slogan of the twentieth century. In the passage from nineteenth to twentieth century, men and women both got out of their stuffy Victorian parlors, their stiff, starched high-necked collars, long black coats and top hats, their bustled and corseted dresses. Together they began to ride bicycles, swim, golf, even smoke. Women also began a valiant struggle to infiltrate traditionally male bastions; to enter the hallowed halls of colleges and universities, to become doctors, lawyers, scientists, to be allowed to vote in a democracy that declared all *men* equal.

Tentatively, they also resorted to divorce as a way out of the life-long misery of bad marriages, although the stigma and economic misery for women was so severe as to dissuade all but the most brave. But as always in periods of rapid change, the old model shattered before a new model could take its place. Emergence from the traditional bailiwick of home, kitchen, and nursery left not only women, but men as well confused, frightened, unsettled. In such a climate the age old misogyny resurfaced, manifested as always by a fear of female sexuality, but with a modern twist—the female archetype known as the femme fatale or vamp.

Sexy and seductive, the femme fatale or vamp was readily identifiable with her blazing red lips, the clinging gowns that mapped out every curve of her body, but cloaked an inner evil—an aggressive, threatening sexuality that renders men helpless and impotent. As such, the vamp is an inversion of the true or normal woman—by nature passive, compliant, driven by maternal feelings, not sexual passion. By contrast, the vamp becomes masculinized, smoking cigarettes or small cigars and speaking in a deep, husky voice, more like a man than a woman.

In her recent memoir, Lauren Bacall recalls that one of the things that won her a role as vamp in the film *To Have and Have Not* was her deep, almost baritone voice. Notable, too, was the contrast between the tough coolness of Bacall's character, Slim, who doesn't flinch when slapped in the face by the police, and the typically feminine behavior of the French wife who faints when Bogart removes a bullet from her husband's shoulder.

Actually, Bacall's character could be sweet and vulnerable beneath her tough exterior. But in general the femme fatale was seen as dangerous and without scruples when it came to satiating her desires. Hence the tendency of artists and writers to portray her as Salomé, or as mythical female monsters such as Medusa or the Sphinx. In that form the femme fatale served as symbol for a pervasive sense of doom that infected fin de siècle artists and intellectuals. Just as the femme fatale lures man to his destruction, so too so the twin phenomena of industrialism and capitalism, the cruel heartlessness of an affluent class prey on the suffering poor to feed its insatiable greed and lust for power.

As fatigue, poverty, crowded and filthy living conditions gave rise to ravaging epidemics of cholera, typhus, tuberculosis, an oppressive sense of moral rot and decay caused artists and intellectuals to wallow in pessimism. The Danish philosopher Søren Kierkegaard gave voice to their malaise when he wrote: "My soul is so heavy that no thought can uplift it any more, nor any wingbeat bear it aloft into the ether. If anything moves it at all, it merely grazes the ground, like a bird flying low before a storm. Oppressiveness and anxiety are brooding over my inner being, sensing an earthquake to come."[1]

As in the epidemic of venereal disease, the femme fatale was a new social evil at which society could point its finger. The very term connotes lethal danger; indeed artists would render her in various guises—as a menacing man-slayer who preys on vulnerable men, as Eve, as the Sphinx, as the evil sorceress Circe who changed men into animals, as the sex-crazed Salome dancing around the head of St. John the Baptist, as the seductive female vampire whose embrace is the kiss of death.[2] Just as the male vampire drains his victims of their life force, their blood, the femme fatale immobilizes her victim with an erotic energy that renders him helpless and impotent. Thus the terrifying aspect of the vamp.

In 1895 the German artist Franz von Stuck portrayed that menace almost obsessively in the form of the ancient Sphinx, half cat, half woman. In *The Kiss of the Sphinx,* the best known of that genre, a humanized, bare-breasted sphinx, her face obscured by her long, disheveled hair, leans forward from her perch on the ledge of a rock to embrace a nude, kneeling man bearing the artist's features.* With lips pressed passionately against his

---

*In 1904 von Stuck did another Sphinx, this time a voluptuous nude stretched out on the ground who, cat-like, stealthily fixes her gaze on her prey, just out of sight. The critic, Fritz von Ostini, noted that although "The cat's body is not there at all, . . . the creature is 'completely a cat' in expression and attitude, false and beautiful,

mouth and huge cat paws enclosing his waist, she embodies the dread creature described by Heinrich Heine in his poem "Sphinx:"

> Terror and lust cross bred!
> In body and claws a lion's form
> A woman in breast and head.
> . . . Her white eyes
> Spoke of desire grown wild
> I yielded, passion-tossed
> And as I kissed that lovely face
> I knew that I was lost
> She drank the breath from out my breast,
> She fed lust without pause;
> She pressed me tight, and tore and rent
> My body with her claws.[3]

Von Stuck's *Sphinx* provoked such an outrage that it was banned from display in any window of an art gallery in Berlin—nothing new to the artist who reveled in controversy. Some years earlier, in 1893, he had infuriated the public with a painting entitled *Sin,* a portrait of a dark-haired woman—seductive, mysterious, vamp-like.* Gazing at the viewer with a brazen, complicitous expression, her black velvet drape falls open to reveal an elongated torso with breasts thrust outward. Coiled around her shoulder is a black, fat-jowled serpent—a clear allusion to Eve. Yet there is a disquieting ambiguity here. She is not merely Eve, but a strange mutation, a shockingly eroticized Madonna.

In his novel, *Glaudius Dei,* Thomas Mann undoubtedly had von Stuck in mind when he writes of an artist who painted a "Madonna, completely modern and free of any conventions. The figure of the Holy mother had an oppressive femininity, bared and beautiful. Her large sultry eyes had dark edges."†[4] At the secessionist exhibition at Munich's Museum for Modern Art, the

---

flattering and dangerous. The name of this Sphinx is—Woman!"

*This woman, too, has features strikingly like his own.

†So too a visitor to the studio: "A woman to drive you insane. The dogma of the immaculate conception is a little unsettling."

painting caused a minor scandal because of its profanation of the sacred.[5] But perhaps its most lasting impression was on the Norwegian painter, Edvard Munch, who lived and worked in Berlin at the time.

Today Munch's most famous work is *The Scream*, a painting that captures the angst of a dislocated, alienated generation. Less familiar is his *Madonna* of 1894, for the shock of its melding of Madonna/whore into a single, striking figure, as in von Stuck's *Sin*, does not resonate with the modern viewer. Indeed, Munch's imagery is more subtle and psychological. Devoid of the serpent with its biblical connotation, his Madonna seems caught in the throes of an ecstasy which could be sexual or spiritual, or both.

In that respect, Munch's art reflects not only the neuroses of his generation, but his own private demons derived from a dark cloud of piety, guilt, and the constant shadow of death that hung over his entire family.

Munch was only five when his intensely pious mother died at age thirty of tuberculosis. In a letter of farewell to her five children she promised that her spirit would keep constant watch over them from heaven.[6] And indeed it did, for each of them wrestled in his or her own way with the residue of her piety. In Munch's paintings her image constantly appears as a gaunt, melancholy, woman, severely dressed in black, who silently, reproachfully observes the artist's rendering of couples engaged in their various dances of love, sex, reproduction.

As to Munch's doctor father, his excessive religiosity seemed to his son to border on insanity at times. A remote man immersed in his medical practice, he constantly rebuked his son for the smallest, most innocent acts of childhood, regaling him with images of hell so vivid that the boy sometimes imagined himself "at the edge of inferno."[7] At age thirteen Munch almost died from a massive pulmonary hemorrhage. As the terrified boy choked on great globs of blood, his father stood by begging him to repent and confess all kinds of nameless sins. Years later

Munch recalled the horror of that day in his diary:

> Fear took hold of him. . . . In a few minutes he would be standing in front of God's judgment seat. . . . He would be condemned forever. . . . He would burn forever in sulphur . . . in hell.[8]

Compounding his guilt was the death from tuberculosis of his beloved sister, Sophie, at age fifteen, the death of an adult brother from pneumonia, and the descent into madness of his sister, Laura. Munch's own salvation lay in his close circle of bohemian artists—all in full rebellion against church, family, bourgeois propriety and morality. Nightly they gathered to drink, smoke, celebrate their cherished ethic of free love, either with the liberated women within their circle or with prostitutes. Their radical manifesto included the injunction "Thou shalt sever thy family roots / Thou canst not treat thy parents badly enough."[9]

But Munch never could sever the ties that bound him to family and Christian guilt. Nightly he abandoned his raucous friends to eat at home where his father regaled him about sin, punishment, and the day of reckoning. Little wonder that Laura went mad, while Munch himself was tortured by a paranoia and ambivalence that marked his relationships with women all his life. For all the declared liberation of his bohemian, free-thinking friends, Munch's demons conjure the cold breath of the Church Fathers railing against the twin perils of female beauty and seductiveness.

Actually the handsome, witty, and famous Munch loved women, and they loved him. Drawn to a series of strong women, some of whom were accomplished in their own right, Munch faced a morbid fear of intimacy and marriage, combined with agonizing jealousies that inevitably proved ruinous. His first lover, the married Millie Thaulow, was a compulsive flirt, deliberately provoking suspicions and jealousy that tormented him even after they parted. Next was Tulla Larsen, wealthy and possessed of some talent as a painter. Loving and solicitous about Munch's nervous disorders, she aspired to become his wife. Yet Munch convinced himself of wholly imagined infidelities. In *The Sin*, a 1901 lithograph/portrait of Larsen, he gives her wild, staring eyes, thin clenched lips, full breasts, unruly, long red hair, whereas in reality she was demure and self-contained.[10]

Munch's last love, Eva Mudocci, was beautiful, a gifted violinist, and wholly committed to her own career, thus averting the marriage crisis. She, too, patiently and lovingly put up with Munch's hypochondria and neuroses. Yet his last portrait of her as *Salomé* portrays her as a malevolent, sex-crazed murderess, precipitating, Mudocci said, "our only row."*

After they parted Munch grew increasingly bitter, resorting to prostitutes with whom there would be no emotional involvement. Even that failed to allay his anxieties which, combined with alcoholism, brought him to the brink of self-destruction at age forty-five. A nine-month stint in a sanatorium seemed to cure him of both addictions—drink and the torturous affairs with women. Relinquishing both their "pain and happiness," Munch declared:

> I have turned my back on a strange world—like the old Italian painters, I have decided that women's proper place is in heaven. Roses can inflict too much damage with their thorns.[11]

Perhaps what saved Munch from madness was his art. Despite numerous tender portraits of women friends that display their beauty and grace, Munch's oeuvre is also notable for a recurring female trilogy: the pure and innocent blond woman, the sensuous, dangerous vamp, and the elderly, threatening woman in black. Some of his most notable works, however, focus on a single figure—the menacing vamp who renders a man helpless.

Such is the case of a painting now known as *Vampire.*†

---

*Another *Salomé* shows Mudocci tenderly resting her head on a sketch of Munch himself.

†Done early in his career in 1893, the year of von Stade's *Sin.*

Originally entitled *Love and Pain*, it portrays a woman with hazy features whose long, red hair completely encircles her male partner, whom she kisses on the neck. With his head buried in her bosom, the man seems collapsed, defeated, caught like a spider in the web of her hair. Munch himself disavowed anything sinister in the kiss, or any reference to a particular woman. Yet his obsession with long red hair was well known to his friends.* Munch also left in his papers an intriguing clue to what it might have meant to him. Reminiscing about a woman whom he does not name, he writes:

> She had been sitting next to me. . . . She had bent her head over mine. . . . The blood-red hair had entwined itself around me like blood-red snakes. . . . Its finest threads had entangled themselves in my heart.†[12]

For Munch's close friend the Polish poet Stanislaw Przybyszewsk, the metaphor was unmistakable—man's victimization by the woman/vamp. In 1897, when Bram Stoker's *Dracula* came out, Przybyszewsk renamed the painting *Vampire*, to his mind "A broken man, and on his neck a Vampire's face . . . He cannot free himself from the Vampire, nor from the pain."[13]

Przybyszewk understood that pain only too well, for his wife, known as Duchna, was notorious for flaunting her many lovers in her husband's face. The playwright Strindberg, whom she rejected, dubbed her "a vampire and a whore;" she also inspired the figure of Eve in Munch's painting *Jealousy*.‡[14] Here

---

A story is told that Tulla Larsen planned an elaborate scheme to coax him into marriage. Knowing his passion for red hair, she pretended to be dead, letting her long red hair fall about her shoulders. The scheme backfired when Munch realized it was a hoax, flew into a rage, and never forgave her.

†When a scholarship in Paris separated him from Millie Thalow, he said "he felt as if strands of her hair still reached him and wove around his heart like threads."†

‡Eventually Duchna met a tragic end after running away with a young friend of the family, Wladislaw Emeryk. The couple was found shot dead in a hotel room, either a murder or a double suicide. Ironically, their death has strong parallels to that of Archduke Rudolph of Austria, who in 1889 shot his young

Eve reaches for an apple, presumably to offer it to a man with Munch's features, while in the lower foreground Przybyszewk's tense, drawn face appears, gazing piteously at the viewer.

Yet Munch was not an inveterate woman-hater. One of his most exquisite portraits is *The Brooch*, a likeness of Eva Mudocci in which her lovely face is framed by a swirl of luxuriant, dark hair (In real life she had shoulder-length hair). Ironically, although he had not yet met Mudocci at the time, the portrait bears a strong resemblance to the painting that became an obsession for him in later years, his *Madonna* of 1894.

Initially entitled *Woman Making Love*, then *Loving Woman*, Munch's *Madonna* is a long-torsoed woman with flowing black hair. As in von Stuck's *Sin*, her raised arms thrust her breasts outward, but beneath her abdomen Munch adds a thin black line emphasizing its roundness and suggesting pregnancy. With head thrown back, dark, heavy lidded eyes half closed, mouth slightly ajar, she seems caught in the throes of an ecstasy. A bright red orb behind her head suggests a halo, yet by its color—the hue of sin—it profanes the Madonna image. Surrounding the figure are characteristic wavy, undulating circles of rust and blue, at the top left corner a glowing red contrasts with the cool blue of the lower right hand corner.

Throughout Munch plays with various contrasts—sacred and profane, woman as at once sensual and spiritual, earthy and otherworldly. For Munch's conservative hometown, Christiana, that ambiguity was shocking and irreverent. Today, however, it is the mystery that intrigues, undoubtedly as Munch intended. Indeed, he deliberately confused the image by giving the figure two nipples on the left breast—one positioned as if she was standing upright, as in an icon of the Madonna, the other as if she were a real woman stretched out in bed, gazed upon by her lover.[15] And although he used a professional model for the

---

lover, Mary Vetsera, then himself in his hunting lodge in what was apparently a suicide pact.

figure, an intriguing diary entry made a decade earlier at the height of the affair with Millie Thaulow offers a tantalizing hint of personal meaning:

> There is something holy in your face, lying there under the lamp of moonlight. Your hair is brushed away from your clean forehead. You have the profile of a Madonna. Your lips part as though in pain and I ask in fear if you are grieved, but you whisper softly . . . I love you.[16]

Later, Munch wrote of his *Madonna:*

> your face holds all the beauty of this earth
> your lips carmine as the ripening fruit move apart as in pain
> the smile of a corpse.[17]

Clearly it meant a great deal to him, for he constantly made variations on the original throughout his life. In some versions she is less sexual and more serene, in one striking alteration a band of sperm, almost like tears, frames the figure, while in the left bottom corner a skeletal fetus scowls.

Undoubtedly Munch's family history had something to do with such recurring images of conception and death. And in an age when women commonly died in childbirth or, weakened by tight corsets, too little exercise and too many pregnancies, from tuberculosis, the metaphor is particularly apt.[18] Yet the great power of this enigmatic work is its apotheosis of the eternal duality of woman—maternal and sensual, loving and menacing, creator and destroyer. At the same time it transcends any stereotype. Neither Madonna nor whore per se, she melds qualities of sanctity and sensuality, tenderness and spirituality, lover and mother. The luxuriant hair that encompasses the figure seems more a soft halo than a trap. Behind the eyes closed in ecstasy lies the mystery of her sexuality, while the sperm- and cadaver-like fetus suggest the inevitable tragedy of love when death lurks in the wings.

During an eight-year period from 1895 to 1903, Munch recast his *Madonna* in countless variations. In some he merged her figure with that of the sinister woman in Vampire, in others he restated the equivalence of sex and death. But in his more tender renderings, perhaps Munch found a measure of peace from the psychic demons that distorted his view of women, even those he loved.

And therein lies the contradiction. On the one hand, Munch was attracted to women, was gracious and charming to them, and appreciated their intelligence, beauty and talent. Indeed, a profound tenderness was intrinsic to his nature.[19] Yet intense relationships evoked inner demons over which he had no control, hence the threatening figures that distort and menace.

Perhaps the latter derived from an overdose in childhood of a Christian piety that tinges anything sexual with the lurid glow of sin. Yet his powerful images convey, as only art can, the dichotomous view of women that was imbedded into the collective consciousness of his time. If his menacing vamps were forged in his own mind, by fusing the two archetypes into one image, as in his *Madonna,* Munch captured the yearning of a modern generation for the new woman—both Madonna and Magdalen, both spiritual and sensual, mother and lover, faithful yet exciting.

Oddly enough, one pathway to that new woman lay in Sigmund Freud's work on neurosis and female hysteria. Freud, in fact found sexual repression to be intrinsic to Western civilization; men and women, Jews and Christians alike. "Civilization," he wrote, "is built on the suppression of instincts." Nor was it "possible for the claims of the sexual instinct to be reconciled with the demands of culture."[20] Yet it was precisely the Victorian codes demanding abstinence outside of marriage, and repression of sexual passions within marriage that were the root cause not only of neurosis, but of the stunted, perverted sexuality described earlier in *My Secret Life*. Such mass neuroses also lay beneath the malaise that gripped fin de siècle artists and writers, resulting in a morbid fear of death, a sense of future calamity, a numbing of the desire to have children.

For Freud the burden of repression lay heavier on women, causing frigidity, buried hostility, the hysterical neurasthenia he saw in many of his female patients. Consciously or not, the pure, high-minded Victorian wife looked to the Virgin Mary as archetype, sublimating libidinal drives into maternal love, gradually retreating from her role as sexual partner. Yet, Freud regarded sex as the vital life force, while female frigidity leads to passivity, an apathy in which "*any* form of thinking, and knowledge loses its value for them." Women's alleged intellectual inferiority, Freud believed, was not at all a matter of biology, but "the inhibition of thought necessitated by sexual suppression."[21]

Freud himself never used the term Madonna/whore, nor did he think in those terms. Rather, he focused on the Oedipal triangle, the psychic trauma when a son is confronted with the father's sexual possession of the mother, object of his own desires. As a result, he projects his fury onto all women as whores.[22] As to women, Freud held that a "woman's value is measured by her sexual integrity and . . . reduced by . . . being like a prostitute." Freud, in fact, regarded prostitution as a sexual perversion, "a striking departure from the normal" for either sex.[23] Consequently, wives should not be "whorish" in bed, but should observe a proper decorum. He himself eventually withdrew from sexual activity when the burden of childbearing became too much for his wife.

Ironically, Freud's general theory of sexuality ultimately exploded the notion that normal women had an attenuated sex drive. Men and women, he wrote, are biologically equal as sexual beings; it is social conditioning that diminishes women's natural libido. As a result, women's vital and creative energies atrophy while men find an outlet for their sexuality with a mistress, a casual affair, or a prostitute.

Freud himself was close to women who had professional

careers and openly asserted their sexual prerogatives as well.* However, the time was not yet ripe for the liberated woman, for the price of freedom was to be branded as fallen woman. Indeed, for most Victorians the ancient Jewish philosopher, Philo, had it right when he wrote: "women outside the boundaries of home and family are a stranger to decency and modesty and temperance and other virtues."[24]

As to the Magdalen, her image was about to flower anew as a renewed interest in the humanity of Jesus resurrected the legend of the Magdalen as his lover. Yet she would retain the peculiar ambiguity that made her at once saint and sinner—a notion exploited by the contemporary media goddess, Madonna. In her signature song "Like a Virgin", Madonna plays on the virgin/whore legend as, with a cross dangling from one ear, she writhes in the throes of sexual abandon. But even a bleached-blonde sex kitten, dressed like the quintessential whore, can be redeemed by love. By virtue of its purifying effect, she too can become

> Like a Virgin
> Touched for the very first time.†

* When Freud's close friend, the writer Lou Andreas Salomé, had her clitoris surgically moved to heighten sexual pleasure, Freud was furious.

† "Like a Virgin" by Tom Kelly and Billy Steinberg. Recorded by Madonna on her 1984 album *Like a Virgin*.

CHAPTER 19

"I DON'T KNOW HOW TO LOVE HIM"

Set me as a seal upon your arm;
For love is strong as death,
passion fierce as the grave.
Its flashes are flashes of fire,
a raging flame.
Many waters cannot quench love,
neither can floods drown it.

Song of Songs 8:6-7

If any one work of art encapsulates the shifting image of the Magdalen as the nineteenth century drew to a close, it might be Rodin's masterpiece *Christ and the Magdalene.* A late work in which the sculpted figures swirl out of raw, natural stone, the nude bodies of Jesus and Mary Magdalen merge in an embrace that seems to supersede the boundaries of death.

In the original plaster study, fresh from the creative hand of the master, the Magdalen's wild, disheveled hair partially covers Jesus bruised body, while her left arm cradles the drooping head. In the smooth, more polished marble version, the two figures melt into one another; as the Magdalen's swooning form mimics Jesus's collapse of death, she seems to absorb his suffering into her own pain-racked body. Here, once again, is the Magdalen for whom love is all, even beyond death. Or, as a long forgotten poet of the Italian Renaissance put it:

> Would . . . that my lord had been crucified in my arms, my hands nailed against his, . . . so that I die with him, and thus neither in life or death departed from him.[1]

Rodin's *Christ and the Magdalene* treats the Magdalen as neither sinner or prostitute, but as the inspired lover who makes Jesus's humanity complete, one whose all-encompassing love reaches beyond death itself. In its powerful eroticism, in the press of nude flesh on flesh, the legend of the Magdalen as Jesus's lover surfaces in contemporary form—not as sinner who must repent her love, but as spiritual partner through whom God's love is funneled. Indeed, the contemporary search for the human Christ coincides with a quest for a new spirituality. As Maurice Denis put it, "we are all preoccupied with God. Today, Christ is living. . . . There has not been for a long time a more passionate epoch than ours for religious Beauty."[2]

If Rodin's sculpture strives after that beauty in a work of art, it may have had personal meaning as well. For some time Rodin wrestled with various names—*Prometheus and an Oceanid, Prometheus Bound, Genius and Pity*—all of which suggest the suffering Christ as metaphor for the suffering artist inspired, supported, consoled by a female muse. By naming it *Christ and the Magdalene* Rodin made the metaphor more specific—the myth of the Magdalen as Jesus's lover—and thereby a powerful image of shared suffering. Possibly, the inspiration was his own anguished relationship with the woman who was both mistress and alter ego for fifteen years, the brilliant sculptor Camille Claudel. If so, the Magdalen figure takes on a new and powerful dimension, for no one understood the pain of the outcast better than she.

During their association their work was sometimes so closely intertwined that certain pieces, most notably key figures in the monumental *Gates of Hell,* are impossible to ascribe to either artist. Yet it has been attributed to him alone. For that reason and others, their affair was fraught with pain for Claudel. For one thing, Rodin would not give up either his casual affairs with his models, or his long time mistress, Rose Beuret. A simple and uneducated woman for whom his art was an unfathomable mystery, she humbly served as housekeeper and cook, kept his clay models damp and took care of petty business matters. Eventually their relationship deteriorated into demanding master, and submissive, long suffering servant. But Rodin would not abandon Beuret to marry Claudel. For a time he juggled two households and two mistresses, each one burning with resentment of the other.

If Rose won the titanic domestic battle, Claudel lost on yet another front—her struggle for independence and recognition as an artist in her own right. While Rodin's growing fame made him an international icon, Claudel slipped into oblivion when she abandoned his studio and her position as his assistant. At a time when no sculptor could survive without government support, a woman, no matter how talented, could not possibly make her way into the intricate labyrinth of official beauracracy. And despite Rodin's numerous efforts to help her win commissions, the plain fact was that the art establishment was militantly and exclusively male.

Worse still, Claudel's profession and the affair with Rodin thrust her into the limbo of fallen woman. Castigated by society, her family bitterly accused her of dishonoring them. Evicted from her family's home, denied recognition of her talent, she shut herself up in her studio, becoming increasingly isolated. Unkempt in appearance, her studio filled with debris and over run by cats, she gradually descended into paranoia and an eccentricity that verged on madness. Finally the family had her committed to a state insane asylum where, initially, she was allowed neither visitors nor mail. Although that ban was eventually lifted, for the last thirty years of her life this gifted sculptor was never again allowed to work at her art.

Even when her condition improved and the doctors offered to release her into the custody of the family, they refused. Despite numerous reports that her mind was absolutely clear by friends who visited her, they regarded her as a permanent stain on their honor. As her mother put it, "She has all the vices. . . . [S]he has done us too much harm."[3] Neither mother nor sister ever visited her in thirty years; her beloved brother, Paul, spoke of her as though she were dead. When finally she died, she was buried in an anonymous grave.

But if her family forgot her, friends did not, nor did reformers outraged by draconian laws that sanctioned incarcerating a person indefinitely without even a psychiatric examination. As journalist Paul Vibert put it,

> Unfortunately victims like the poor, great artist Camille Claudel are thrown brutally into an asylum and locked away for life . . . and no one can do anything to liberate this brilliant sculptress.[4]

Vibert believed that Rodin's prestige might have saved her, but he did little to help.

Perhaps, then, his *Christ and the Magdalene* mirrors a nagging guilt manifested by a Magdalen who is actually Claudel, crucified on the cross of her lover's success. All we can say for certain is that this striking piece gives the Magdalen legend a contemporary twist in its powerful eroticism and its implication of a shared fate. Indeed, in a world freed of ancient superstitions and the wholesale guilt of Original Sin, one would expect that the Magdalen would be restored to her rightful place in

Christianity. Yet mention of her still evokes a sly wink from those who continue to see her as the prostitute redeemed by Jesus's love.

That Magdalen legend, however, so firmly ensconced in Europe, has never quite crossed the Atlantic. In largely Protestant America, where reformers threw prostitutes into jail cells, not Magdalen Homes, she slipped into relative obscurity. Even the influx of Catholics in the nineteenth century failed to rejuvenate her cult, for saint worship with its relics and processions never really flourished in America as in Europe. Not until the tumultuous sixties was her legend rehabilitated; not in the Church, but in the theater via the rock musical, *Jesus Christ Superstar.*[*]

With its hit tunes and biblical figures as flower children, *Jesus Christ Superstar* reached an audience that included hard-core cynics and non-believers. A generation of strangers to the Gospels suddenly confronted the mystery of Jesus, and the relevancy of his parables for a jaded world searching for some kind of spiritual rejuvenation. Yet by portraying Jesus as a man with his feet very much on this earth, Webber and Rice succeeded in stripping away eons of myth.

By focusing on the triad of Jesus, Judas, and Mary Magdalen, *Jesus Christ Superstar* sharply contrasts the idea of false love, as in Judas, and true love, as in the Magdalen. When first we meet her she tenderly cares for an exhausted Jesus, bathing his feet and anointing him with oil. Like a mother, she croons a gentle lullaby, admonishing the weary man to put his worries and problems to rest; as the balm of sleep approaches she cradles him in her arms.

Galled by her devotion, Judas reprimands Jesus for consorting with such a woman in such an intimate way, letting her kiss him, stroke his hair, wasting money on expensive oils that could have been given to the poor. To that Jesus replies that

---

[*]By the team of Webber/Rice.

only the Magdalen understands him. Only she gives him what he really wants and needs, nor should Judas criticize her unless his "slate is clean."

This Magdalen, however, is a painfully ambivalent post-Freudian figure who ponders the shift from the defiantly sexual woman she was, and the unfamiliar woman she has become. Attracted to Jesus, she recognizes that this is something wholly different. Tormented by doubt, in the hit tune "I Don't Know How To Love Him" she muses on the strange paradox of this man who, after all, is just a man like all the others, yet who moves her as none other has.

In time-honored fashion, she is transformed, inexplicably and fundamentally changed, a stranger even to herself. Confused, torn between her former careless sensuality and the dignity of her reawakened person, she wavers between fear of this new found emotion and a powerful and unremitting love, wholly different from anything in her past. Rent by the age-old quandary of woman, she reverts to safe, non erotic, maternal love, as she rocks the sleeping Jesus in her arms.

In fact, *Jesus Christ Superstar* never explicitly identifies the Magdalen as Jesus's lover, leaving it to the audience's imagination and the director's discretion. In some productions the erotic connection is strongly implicit, but in the filmed version Mary Magdalen is closer to the Gospel figure. Aware of the terrible fate that awaits him, she anoints him in preparation for his death. Most of all, she is in a quandary, confused by her erotic attraction to a man who has revealed to her the higher, more sublime meaning of love. Quite literally she is at a loss as to "how to love him." Now that she has confronted a spiritualism so all-encompassing, sexual love can never be the same for her.

Not so the Mary Magdalen of Martin Scorsese's controversial 1988 film *The Last Temptation of Christ.* Its scorching portrayal of Jesus as deeply flawed, insecure, painfully ambivalent about his mission created a furor. As to Mary Magdalen, not only does she revert to the sinner/whore, at times she takes on aspects of an ancient fertility goddess. If *Jesus Christ Superstar* merely alluded to the notion of Jesus's sexuality, Scorsese faced the issue head on, bluntly showing Jesus on screen having sex with Mary Magdalen.

Based on the novel by Greek writer Nikos Kazantzakis, Scorsese's film sticks rather closely to its source. Like Kazantzakis, Scorsese, a lapsed Catholic who was briefly headed for the priesthood in his youth, has struggled with his faith throughout his life. Kazantzakis' Jesus, however, is even more transparently a self-portrait of the author, a man tormented by an agonizing internal split—"from my youth onward . . . the incessant, merciless battle between the spirit and the flesh."[5]

All his life Kazantzakis sought a resolution to that wrenching dichotomy, initially in a tiny, bare cell in a Macedonian monastery on Mount Athos from which even female animals, cows and hens, were strictly excluded. When spiritual peace eluded him there, he abandoned his monk's cell, turning successively to Nietzsche, Buddha, Lenin, Odysseus, and finally back to Christ.

Kazantzakis, who married twice, wrote that he eventually reconciled "these two primordial forces . . . so contrary to each other, to make them realize they are not enemies but, rather, fellow workers" in harmony with one another.[6] Not so the tormented Jesus of his novel, who reconciles them only with his death.

As in the novel, Scorsese's Jesus (Willem Dafoe) is a man tormented by weakness, indecision, anger, one who longs for ordinary things—a wife, family, the comforts of home and hearth—one who aspires to life rather than death. At the very center of that conflict is Mary Magdalen (Barbara Hershey) who personifies all that is desirable and sensual in woman. Like the pagan goddesses of antiquity, she entices man to fulfill his destiny by procreating his species. Her body, with its exotic henna tattoos on face, hands and legs, exudes the musky aroma of the seraglio; whenever she appears the tinkling sound of jangling arm and ankle bracelets are heard.

Yet, like Jesus, she suffers from a profound self-loathing. In fact, Jesus has so debased himself that even God hates him. Not only does he work on the Sabbath, when voices urge him to begin his mission, Jesus protests that he is "a coward, an illiterate and idler, a hedonist who loves good food, wine and laughter." Worse still, he makes the crosses used by the detested Romans to crucify Jewish Zealots. Even his mother temporarily deserts him when he is cursed by fellow Jews.

Above all, this Jesus is tormented by sexual longings that will dissuade him from his mission. They keep him awake at night and make his "blood [boil] furiously." Yet the mere thought of a woman brings a demon that digs its barbed claws into his head, as its "frenzied wings beat above him, tightly covering his temples."[7]

Desperate to exorcise his demons, Jesus retreats to a desert monastery. But first he must seek forgiveness from Mary Magdalen, for he is the cause of her degradation. As young children of three and five, they had innocently joined their naked young bodies together. Forever haunted by the overwhelming sweetness of that encounter, Mary Magdalen seeks oblivion by defiling herself with men of every stamp; old and young, Jewish and gentile, noble and common, rich and poor. Insatiable in her greed for customers, she even plies her trade on the Sabbath. In dreams she appears to Jesus as a demon of lust incarnate.

At Magdala, Jesus takes his place behind a line of clients who refer to themselves as "pilgrims" and "worshippers." Exuding the reverence with which they would approach a sanctuary, some even sway in prayer "before entering Paradise."[8] Stolidly, Jesus watches as her naked body undulates in each embrace. When at last they leave, he begs her forgiveness, but her bitterness is too profound. Her only salvation, she says, lies in the "Mud-shame, filth" of her debasement. *[9]

In the desert Satan comes to tempt Jesus in several guises, one of which is Mary Magdalen in the body of a cobra. When none of them succeed, Jesus staggers out of the desert to take up his mission. First, however, he comes to the home of Mary and Martha of Bethany, who take the ragged, starving man into their home. To dissuade him they remind him that, as a man, God wants him to have a home and children. But Jesus has passed through the fire of temptation: his resolve now is firm.

Jesus's mission begins when he stumbles onto a horrendous scene: Mary Magdalen encircled by a mob hurling stones at her for plying her trade on the Sabbath. As the rabid crowd howls for her death, Jesus dissuades them by paraphrasing the famous adage about casting the first stone. The crowd disperses as each one confronts his own guilt, and a wholly transformed Mary Magdalen becomes a devoted follower. From then on they refer to one another as brother and sister. A newly confident Jesus delivers the Sermon on the Mount, recruits his disciples, teaches, and performs miracles.

Having returned to the Jesus of the Gospels, the film takes another astounding turn at the crucifixion scene. In a riveting dream sequence, an angel comes and rescues Jesus from the Cross. Freed from his destiny, Jesus is granted his wish for an ordinary life. Breaking the most sacred taboo in Christianity, he and Mary Magdalen make love in a scene of great tenderness. She becomes pregnant, but just as her swollen belly is about to produce its fruit, a blinding light envelops her, and she dies. Even in a dream world, she must pay the price for her former life.

A grief-stricken Jesus is consoled by the guardian angel who assures him that all women are one. As proof, he leads Jesus to the house of Mary and Martha. The former is merely Mary

---

*In the novel her bitterness melts. After making a warm fire and a simple meal, like a mother, she rocks Jesus to sleep at her breast. At daybreak she awakes to find him tenderly caressing her face.

Magdalen with another face. Thus, it will be the safe, domestic woman who bears Jesus's son. Changing his name to Lazarus to conceal his identity, Jesus exults in the serenity of married life until Martha's virginity threatens their tranquility.

This time an African angel appears to say that African people are more open and honest about sexuality.[10] Their God neither scolds nor inculcates guilt in his people; besides, all women are essentially the same, only with different faces.[11] That night when Martha creeps into Jesus's bed, he understands that "name, shape, color, beauty or ugliness" is irrelevant, that her childless womb has been "suffocating" with its unborn progeny. Like the patriarchs of old, Jesus lives with his two wives, the little house bursting with their progeny.[12] Wholly contented, the sisters give not a hoot for paradise, for as Mary puts it, "I'm a woman. . . . Let's leave the eternal joys to the men." Perplexed, Jesus asks how can you "lock yourself up in that space"? To that Mary answers that women are only happy within boundaries: "You know that, rabbi. A woman is a reservoir, not a spring."[13] Sitting by the hearth at night, the women respectfully maintain silence, knowing that "at times a woman's speech gladdens a man; at times it makes him furious."[14]

Only as an old man, when some of his former disciples recognize him beneath the coarse features of a common peasant, is Jesus's serenity destroyed. When they curse him as "Coward, Deserter, Traitor," the dream evaporates. Waking on the cross, Jesus exultantly recognizes his triumph over temptation. Crying out "It is accomplished," he dies, his destiny fulfilled.

For all the uproar over Scorsese's unorthodox Jesus, it was the explicitly depicted intercourse with Mary Magdalen that evoked a firestorm from Christians of every stamp, from Catholics to Protestant fundamentalists. In cities like Boston with a heavy Catholic population, pickets paraded outside the theater, heckling patrons every night of its run. A bomb was set off at the Paris Cinema in the New York, injuring thirteen people. Clearly, in our allegedly secular world, the notion of Jesus as a sexual man remains the ultimate blasphemy.

For feminists, however, the offense lay elsewhere: not only in the insult to women as nonentities—nameless, brainless, and inert—but also in reviving the myth of the Magdalen as whore. While Jesus is treated in a radically contemporary way, the Magdalen looks back to the ancient dichotomy.[15] Especially in America, where her cult was virtually unknown, the sultry, exotic character played by Barbara Hershey seized the popular mind at a particularly crucial juncture for women in the church. Precisely when feminist scholars have revived the authentic gospel figure as an important model for women in the ministry, Scorsese's film only reinforced the legend that denigrates her.

If Scorsese's Jesus struggles with his sexuality in a wholly modern way, his Magdalen remains trapped by the age-old cliché. Despite her conversion she must be reviled, punished, transmuted into a domestic doormat. Finally bound in sexual and spiritual union to the man she loves, her identity is blurred, her face indistinguishable from that of all womankind.[16] Perhaps it is precisely that notion that sums up the problem of the Magdalen today.

For those who would see Jesus as having been a 'man in all his parts', she is the necessary compliment to his humanity. In D. H. Lawrence's erotic novella *The Man Who Died,* she is the woman who resurrects Christ in the literal sense, the woman whose touch makes him a fully sexual man. For the French novelist, Marguerite Yourcenar, she is a woman whose redemption saves her from sin, but deprives her of a fulfilled sexual or domestic life. Rather, she sublimates her natural urges to become disciple, healer, and domestic drudge all in one. Some theologians, both male and female, have argued that she may have been Jesus's wife—according to William Phipps, an unfaithful one at that.[17] And with the phenomenon of Dan Brown's mystery novel, *The Da Vinci Code,* a new myth emerges.

She is unequivocally wife and a mother whose progeny can be traced to this very day. More important, emerging from years of obscurity, she even appeared on the cover of *Newsweek* which has dubbed her "The year's surprise 'It' girl."

Unfortunately, Brown's sensational claim obscures the real work of scholars, and the crucial role model the Magdalen provides for women in the ministry today. Clearly, Jesus and some of his followers held her in high regard. As first witness to the resurrection she stands at the very crossroad between Judaism and Christianity. In the Gnostic Gospels her firm conviction stands in stark contrast to the sometimes panicky, indecisive male apostles; as wise woman and teacher she shatters the notion that women were wholly excluded from study and prayer in the early Church. Yet for all that she remains mysterious and elusive, a figure intricately connected to the age-old feminine polarity that categorizes certain kinds of women as marginal.

For Sandra Rushing, in her book *The Magdalene Legacy*, she is a deeply sympathetic figure, struggling to comprehend Jesus's altered form after the resurrection. In that incredibly charged moment in the garden, unable to touch him, to throw her arms about him and cling to him as instinct demands, she herself is transformed. Transmuting the love she has known into a

> new and vital spirituality . . . Mary Magdalene learns that she must, herself, rise up as an independent woman of faith, as a leader of the early Christian movement. She can no longer deny her own spirituality, her own strength, nor can she project them onto Jesus. He cannot carry her psychic projection of perfect brother, or father, or even love-husband. She must stand in the Judean dust and grieve for her companion, for in that grieving will be born the timeless aspects of her leadership of his followers.[18]

And in that grieving sorrow turns to strength, bereavement to the balm of a new life. Companion, apostle, lover, whichever identity we choose, in restoring the authentic persona her tears lose the bitterness of shame, her pain and sorrow become a pathway to strength and self-reliance. Rather than the repository for centuries of degradation of women, the fanaticism that has made women the scapegoat for the natural sexual drive of men, the Magdalen offers an image of independent woman searching for a place outside traditional categories. Like the Virgin Mary, she too may be a mother. Unlike the Madonna, she may be a widow, a divorced woman, a single mother, a welfare mother. Indeed, Mary Magdalen may yet be patron saint for those whom society still casts out into its periphery—not sinners, but human beings as Jesus saw them—struggling with the mysterious, complex nature of woman.

EPILOGUE

March 2002: a small courtroom in Sokoto, regional capital in northern Nigeria. At noon the sweltering hot, densely crowded room buzzed with flies drawn to the musky odor of human sweat. For the most part they were reporters waiting for the decision of the Islamic court in the much publicized case of Sufiyatu Huseni, a tiny, wizened woman of thirty five who looked decades older. An impoverished and illiterate mother of three, she had appealed a sentence of death by stoning for the crime of adultery.

About one year earlier Sufiyatu had returned to her native village, Tunger Tudu, after divorcing her husband who could not support her and their two children. Hardly better off in her blind father's mud and straw hut, Sufiyatu attracted the attentions of sixty year old Yakubu Abubakar. When she rejected his advances he took her by force when she was in the bush alone. Sufiyatu became pregnant, and someone reported her to the police in nearby Sokoto.

Shortly thereafter Sokoto fell under the jurisdiction of Islamic fundamentalists who tried her according to Sharia—strict Islamic law. At the hearing Abubakar denied all charges against him, and Sufiyatu was sentenced to death by stoning as soon as her baby girl was weaned. Her only hope lay in appeals from human rights organizations who made her case an international *cause celebre.*

In an article for The New York Times, "Death by Stoning," reporter R. Dowden asked the attorney general of Sokoto State, whose young daughters were sitting at his feet, how the execution would be carried out. Sufiyatu, he said, would be tied to a tree or, more likely, buried in a pit up to her neck, then pelted with stones about the size of a fist—in other words, slowly and brutally battered to death. He himself would gladly throw the first stone.[1]

Fortunately, with the spotlight of the entire world trained on the tiny courtroom, Sufiyatu won her appeal. The verdict was overturned and human rights organizations breathed a deep sigh of relief. Yet the very next day another 'adulteress' was tried and sentenced to stoning—this one, like others before and after, virtually certain to be carried out.

Of course, such a case devolves upon an extreme Islamic fundamentalism that has little or nothing to do with a modern democracy. Yet it is a vivid reminder of the tenacity of ancient codes that scapegoat women, even in the case of rape. Death by stoning may be an aberration in today's world, yet the age-old dichotomy still pertains in deeper, hidden forms. Closer to home, perhaps, is a different sort of tragedy, the case of Andrea Yates, the Texas mother who, one by one, drowned all five of her children. Although spared the death penalty, the heartbreaking infanticide riveted a nation struggling to conceive how this seemingly model mother could commit such a horrendous act. One answer, of course, is that Yates was psychotic at the time. But Professor Victoria Brown of Grinnell College saw something deeper, something drawn from a Jungian collective unconscious that impelled Yates toward the tragedy. In Brown's opinion, Yates had internalized a profoundly religious "image of woman as [the Virgin] Mary. That is how she redeems herself from original sin, that is how she is valuable to the community—as the self-sacrificing mother."[2]

Times reporter Anne Taylor Fleming agreed, contending that Yates's desperate struggle to be the perfect mother, even home schooling her children, was partially mandated by a "historically and religiously ordained role, motherhood."[3] Yet despite her post-partum psychoses, delusional states and suicide attempts, neither her husband nor parents recognized the danger at hand; the burden on an already fragile psyche of trying to live up to a superhuman ideal of perfection.

Nor is that drive to perfection unknown to a whole segment of today's women. The powerhouse 'Martha Stewart' suburban wife and mother—cook, chauffeur, PTA maven, and fashion plate with a Jane Fonda body, all the while keeping her white kitchen floors gleaming—is as much a myth as the Madonna ever was. In reality, that illusory ideal of perfect wife and mother can lead to anxiety, depression, the suburban valium stupor, or in its extremity the 'Maternal Madness' that gripped Andrea Yates.

Conversely, the Virgin's polar opposite pertains even yet, as does the world's oldest profession. Thanks to the tell all revelations of the Beverly Hills madam, we know that prostitution with a certain patina of elegance continues to be the option of choice for the rich and powerful. As to street prostitution, one need only look around the central bus terminal in any major city, or in Boston's so called combat zone, Berkeley's University Avenue, or New York City's downtown meat packing district (prostitutes having been evicted from Times Square by Mayor Giuliani and its conversion to 'Disney Square').

These women may not be called Magdalens, but society's attitude toward them remains the same. Only recently, in Springfield, Massachusetts, Mayor Albano announced an all-out campaign against prostitution in that city on grounds that it had become a public nuisance. So many women were plying their trade in the down town area that business was being driven away from Springfield's rejuvenated city center. His solution, a mandatory one-year jail sentence for convicted prostitutes, roused the ire of Springfield's NOW chapter. As always, they asserted, the law punishes women already driven by desperation, while letting their partners go scott-free.

On a wholly different level, an updated version of the proverbial man-eating vamp has emerged—the high powered female executive who stalks her prey in the corporate board room. In the film *Fatal Attraction*, Glen Close plays a successful career woman driven to murderous derangement by sexual frustration and the empty apartment to which she returns nightly. More menacing still is Sharon Stone's character in *Basic Instinct*, the female monster of the nineties. Driven by competitive instincts nurtured by an inverse world in which women assume male roles, she threatens to destroy her happily married colleague if he resists her sexual demands. Interestingly, the wife whom he refuses to betray is played as her polar opposite—the proverbial, well-scrubbed girl next door.

Out in the real, grinding work a day world, few women have time for such seduction dramas. More typically they struggle to juggle the double whammy of demanding careers and the never-ending needs of home, husband, children. Although record numbers of women have entered the work force, no significant steps to deal with that reality has been pursued either publicly or privately. Day care remains overcrowded and too expensive for mid- to lower-income families. Despite the trailblazing maternity and family leave bill passed by the Clinton administration, we have yet to see the flexible working hours common in several European nations that would alleviate the problem of latch key children and the burden of guilt that falls on the shoulders of working mothers.

At the same time, stay at home moms earn little respect in today's society, while women who have fought their way into competitive professions are faced with wrenching decisions when the biological clock begins running out. Welfare mothers, on the other hand, have no choice; either leave their children or lose benefits, despite the trauma to households that have already lost their fathers. Soaring rates of divorce, the fifty-fifty property split, and the abolition of alimony have also taken a serious toll on the family. Survival now depends upon a working mother, yet women who have not pursued professions face a daunting experience in the workplace, not to mention the awesome responsibility of single parenthood. Little wonder that the fastest growing category of poverty today is single mothers and their children, to whom society turns a blind eye.

Perhaps, then, an updated Madonna figure might serve us well; not the untouchable virgin set on a pedestal, but an icon for the dignity and worth of motherhood and its superhuman demands—the physical burden of pregnancy, the sleepless nights with small infants, the unremitting demands of family in a unrelenting, competitive world. Certainly Mary's all embracing, all forgiving love reminds us of that vital nurture for which we continue to yearn, even as adults. If there is a myth that never dies, it would be that of motherhood, although amended by the extraordinary phenomenon of modern fathers who share in the nurturing from the very beginning.

Not all women are cut out to be mothers; but even for Catholic women who have elected a religious vocation instead, the traditional Madonna icon does not suffice. Many nuns today live very much in the world, relinquishing their habits and convent cells to actively serve the poor and the needy. For them, as well, the figure on the pedestal needs replacing with one that corresponds with modern realities.

One such woman is the now-famous Sister Helen Prejean, whose conflicted relationship with a convicted rapist and murderer became the subject of the novel and film *Dead Man Walking*. The film opens with a flashback—Sister Prejean's induction into the convent when, as bride of Christ, she exchanges her wedding gown for a nun's habit. Thirty years later she wears ordinary street clothes and lives in an apartment close to the poor families she serves. As her relationship with the killer, Poncelet, evolves, he perceives the loneliness that envelops her when cheerful voices and the odor of a family barbecue waft into her solitary room on a Sunday. But when he cruelly badgers her about her celibacy, she responds that there are other ways of experiencing intimacy. Perhaps she has no lover, but like the Virgin she offers even a callous murderer her unconditional love.

Only at the eleventh hour, just before his execution, does that love work its miracle. Breaking through his hardened shell, Poncelet confesses, weeping the cleansing tears of penitence. Unlike the cold, harshly judgmental prison Chaplain, Sister Prejean's love has touched this man debased by such horrendous crimes, compensating perhaps for what is denied her by her celibacy.

Dead Man Walking also reminds us of the chasm that yet remains between ordained men and women in the Church today. Sister Prejean could not be a prison chaplain, since nuns cannot administer the sacraments or officiate at Mass. Indeed, even as nuns become more worldly, maintaining demanding, high-powered professions, that inequity becomes more glaring and more frustrating.

A case in point would be the Sisters of Mercy in Pittsburgh. In days past the sisters gave up all personal identity on assuming the veil, taking the Blessed Mother's name. Today they use their own names, wear street clothes, jewelry and makeup, drive their own cars, and hold down exacting, professional jobs. Yet in accordance with the vow of poverty, chastity and obedience, the sisters must turn over their salaries to the church which allows them a meager monthly allowance. Priests, on the other hand, receive a more liberal allowance, better housing and maids and cooks to care for their personal needs.

Each of the Sisters must wrestle in her own way with that partiality. But for Sister Michelle Smolin, a strikingly attractive lawyer who, as public defender, represents Pittsburgh's poor and dispossessed, the most dogged problem is the Dogma of the Immaculate Conception. As Smolin sees it,

> the very concept of Mary's immaculate conception . . . [is] inherently disrespectful to women, for if Mary was conceived without original sin she is robbed of her humanity, and the implication is that all women are unworthy.

Yet the Dogma of the Immaculate Conception remains one of two Catholic doctrines declared infallible. To question it is not only to invite excommunication, but to demystify a great miracle, to thereby question all miracles and deny that some things are not given to human understanding. Nor can the Church risk tampering with Mary's legend, for the notion of pure, unsullied womanhood—mother, sister, wife combined in one—is, after all, its own creation. More explosive by far is a larger question—one that, at the moment, threatens the entire edifice of the church. A veritable eruption of shocking revelations about sexual abuses of minors by the clergy has forced not only the church, but society at large to face the psychological and moral ramifications of celibacy. Parish by parish, city by city, clergy are either accused of child molestation, or have confessed to crimes long hidden within the administrative and legal apparatus of the Church. Like a poison that, once released, leaves its residue in the atmosphere, this problem resists conventional methods of resolution. The pain and damage done to innocent victims is too great. Clearly, the call for debate on a celibate, exclusively male clergy is at hand.

Central to that debate is not only the issue of Mary's virginity, but the larger issue of Jesus's position on celibacy. Nowhere in the Gospels does Jesus make virginity an absolute condition for admission to the Kingdom—not for women or men, and certainly not for mothers. As we have seen earlier in this book, in his own time and place such an idea would be absolutely untenable for a Jew. Rather, it was the Church Fathers who created the intellectual and emotional climate that made celibacy a condition for holiness and, eventually, a requirement for priests and nuns. As to the historical Jesus, of whom we know so little, we have no idea whether he himself was celibate, or whether, like his great counterpart Hillel, it was taken for granted that at some point he had been married.

For those who continue to seek the human Jesus, the capacity to give and take love is a given. That love need not be sexual, however the legend of the Magdalen as Jesus's lover or wife has proven as tenacious as the Madonna legend. Yet, like the Madonna, an updated Magdalen could be a major factor in the vehement debate about women's place in the Church today. By stripping away layers of mythology, the Magdalen bears witness to the vital presence of women in the original Jesus movement, and in the evolving Church. As apostle, teacher, preacher, evangelist, prophet, mystic, she transcends the traditional restrictions on women as active participants. Rather she presents a model for partnership, for women as equal before the Lord, as Jesus himself demanded.

Most important, as a woman whose marital status remains uncertain, the Magdalen stands for woman in all her diverse categories: single women, single mothers, working women, widows, companions, lovers. Yet the stubborn legend that she was a prostitute endures, as do male fantasies about the archetypal sexually desirable woman. However, in a climate purged of negative attitudes toward sexuality, that vital force in both men and women becomes vibrant and creative.

In that respect, whichever identity she assumes the Magdalen's tears must lose the bitterness of shame. Rather than a symbol for repentance and scapegoat for male desire, a modern Magdalen must offer a model of independent woman; capable, respected, indispensable partner to man as she was in the Creation story before the Fall. As alternative to the Madonna, she must resonate with women whom, even now, society reflexively casts into the periphery—single, divorced, widowed women, mothers without partners who must fend for themselves and their children. Through her we are yet reminded of Jesus's great compassion for the difficult lot of women on the fringe.

Indeed, her legend reminds us of Jesus's exceptional empathy for women, whom he refused to regard as chattel or as intrinsically sinful. In this we must be careful not to project a contemporary consciousness. Like every great figure, Jesus was a man of his own time, even while he rose above it. Yet, the gospel writers have given us ample reason to believe that Jesus neither feared, rejected, nor looked down upon women, that he appreciated their intelligence and loyalty, that he included them in his teachings and, possibly, in their dissemination as well.

Nor did he condemn either men or women for their sexuality. Rather, he taught the deeper meaning of love through that nameless woman in Luke with whom the Magdalen has been confused—she who wept at his feet, kissed and dried them with her hair, anointed him with sweet myrrh. Castigated by his shocked Pharisee host, Jesus responded with, perhaps, the greatest of his teachings about human frailty. Her transgressions were not an incurable disease or a ticket to damnation. Rather, "her great love proves that her many sins have been forgiven." In such fashion the two Marys remain as potent symbols of womankind—archetypes representing woman's myriad roles as wife, mother, lover, creator, nurturer, scholar, and teacher, possessing both wisdom and spirituality.

Viewed in this way as complementary rather than separate categories, they fulfill a role even yet—a holistic view not only of woman, but of our universal and fundamental humanity.

BIBLIOGRAPHY

Auerbach, N., *Woman and the Demon,* Harvard Univ. Press, 1982.

Aretino's Dialogues, Rosenthal, R., trans., London, 1972.

Augustine, Saint; *The Confessions of Saint Augustine,* Modern Library,1949.

_______________ *The City of God,* from *The Fathers of the Church,* Collected Works, Catholic University of America Press, 1963.

_______________ *Treatise on Marriage and Other Subjects,* from *Fathers of the Church,* as above.

Baeck, L., *Judaism and Christianity,* Meridian, 1948.

Baker D. and Murphy J, eds. *The Late Medieval Religious Plays of Bodelian Mss. Digby 133 and e museo 160,* Oxford U. Press 1982.

Banti, A., *Artemesia,* Univ. Nebraska press, 1953 1st, 1988 2nd

Bauer, G., *Bernini in Perspective,* Prentice Hall, 1976.

Baxandall, *Painting and Experience in Fifteenth Century Italy,* Oxford U.P., 1988.

Bell, R., *Holy Anorexia,* Univ. Chicago Press, 1985.

Bell, S., *Women From the Greeks to the French Revolution,* Stanford U. Press, 1973.

Belting, H., *A History of the Image Before the Era of Art,* Univ. Chicago P., 1994.

Biale, D., *Eros and the Jews,* Basic Bozoks, 1949.

Bischoff, U., *Munch,* Taschen, 1993.

Bornkamm, G., *Jesus of Nazareth,* Harper and Row, 1960.

Boulding, E., *The Underside of History, A View of Women Through Time,* Westview Press, 1976.

Boyarin, D., *Carnal Israel,* Univ. Calif. Press, 1993.

Brading, D.A., *Mexican Phoenix: Our Lady of Guadalupe,* Cambridge University Press, 2002.

Brown P., *The Body and Society; Men, Women and Sexual Renunciation in Early Christianity,* Columbia U. Press, 1988.

_______ *The World of Late Antiquity,* Norton, 1971.

Bruce, F.F., *New Testament History,* Anchor Books, 1972.

Brundage, J., *Law, Sex, and Christian Society in Medieval Europe,* Univ. Chicago, 1987.

Burkett, W., *Ancient Mystery Cults,* Harvard U. Press, 1987.

Cameron, R., *The Other Gospels, Non-Canonical Gospel Texts,* Westminster, 1982.

Campbell, J. ed., *The Portable Jung,* Viking, 1971.

Carlton, C., *Royal Mistresses,* Routledge, 1990.

Catherine of Sienna, *The Dialogue,* Paulist Press, 1980.

Clark, E., *Women in the Early Church,* Michael Glazier Inc., 1983.

Clark, G., *Women in Late Antiquity,* Oxford U.P., 1994.

Cleugh, J., *Love Locked Out, An Examination of Sexuality in the Middle Ages,* Crown Pub. 1963.

Colledge and McGinn, trans. *Meister Eckhart,* Paulist Press, 1981.

Collins, W., *Armadale,* Oxford U. Press, 1989.

________ *Basil,* Oxford U. Press, 1990.

Countryman, W., *Dirt, Greed and Sex; Sexual Ethics in the New Testament,* Fortress, 1988.

Crashaw, R., *Complete Poetry,* G. Williams, ed., Anchor, 1970.

Crosson, D., Jesus, *A Revolutionary Biography,* Harper, 1989.

________ The *Historical Jesus,* Harper, 1991.

________ *Four Other Gospels,* Winston Press, 1985.

Cushman, L., *The Devil and the Vice in English Dramatic Literature Before Shakespeare,* F. Casso, 1970.

Filoramo, G., *A History of Gnosticism,* Blackwell, 1990.

Dante, *The Portable Dante,* Viking, 1952.

Dart, J., *The Jesus of Heresy,* Harper and Row, 1988.

de Case and Sanders, *Rodin's Sculpture,* C. Tuttle, 1977.

Denny, N., *Medieval Drama,* E. Arnold, 1974

de Vex, R., *Ancient Israel,* McGraw-Hill, 1961.

de Voragine, Jacobus *The Golden Legend,* Princeton U. Press, 1993, Vol.

Durant, W., *The Reformation,* Simon and Schuster, 1957.

Elliot, J.K., *The Apocryphal New Testament,* Oxford U. P., 1993.

Epstein, S., *Edvard Munch,* Allen Memorial Art Museum, Oberlin, OH. 1983.

________ *Edvard Munch, Master Prints from the Epstein Family Collection,* National Gallery of Art, 1990.

Forge A., *Fragile Lives,* Harvard U. Press, 1993.

Ford, John, *'Tis Pity She's a Whore',* S. Barker, ed., Routledge, 1997.

Fromm, E. *The Dogma of Christ,* Anchor Books, 1966.

Fromm, E., *You Shall Be As Gods, A Radical Interpretation Of The Old Testament And Its Tradition,* Holt, Rinehart and Winston, 1966.

Frymer-Kensky, T., *In the Wake of the Goddesses,* Free Press, 1992.

Garrard, M, Artemesia Gentileschi: The Image of the Female Hero in Italian Baroque Art, Princeton, 1989.

Gadon, E., *The Once and Future Goddess,* Harper and Row, 1989.

Glasscoe, M., ed., *The Medieval Mystical Tradition in England,* D. S. Brewer, 1984.

Grant, R., *The Secret Sayings of Jesus,* Doubleday, 1960.

______, A Sourcebook of Heretical Writings From The Early Christian Period, Harper, 1961.

Grimal, P., *Love in Ancient Rome,* U. Oklahoma P., 1912.

Harriman, H., *Women in the Western Heritage,* Dushkin, 1995.

Harrison, F., *The Dark Angel,* Universe Books, 1977.

Haskins, S., *Mary Magdalen, Myth and Metaphor,* Harcourt Brace, 1993.

Hawthorne, N., *The Scarlet Letter,* Signet, 1959.

Hemmings, F., *The Life and Times of Emile Zola,* Scribner, 1977.

________________ Heresy *In the Middle Ages,* Manchester U. P., 1967, Vol. 11, See Ch.VI, "The Older Heresies and the Flagellants".

Hervieux, J., *The New Testament Apocrypha,* Hawthorn Books, 1960.

Heyn, D., *The Erotic Silence of the American Wife,* Turtle Bay, 1992.

Horsley, R., *Sociology and the Jesus Movement,* Crossroad, 1989.

Hufton, O.H., *The Poor of Eighteenth Century France,* Oxford U. Press, 1974, see Ch. XI, Prostitution.

Hunter, D., *Marriage in the Early Church,* Fortress P. 1992.

Hunter-Steibel, P., Catalogue for *Chez Elle, Chez Lui, At Home in 18th Century France,* Rosenberg and Steibel, 1987. p. 22.

Huxley, A., *The Devils of Loudon, Harper, 1953.*

Kautsky, K., *Foundations of Christianity,* Russell, 1953.

Kazantzakis, *The Last Temptation of Christ,* Bantam 1963.

Kearney, P., *A History of Erotic Literature,* Macmillan, 1982.

Kertzer, D., *Sacrificed for Honor, Infant Abandonment and the Politics of Reproductive Control,* Beacon Press, 1948.

Keuls, E., *The Reign of the Phallus, Sexual Politics in Ancient Athens,* Harper and Row, 1985.

Kinsley, D., *The Goddesses' Mirror,* State Univ. of New York Press, 1989.

Klapisch-Zuber, C., ed., *A History of Women in the West,* Harvard Univ. Press, 1992.

Klein, E., *All Too Human,* Pocket Books, 1996.

Klingman, W., *The First Century,* Harper Perennial, 1990.

Kraemer, R., ed., *Maenads, Martyrs, Matrons, Monastics,* Fortress P., 1988.

_________*Her Share Of The Blessings, Women's Religions Among Pagans, Jews, And Christians In The Greco-Roman World,* Oxford U.P., 1992.

_________*Women In Scripture, A Dictionary of Named And Unnamed Women in the Hebrew Bible and*

Apocryphal/Deuterocanonical Books and the New Testament, Houghton Mifflin, 2000.

LaPorte, J., *The Role of Women in Early Christianity,* Mellen Press, 1924.

Laquer, T., *Making Sex,* Harvard U. Press, 1990.

Layton, B., *The Gnostic Scriptures,* Doubleday, 1987.

Lees, C., *Medieval Masculinities,* U. Minnesota Press, 1994.

Leff, G., *Heresy in the Late Middle Ages,* Manchester U. Press, 1967, Vol 1 and 11.

Lewis, R. W. B., *Edith Wharton, A Biography,* Harper and Row, 1975.

Leyerle, B., *Theatrical Shows and Ascetic Lives,* Univ. California Press, 2001.

Lieu, J. et al, ed., *The Jews Among Pagans and Christians,* Routledge, 1992.

Lincoln, V., *Teresa: A Woman, A Biography of Teresa of Avila,* SUNY Press, 1984.

Lucie-Smith, *Sexuality in Western Art,* Thames and Hudson, 1991.

MacHaffie, B., *Readings in Her Story,* Fortress P. 1992.

Maeterlinck, M., *Mary Magdalene,* Dodd, mead and Co., NY, 1910.

Mahony, P., *Maurice Maeterlinck, Mystic and Dramatist,* Institute for the Study of Man, 1984.

Mahood, L., *The Magdalenes, Prostitution in the Nineteenth Century,* Routledge, 1990.

Malvern, M. *Venus in Sackcloth: the Magdalen's Origins and Metamorphoses,* Carbondale, 1975.

The Illustrated Mayhew's London, ed. Weidenfeld and Nichols, Canning, London, 1986.

McHaffie, *Readings in Her Story,* Fortress Press, 1949.

McNamara, J., *A New Song, Celibate Women in the First Three Christian Centuries,* Haworth P. 1983.

__________*Sisters in Arms: Catholic Nuns Through Two Millennia,* Harvard U. P.1996

Marcus, S., *The Other Victorians,* Basic Books, 1964.

Marsh, J., *Pre-Raphaelite Women,* Artus, 1987.

Mason, M., *The Making of Victorian Sexuality,* Oxford U. Press, 1994.

McGinn, B. ed., *Meister Eckhart, Teacher and Preacher,* Paulist Press, 1986.

_________*Meister Eckhart, The Essential Sermons,* 1981.

Mendgen, E., *Franz Von Stuck,* Taschen, 1995.

Miles, M., *Desire and Delight, A New Reading of St. Augustine's Confessions,* Crossroad, 1992.

Millet, B., ed., *Hali Meidhad,* Oxford Univ. Press, 1982.

Moore, J., *Love in Twelfth Century France,* Univ. Pennsylvania Press, 1972.

Mort, F., *Dangerous Sexualities,* Routledge, 1987.

Moss, A., *Women of Scripture,* Methodist Publishing House, 1999.

Mulder-Bakker, A., *Sanctity and Motherhood, Essays on Holy Mothers in the Middle Ages,* Garland, 1995.

Murray, J., *Strong Minded Women,* Pantheon Books, 1982.

My Secret Life, vol. 1-VI, Vol. VII-XI, Grove Press, NY, 1966.

Nash, J., *Veiled Images: Titian's Mythological Paintings for Phillip 11,* Philadelphia Art Alliance Press, 1949.

Nagle, B., *The Ancient World,* Prentice Hall, 1996.

Nelson, A., *Medieval English Stage,* Univ. Chicago Press, 1974.

Neusner, J., *Judaism in the Beginning of Christianity,* Fortress, 1993.

________ *Judaic Law From Jesus to the Mishnah,* Scholar's Press, 1993.

New English Bible, Oxford U.P., 1970.

Olson, Carl, *The Book of Goddess Past and Present,* Crossroad, 1989.

Osborne, L., *The Poisoned Embrace, A Brief History of Sexual Pessimism, Vintage, 1993.*

Oxford Study Bible, Oxford U. Press, 1992.

Packer, L., *Christina Rossetti,* U.C. Press, 1963.

Pagels, E., *The Gnostic Gospels,* Vintage, 1989.

_________ *Adam and Eve and the Serpent,* Vintage, 1988.

Paz, O., *Sor Juana,* Harvard U. Press, 1988.

Pearl, S., *The Girl with the Swansdown Seat,* Bobbs-Merill, 1955.

Perkin, J., *Women and Marriage in Nineteenth Century England,* Lyceum, 1989.

Pevsner, N., *Mary Through the Centuries,* Yale U. P., 1996.

Phillips, J., *Eve, The History of an Idea,* Harper and Row, 1984.

Phipps, *Genesis and Gender,* Praeger, 1989.

Pognon, E., ed. *Boccaccio's Decameron,* Crown Publishers, 1978.

Potter, R., *The English Morality Play,* Routledge, 1975

Price, R., *Three Gospels,* Scribner, 1996.

Prosser, E., *Drama and Religion in the English Mystery Plays,* Stanford U. Press, 1961.

Pullan, B., *Rich and Poor in Renaissance Venice,* Oxford U., P., 1971.

Quaife, G., *Wanton Wenches and Wayward Wives,* Rutgers U. Press, 1979.

Ranke-Heinemann, *U. Eunuchs for the Sake of Heaven,* Penguin Books, 1990.

Ruether, R., *Religion and Sexism,* Simon and Schuster, 1974.

________ *Mary, The Feminine Face of the Church,* Westminster, 1977.

Richardson, S., *Pamela,* W.W. Norton, 1958.

__________ Clarissa, Riverside, 1962,

Robinson, J., ed., *The Nag Hammadi Library in English,* Leiden, 1984,

Rogers, K.M., *The Troublesome Helpmeet; A History of Misogyny in Literature,* Univ. Washington Press, 1966.

Rose, P., *Parallel Lives,* Vintage, 1984.

Ros, M., *Night of Fire,* Sarpedon, 1991.

Rushing, S., *The Magdalene Legacy, Exploring the Wounded Icon of Sexuality,* Bergin and Garvey, 1994.

Ruskin, J., *Sesame and Lilies,* Sibley and Ducker, 1977

Sagan, E., *Freud, Women and Morality,* Basic Books, 1988.

Saldarini, A., *Matthew's Christian-Jewish Community,* U. Chicago Press, 1994.

Salisbury, J., *Church Fathers, Independent Virgins,* Verso, 1991.

Sanders, E.P., *The Historical Figure of Jesus,* Allen Press, 1993.

________ *Jesus and Judaism,* Fortress Press, 1985.

Sandmel, S., *A Jewish Understanding of the New Testament,* University Pub., 1956.

Schussler, Fiorenza E., *In Memory of Her,* Crossroads, 1989.

Sheed, F. J., *Confessions of St. Augustine,* trans., Sheed and Ward, 1943.

Southwell, R., *Mary Magdalen's Funeral Theares,* Delmar, NY, 1975.

St. Teresa of Avila, *Vida,* Burns and Oates, 1962.

Stevenson, J., *The Catacombs,* T. Nelson, 1978.

Suetonius, *The Lives of the Twelve Caesars,* Modern Library, 1931.

Thurston, B., *The Widows: A Woman's ministry in the Early Church,* Fortress Press, 1973.

Tillyard, S., *The Lives of the Twelve Caesars,* Modern Library, 1931.

Tomalin, C., *Mrs. Jordan's Profession, The Actress and the Prince,* Alfred A. Knopf, 1995.

________ *The Invisible Woman,* A. A. Knopf, 1991.

Torjsen, K., *When Women Were Priests,* Harper, 1993.

Trudgill, E., *Madonnas and Magdalens,* Holmes and Meier, NY, 1976.

Tuttle, R., *Mysticism in the Wesleyan Tradition,* Francis Asbury Press, 1989.

Vermes, G., *Jesus the Jew,* Fontana/Collins, 1973.

Voragine, Jacobus, *The Golden Legend,* Princeton U. Press, 1993.

Walker, B., *The Woman's Encyclopedia of Myths and Secrets,* Harper's, 1983.

Warner, M., *Alone of All Her Sex, The Myth and the Cult of the Virgin Mary,* Vintage, 1983.

West, S., *Fin De Siecle,* Overlook Press, 1993.

Wilson, I., *Jesus; The Evidence,* Harpers, 1984.

Witherington, B., *Women in the Earliest Churches,* Cambridge U. Press, 1988.

Woolf, R., *The English Mystery Plays,* Univ. California Press, 1972.
Young, K., *The Drama of the Medieval Church,* 1993 reprint, Oxford, 1962.
Young-Breuhl, *Freud on Women,* W.W. Norton, 1990.
Zola, E., Nana, Oxford U. Press, 1992.

ENDNOTES

Preface

1. Klein, E. *All Too Human*, Packet Books, 1996.

Chapter One

1. Faxon A., *Women and Jesus*, Pilgrim Press, 1973, p. 62.
2. Crossan, D. *Jesus: A Revolutionary Biography*, Harper, 1989, pp. 110-11.
3. Schussler Fiorenza, E., *In Memory of Her*, Crossroad, 1989, p. 173. Also see Introduction and Ch. 5 for in depth discussion of women as missionaries. (Quotation from p. 161)
4. Torjesen K., *When Women Were Priests*, Harper, 1993. p. 54
5. Crossan, p. 192. Crossan has also speculated that Mark, the earliest and most authentic of the Gospel writers, could have been a woman.

Chapter Two

1. Brading, D.A., *Mexican Phoenix, Our Lady of Guadalupe*, Cambridge University Press, 2002.
2. Ros M., *Night of Fire*, Sarpedon, 1991. p. 63.
3. Klingman W., *The First Century*, Harper Perennial, 1990, p. 174.
4. For an in-depth discussion of Roman law on this issue see Clark, Gillian., *Women in Late Antiquity*, Oxford U. Press, 1993, Ch. 1, "Law and Morality", especially pp. 18-19.
5. For a compelling discussion of the Temple, see Klingman as above.
6. Vermes, G., *Jesus the Jew*, Fontana/Collins, 1973, pp. 218-19.

Chapter Three

1. From Philo, *On The Contemplative Life*. Quoted in R. Kraemer, ed., *Maenads, Martyrs, Matrons, Monastics,* Fortress Press, 1988, p. 27.
2. Biale D., *Eros and the Jews,* Basic Books, 1992, p. 34.
3. Genesis 22:7.
4. Ruth 2: 9-10.
5. Biale, p. 131
6. Boyarin D., *Carnal Israel,* Univ. Calif. Press, 1993, p. 113.
7. Ibid, p. 114.
8. Biale, p. 101
9. Ibid, p. 103.
10. Ibid, p. 80
11. Ibid, p. 5.
12. Kraemer, p. 43.
13. Boyarin, p. 110.
14. Ruether R., *Religion and Sexism,* Simon and Schuster, 1974, p. 97.
15. Biale, p. 134.
16. Ibid, p. 104.
17. Ruether, p. 94.
18. Ibid, p. 94
19. Biale, p. 133.
20. Salisbury, J., *Church Fathers, Independent Virgins,* Verso, 1991, p. 19.
21. See *Mark* 7:1-8. Also see Sanders, *Jesus and the Jews,* p. 180-81.
22. McNamara, J., *A New Song,* Haworth Press, 1983, p. 9.
23. In the seventeenth century the Sabbatai Zevi was so widely accepted by Eastern European Jews as the Messiah that many of them sold all their goods, properties, and liquidated their assets in the belief that the last days had come. The economic effect was felt throughout Europe.
24. Brundage J., Law, Sex and Christian Society, Univ. Chicago, 1987, p. 110.

25. For a detailed discussion of the celibacy controversy see Haskins, S., *Mary Magdalen, Myth and Metaphor,* Harcourt Brace, 1993, p. 89. Note that at the 5th Council at Carthage higher clergy had to separate from their wives or lose their office.

Chapter Four

1. Ranke-Heinemann, U., *Eunuchs for the Sake of Heaven, Women, Sexuality, And The Catholic Church,* Penguin Books, 1990, p. 15. Also see R. Grant, A Sourcebook of *Heretical Writers From the Early Christian Period,* Harper, 1961.
2. Brundage, fn. 68, p. 64.
3. Hunter, D. *Marriage in the Early Church,* Fortress Press, 1992, p. 40.
4. Quoted in Bell, S., *Women: From the Greeks to the French Revolution,* Stanford U. Press, 1973, p. 85. Also see Rogers K. M. *The Troublesome Helpmate: A History of Misogyny in Literature,* University Washington Press, 1966.
5. Brown P. *The Body and Society; Men, Women and Sexual Renunciation in Early Christianity,* Columbia U. Press, 1988, p. 168.
6. Ibid, p. 171.
7. Cleugh, *Love Locked Out,* Crown Press, 1963, p. 11.
8. Ranke-Heinemann, p. 57.
9. Salisbury, p. 18.
10. Clark, Elizabeth, *Women in the Early Church,* Michael Glazier, 1983, p. 119.
11. Ibid, p. 124
12. 1st Thessalonians 4:31, 1st Corinthians, 7:1, Galatians 5:19.
13. 1st Corinthians 7:9 - 35.
14. 1st Corinthians, 7: 36- 38. For more on the celibate marriage see Leyerle, B Theatrical Shows and Ascetic Lives, Univ. California Press, 2001, p. 79.
15. Clark, p. 30.

16. Hunter, pp. 41-2, from Clement, *The Instructor Book Two.*
17. Ibid, p. 54.
18. Brown, p. 126.
19. Clark, p. 53.
20. Salisbury, p. 19.
21. Ibid, p. 21.
22. Xenophon, Mem., 2:2:4, Quoted in Blundell, *Women in Ancient Greece,* Harvard U. Press, 1995, p. 102.
23. Brundage, p. 17.
24. Ibid, p. 18.
25. Suetonius, *Lives of the Twelve Caesars,* Modern Library, 1931, pp. 145-6.
26. Ibid, pp. 258-9.
27. Ranke-Heineman, p. 11.
28. Ibid, pp. 12-13.
29. Ibid, p. 50.
30. Haskins, p. 75.
31. Ibid, p. 142.
32. Nash, J., *Veiled Images: Titian's Mythological Paintings for Phillip 11.* Philadelphia Art and Alliance Press, 1949, p.47.
33. Brown, p. 392.
34. Ibid, p. 394.
35. Ibid, p. 394.
36. Clark, E., Ed., St. Augustine On Marriage and Sexuality, Catholic University of America Press, 1996, pp. 13-14.
37. See Brown, p. 401.
38. Clark, p. 65.
39. Epistle to the Romans, vii, 23-4.
40. Salisbury, p. 43.
41. Pagels, *Adam and Eve and the Serpent,* Vintage, 1988, p. 134.
42. 42., Ibid, pp.1 33-134.
43. Hunter, p. 77.
44. Ibid, p. 82 and 92.
45. Ibid, p. 90.

46. Ibid, p. 99.
47. Actually, Pelagius' position was ambivalent. When a prominent Roman matron, Celentia, asked him to defend a vow of chastity in defiance of her husband, Pelagius backed down, citing Paul: "A wife does not have power over her own body" - and the danger that her husband may be driven to the greater sin of fornication. Yet he will pray that her husband will voluntarily choose chastity, for the decision must be mutual.
48. Hunter, p. 136.
49. Brown, p. 407
50. See Pagels, Ch. V1, "The Nature of Nature"
51. Ibid, p. 146.
52. For more on the flagellants see Leff, G., *Heresy in the Middle Ages,* Manchester U. P. 1967, Vol 11. Ch. VI, "The Older Heresies and the Flagellants".
53. Fromm, E., *You Shall Be As Gods, A Radical Interpretation Of The Old Testament And Its Traditions,* Holt, Rinehart, and Winston, 1966, pp. 168-169.
54. Osborne, L., *The Poisoned Embrace,* Vintage, 1993, p. 35.
55. Warner, M., Alone Of All Her Sex, Vintage, 1976, p. 64.
56. Brundage, p. 64.

Chapter Five

1. Osborne, p. 34.
2. The *Infancy Gospel of Thomas*: this and all Gnostic texts taken from Robinson J. , editor, *The Nag Hammadi Library in English,* Leiden, 1984, p. 125. Also see Evans, et al editors, *Nag Hammadi Texts and the Bible,* Yale U. P., 1993.
3. In Gnostic writings, laughter and crying symbolize the two polarities, good and evil.
4. Robinson, *Protovangelium of James,* p. 11.
5. Warner, p. 29.
6. Robinson, *Gospel of Philip.*

7. Bell, p. 87.
8. Jerome, *A Girl's Education*, quoted in Lualdi, K. *The Making of the West*, Bedford/St. Martins, 2003, pp. 62-3.
9. Clark, Eliz., p. 126.
10. Salisbury, p. 77.
11. Ibid, p. 76.
12. Ibid, p. 79.
13. Kraemer, p. 117.
14. Torjesen, p. 23.
15. Ruether, p. 102.
16. Warner, p. 58.
17. Torjesen, p. 23.
18. Clark, Eliz., p. 38.
19. N. Pevsner in *Mary Through the Centuries* argues, to the contrary, that Mary's obedience was, in fact, a liberating construction; one would have to assume that the choice was made for her by male theologians and scholars.
20. Haskins, p. 80.

Chapter Six

1. See Blundell, p. 30. She says that these 'breasts' may be either fruits or the testicles of bulls sacrificed to her.
2. Ruether, R., Mary, *The Feminine Face of The Church*, Westminster, 1977, p. 16.
3. Haskins, pp. 143-4.
4. Ibid, p. 143.
5. See Huxley, A., *The Devils of Loudon*, Harper, 1953.
6. Pognon, E., ed. *Boccaccio's Decameron*, Crown Publishers, 1978, pp. 14-15.
7. Warner, p. 200.
8. Bell, p. 135.
9. Ibid, p. 133-8.
10. Warner, p. 137.
11. *The Portable Dante*, Viking Press, 1947, p. 548.

12. Ibid, p. 283.
13. Ibid, p. 539-40.
14. Ibid, p. 544.
15. For an excellent discussion of early iconography see Belting, H., *A History of the Image Before the Era of Art*, U. Chicago, 1994.
16. Baxandall, M. *Painting and Experience in Fifteenth-Century Italy*, Oxford, 1988, p. 57.
17. The tradition, of course, derives from the ancient world, the model being Isis suckling her infant.

Chapter Seven

1. From Table Talk, from *Luther's Works*, Brandt, W., ed. Fortress Press, 1962.
2. Quoted in Dackerman, S., *Chaste, Chased and Chastened*, Harvard University Art Museums Gallery Series, No. 6, 1993, p. 4.
3. From Luther, *Werke*, quoted in W. Durant, *The Reformation*, Simon and Schuster, 1967, p. 415.
4. From Luther, *On Marriage*, quoted in J. MacHaffie, *Readings in Her Story*, Fortress Press, 1992, p. 71.
5. Ibid, p. 71.
6. Durant, p. 415.
7. Ibid, p. 5.
8. Martin Luther, *The Estate of Marriage*, from *Luther's Works*, Vol. 45, W., Brandt, ed., Fortress Press, 1962, pp. 38-46, Also quoted in MacHaffie, p. 68.
9. Ibid, p. 69.
10. Ibid, p. 69.
11. MacHaffie, p. 70.
12. Ibid, pp. 70-71.
13. Quoted in MacHaffie, p. 73. From John Calvin, *Commentaries on the First Book of Moses Called Genesis*, trans. J. King, Vol 1, Edinburgh, 1947.

14. Ibid, p. 73.
15. Ibid, p. 74.
16. Ibid, p. 83.
17. Durant, p. 474.
18. Dackerman, p. 3.
19. Hunter-Stiebel P., Catalogue *for Chez Elle, Chez Lui, at Home in 18th Century France,* Rosenberg and Stiebel, 1987, p. 22.
20. Ibid, p. 23.
21. Ibid, p. 36.
22. Richardson S., *Pamela,* W.W. Norton, 1968, p. 164.
23. Richardson S., *Clarissa,* Riverside, 1962, p. 477.

Chapter Eight

1. Quoted in Marsh, J., *Pre-Raphaelite Women,* Artists, 1987, p. 61.
2. Ruskin, J., Sesame *and Lilies, Sibley and Ducker,* 1977, p. 83.
3. Ibid, p. 88.
4. This material taken from Ch I, "Effie Gray and John Ruskin", in P. Rose, *Parallel Lives,* Vintage Cooks, 1984, and is well worth reading in entirety. See pp. 55-6 for Ruskin's revulsion for his wife's pubic hair.
5. Actually, this period saw a revival of Catholicism that Protestants called an epidemic.
6. Packer, L., *Christina Rossetti,* U.C. Press, 1963, p. 103.
7. Ibid, p. 49.
8. Ibid, p. 130.
9. Ibid, p. 102.
10. Ibid, p. 128.
11. Ibid, p. 103.
12. Ibid, p. 72.
13. Marsh, p. 34.
14. Murray, J., *Strong Minded Women And Other Lost Voices From Nineteenth Century England,* Pantheon, 1982, p. 114. She writes, "My darling mother (kept) me ignorant as a baby...."
15. Rose, p. 58.

16. Perkin J., *Women and Marriage in Nineteenth Century England.* Lyceum, 1989, p. 150.
17. Lewis, R.W.B., *Edith Wharton, A Biography,* Harper and Row, 1975, p. 53.
18. Ibid, p. 54.
19. See the Epilogue to Lewis' Biography for a remarkable and hitherto unknown graphic description by Wharton of her sexual awakening.
20. Murray, p. 128.
21. Ibid, p. 129.
22. Ibid, p. 131.
23. Ibid, p. 129.
24. Brundage, pp. xx, xix.
25. Warner, p. xx.
26. *The New York Times Magazine,* March 31, 1996, p. 62.
27. Bell, R. *Holy Anorexia,* Univ. Chicago, 1985, pp. 43-53.
28. Ibid, pp. 76-7 and 124.
29. Campbell J., ed., *The Portable Jung,* Viking Press, 1971, see Chs. 3 and 4.

Chapter Nine

1. Klingaman, p. 157.
2. See Crossan, *Jesus, A Revolutionary Biography.*
3. See Crossan, as above, "The Dogs beneath the Cross", also pp. 125-6 for quotes from Josephus.
4. For a brilliant discussion of this historical malapropism, see Crossan, as above.
5. From NPR program "Fresh Air", interview with Terry Gross.

Chapter Ten

1. Grant R., *The Secret Sayings of Jesus,* Doubleday, 1960, p. 29.
2. Ibid, pp. 44.
3. Some scholars believe that the whitewashing of Pilate may be an interpolation, since the extant Gospel of Peter is a copy

made in the eighth or ninth century from the original papyrus.
4. Robinson, J. ed., *The Nag Hammadi Library in English,* Harper and Row, 1977, pp.121-130.
5. Dart, J., *The Jesus of Heresy and History,* Harper and Row, 1988, p. 114.
6. Robinson, *Dialogue of the Savior.*
7. Ibid, see Gospel of Philip.
8. Acts 20:36: "... they folded Paul in their arms and kissed him." "Greet one another with the kiss of peace." is found in Romans 16:16, 1st Cor. 16:20, 2nd Cor. 13:12, 1st Thess. 5:26, 1st Peter 5:14.
9. Dart, p. 116.
10. Robinson, *The Sophia of Jesus Christ.*
11. Ibid, see Gospel of Philip.
12. Ibid, see Gospel of Mary.
13. This story is the subject of a painting displayed in the Cathedral of St. John the Divine in New York City.
14. Dart, p. 207.

Chapter Eleven

1. Haskins, p. 12.
2. Torjesen, p. 19.
3. See discussion in Schussler-Fiorenza, p. 127.
4. From de Voragine, quoted in Walker, p. 613.
5. Walker, p. 459.
6. Ibid, p. 455.
7. Ibid, p. 202.
8. Ibid, p. 89.
9. Pearson, B., *Gnosticism, Judaism, and Egyptian Christianity,* Fortress press, 1990, pp. 84 and 87.
10. Haskins, p. 18.

Chapter Twelve

1. Quoted in J. Phillips, *Eve, History of an Idea,* Harper, 1984, p.70.
2. Jacobus de Vorgine, *The Golden Legend,* Princeton U. Press, 1993, Vol 1, p.185.
3. Denny, N. *Medieval Drama,* E. Arnold, 1974, p.19, "Saint's Legend as Mimesis".
4. Voragine, p.227-8.
5. Haskins, pp. 119-120
6. From the Magdalen Chapel, Assisi, reproduced in Haskins, plate 45.
7. Philadelphia Museum of Art, Johnson Collection.
8. R. Potter, *The English Morality Play,* Routledge, 1975, p.19.
9. Voragine, p. 375.
10. Ibid, p. 375 - 381.
11. Haskins, p. 135.
12. Haskins, p. 145. Banner of the Flagellants of Borgo San Sepolcro, late 14th c. Metropolitan Museum of Art, New York.

Chapter Thirteen

1. For discussion of altars in medieval drama see Young, K., *The Drama of the Medieval Church,* Oxford: Clarendon, 1962, pp. 212-14.
2. Ibid, p. 21.
3. For more on this see Nelson, *Medieval English Stage,* U. Chicago Press, 1974.
4. M. Malvern, *Venus in Sackcloth, The Magdalen's Origins and Metamorphoses,* Carbondale, 1975, p.102.
5. Ibid, p. 104.
6. Denny, N., *Medieval Drama,* E. Arnold, 1974, p. 105.
7. Ibid, p. 107.
8. Ibid, p. 107.
9. Ibid, p.p. 121-122
10. Ibid, pp. 127 - 144.

11. Ibid, p. 142.
12. Ibid, p. 127.
13. Ibid, p. 132.
14. Cleugh, pp. 32-3.
15. Haskins, p. 167.
16. Ibid, p. 166.
17. Ibid, p. 164.
18. Ibid, p. 164. Also see Malvern, pp. 105-108.
19. Malvern, p. 116.
20. Ibid, p. 117.
21. Ibid, p. 118. Another English dramatist, the so-called Chester playwright drew from Luke's story of the sinner who wept and anointed. In Christ Visiting The Home of Simon the Leper, The Magdalen, Lazarus and Martha welcome Jesus to their home. Immediately, however, the Magdalen pours out her confession: "…from the lord, may I not conceale / my fylth and my feale (fault) / forgeue me that my flesh so feayle, / to thee has done amisse!" Anointing Jesus with the precious oil, she pleads for mercy: "…full of synne and sorrow am I, / but therefore, lord, I am sorry; / amend me through thy great mercy, / that make to thee my mone!" Jesus responds, "…for her great love…her many sins have been forgiven;" signaling an ecstatic outpouring of joy and relief: "…My Christ, my comfort, and my kinge! / I worship thinge; / for now my heart is in lykinge, / and I at my above thee in all." Once again, a largely illiterate audience has added an important text to their understanding of Christianity.

Chapter **Fourteen**

1. For more on this see Leo Steinberg, *The Sexuality of Christ in Renaissance Art and Modern Oblivion*, Pantheon, 1983
2. Cleugh, p. 32
3. Lawner, L., *Lives of the Courtesans*, Rizzoli, 1987, p. 75.
4. Boulding, p. 542.

5. Lawner, p. 32
6. Rowdon, M., *The Silver Age of Venice*, Praeger P. 1970, p. 99.
7. Pullan, *B. Rich and Poor in Renaissance Venice*, Oxford U. Press, 1971, p. 60.
8. Ibid., p. 94.
9. Ibid., p. 285.
10. Quoted in Haskins, p. 466.
11. Lawner, p. 167.
12. Haskins, p. 241.
13. Nash, p. 60.
14. Artemesia's court testimony (at the time she was illiterate) has left a graphic description. Forcing her into the bedroom, Tassi stuffed a handkerchief into her mouth. Pinning her down with one hand, "... with his penis pointed at my vagina, he began to push it inside. I felt a strong burning and it hurt very much, but because he held my mouth I couldn't cry out." Fighting vigorously, she tore skin from his penis and attacked him with a knife, managing to inflict a slight chest wound. Later, Tassi soothed her by swearing that he would marry her, "as soon as I get of the labyrinth I am in. (but) ... when I take you (as my wife) I don't want any foolishness." Aware that she would no longer marriageable to anyone else, Artemesia testified that she later yielded, "...lovingly, many times to his desires, since many times he has also reconfirmed this promise to me." Only later did she learn that Tassi was already married (See Garrard, Mary D., *Artemesia Gentileschi, The Image of the Female Hero in Italian Baroque Art*. Princeton University Press, 1989).
15. There is a striking conjunction here to an earlier *Penitent Magdalen* of Caravaggio (1596 / 98), an intimate member of Orazio's circle who profoundly influenced Artemesia. Known for an almost shocking realism, Caravaggio's saints often resemble common peasants with the dirt of the fields still under their fingernails. In this case, Caravaggio's Magdalen is

utterly human, utterly degraded. Disheveled and unkempt, she sits dejectedly on the floor of a starkly empty room with dark, bare walls, gazing despondently at her empty arms that form a circle, as if cradling a child. Loosely scattered about the floor are her cast-off jewels and the tell tale perfume jar. A single tear trickles down her nose, perhaps a tear of contrition, or possibly something more mundane – a mother's sorrow for her lost infant. Strangely enough, she bears a striking resemblance to the Madonna of Caravaggio's *The Rest on the Flight into Egypt* of the 1596 / 98. Richly dressed, with luxuriant red hair falling down her shoulders and breast, the Madonna's head inclines downward, as does the Magdalen's. Yet the former gently cradles her sleeping infant, whereas the latter seems to mourn a lost child.

16. Haskins, p. 288.
17. Ibid, p. 288.
18. Ibid, p. 285.

Chapter Fifteen

1. Quoted in Haskins, p. 486.
2. From Martin Luther, *Table Talk.* Ed. T.H. Lennon, Phil. 1957, p. 751.
3. Durant, p. 419.
4. Ibid, p. 419.
5. Ibid, p. 420.
6. Ibid, p. 374.
7. Ibid, p. 375.
8. Ibid, p. 374.
9. For more on this see *The Medieval Mystical Tradition in England*, M. Glasscoe, ed., 1984.
10. Southwell, R., *Marie Magdalenes Funeral Teares, 1591,* reproduction, Delmar, N.Y., 1975. Preface.
11. Ibid, pp. 43- 69.

12. See G. Tuttle, *Mysticism in the Wesleyan Tradition,* Asbury Press, 1989.
13. *The Complete Poetry of Richard Crashaw,* Anchor Book, 1970, p. 56.
14. Ibid, p. 131.
15. J. Ford, *'Tis Pity She's a Whore,* S. Barker, Ed., Routledge, 1997, pp. 67, 97, 104.

Chapter Sixteen

1. Cleland J., *Memoirs of a Woman of Pleasure,* G.P. Putnam, 1963, p. 293.
2. Ibid, p. 296.
3. Farge, A., *Fragile Lives,* Harvard U. Press, p. 71.
4. Carlton, C., *Royal Mistresses,* Routledge, 1990, p. 77.
5. Ibid, p. 105.
6. Ibid, p. 119.
7. Trudgill, E., *Madonnas and Magdalenes,* Holmes and Meier, N.Y., 1976, p. 6.
8. Ibid, p. 131.
9. Carlton, p. 148.
10. Pearl, C., *The Girl with the Swansdown Seat,* Bobbs-Merrill, 1955, p. 17.
11. Ruskin, p. XXVII.
12. Trudgill, pp. 13-14.
13. Ibid, p. 14.
14. Harrison, F., *The Dark Angel,* Universe Books, 1977, p. 14.
15. Ibid, p. 22.
16. Marcus, S. *The Other Victorians,* Basic Books, 1964, pp. 18 and 22-3.
17. Laquer, W., *Making Sex,* Harvard U. Press, 1990, p. 210.
18. Trudgill, p. 62.
19. For a full discussion of this revisionist viewpoint see, Peter Gay, *A Bourgeois Experience,* Oxford U. Press, 1987 or Norton 1999.

20. Rose, p. 123.
21. Collins, *W., Basil,* Oxford U. Press, pp. 91 and 192.
22. Ibid, p. 30.
23. Ibid, p. 46.
24. Ibid, p. 327.
25. Ibid, p. 329.
26. Ibid, p. 344.
27. Trudgill, p. 123.
28. Marsh, *Pre-Raphaelite Women,* P. 84.
29. Ibid, p. 84.
30. Ibid, p. 86.
31. Twenty years later, Rosetti did a portrait, almost a twin to Sandy's, of a Magdalen much closer to his 'carnal woman' – "glamorized, full throat, loose hair etc." See Marsh, p. 89.

Chapter Seventeen

1. Trudgill, p. 134.
2. *My Secret Life,* Vol 1-11, Grove Press, 1966, p. 7.
3. Ibid, Ch V111, pp. 124-135.
4. Ibid, p. 129.
5. Ibid, p. 676.
6. Ibid, p. 1391.
7. N. Boyd, *Three Victorian Women Who Changed Their World,* Macmillan, 1982, pp. 80, 89.
8. Zola, E. *Nana,* Oxford University Press, 1992, p. 26.
9. Ibid, p. 25.
10. Ibid, p. 190.
11. Ibid, p. 425.
12. Pearl, pp. 48 and 71.
13. *The Illustrated Mayhew's London,* J. Canning, Ed., 1986
14. M. Mason, *The Making of Victorian Sexuality,* J. Canning, 1994, p. 10.
15. L. Mahood, *The Magdalenes, Prostitution in the Nineteenth Century,* Routledge, 1990, p. 67.

16. Pearl, p. 66.
17. Ibid, p. 57.
18. Haskins, p. 323.
19. Ibid, p. 323.
20. Ibid, p. 310.
21. Ibid, p. 314.
22. Tomalin, C., *The Invisible Woman*, A. Knopf. 1991, pp. 87-90.
23. Haskins, p. 326-7. Also see Jonas Hanway, *Thoughts on the Plan for a Magdalen House for Repentant Prostitutes*, 2nd ed. London, 1759.
24. A Darling, *Lola Montez*, Stein and Day, 1972, p. 187.
25. Ibid, p. 224.
26. Pearl, p. 64.
27. Ibid, p. 62.
28. Chadwick, W. *Women, Art, And Society*, Thames and Hudson, 1990, p. 176.
29. Marcus, pp. 6-7.
30. Mayhew, p. 109.
31. Mahood, p. 180.
32. Ibid, p. 80.
33. Ibid, p. 91.
34. Quoted by Nancy Ramsey, New York Times, Sunday, July 27, 2003, Arts and Leisure, p. 7, writing on the film *The Magdalene Sisters.* Originally a documentary, then a drama, the film is based on the real experiences of inmates in the so-called 'laundries' in nineteenth century Ireland, exposing the sadistic cruelties inflicted upon women locked up in these so called 'reformatories', many for life.

Chapter Eighteen

1. Bischoff, U., *Edvard Munch, 1863-1944*, Taschen, 1993, p. 54.
2. Mendgen, E. *Von Stuck*, 1863-1928, Taschen, 1995. p. 24.
3. Ibid, p. 24. From *The Complete Poems of Heinrich Heine*, Oxford, 1982.

4. Mendgen, p. 42.
5. Ibid, p. 19.
6. Epstein, S., *The Prints Of Edvard Munch, Mirror Of His Life,* Oberlin College, 1983, p. 12.
7. Catalogue, *Munch and Sorenson,* National Academy of Design, New York, 1955, p. 46.
8. Epstein, p. 15.
9. Ibid, p. 32.
10. For the discussion of Munch and women I am most grateful to Sarah G. Epstein, America's foremost collector of Munch lithographs, for her invaluable insights on Munch's relationships, and the materials she made available to me. For a portrait of Tulla Larsen done by her artist-husband, Arne Kavli in 1904, see Epstein, Mirror, p. 89. Here her appearance is cool and notably demure. For The Sin see Berman, P., and Van Nimmen, J. *Munch and Women, Image, and Myth,* foreword by S. Epstein, Art Services International, 1997, pp. 204-205.
11. Epstein, *Mirror*, p. 96.
12. Ibid, p. 39.
13. *Munch and Women*, p. 20.
14. Epstein, S. *Edvard Munch, Master Prints From The Epstein Collection,* National Gallery of Art, 1990, p. 24.
15. See Epstein, *Mirror*, p. 53.
16. *Munch and Sorenson*, p. 36.
17. Epstein, Mirror, p. 52.
18. Interestingly, in his discussion of men with a compulsion to have sex with prostitutes, Freud wrote: "Birth is both the first of all dangers to life and the prototype of all later ones that cause us to feel anxiety...". From *Freud on Women.*
19. Again, Sarah G. Epstein interviewed several people who knew the artist well, including one of his former models, all of whom described him as witty, charming, and polite to

women. In her opinion, paintings such as *Vampire* reflect painful episodes concurrent with particularly relationships.

20. Freud, S. *Collected Works,* See "Civilized Sexual Morality And Modern Nervous Illness", p. 167.
21. Ibid, p. 177.
22. See Freud's case study of the 'Rat-Man'.
23. From "A Special Type of Choice of Object Made By Men", in "Contributions to the Psychology of Love", *Standard Edition Complete Psychological Works of Freud,* Vol 11, p. 166.

24 Torgesen, p. 142.

Chapter Nineteen

1. de Caso and Sanders, *Rodin's Sculpture,* C.E. Tuttle, 1977, p. 93.
2. Ibid, p. 93, From "Notes on Religious Painting". In that Rodin was not alone, as the quest for Jesus the man raised the issue of his sexuality. However, for the stridently anti-clerical 'Decadent' school of art, with its frontal attack on traditional Christian morality, that humanity was often depicted in a deliberately coarse, patently blasphemous manner. Thus, in *Calvary,* by the Belgian painter, Felicien Rops, a devil with a large and erect penis hangs upon the cross, and in his *St. Mary Magdalen* the saint masturbates beneath a large, disembodied, "haloed penis" nailed to the cross. Lovis Corinth's *Deposition* of 1895, however, is less offensive. While Jesus' mother is depicted as a wrinkled, toothless, swarthy old woman, his Magdalen literally collapses onto the body of the dead Jesus who, nonetheless, appears to encircle her tenderly in his mangled arms. In its flesh on flesh embrace, Corinth's *Deposition* seems to anticipate Rodin's *Christ and the Magdalen.*
3. Grunfeld, F., *Rodin, a Biography,* Henry Holt, 1987, p. 241.
4. Ibid, p. 241.

5. N. Kazantzakis, *The Last Temptation of Christ,* Bantam Book, 1965, p. 1.
6. Ibid, p. 1.
7. Ibid, p. 25.
8. Ibid, p. 83.
9. Ibid, p. 87.
10. Ibid, p. 442.
11. Ibid, p. 446.
12. Ibid, p. 456.
13. Ibid, p. 458.
14. Ibid, p. 465.
15. Scorsese himself conceded in interviews that the struggle between flesh and spirit intrinsic to the novel was one that he understood very well. As a Catholic who studied for the priesthood at one time, he understood only too well the deeply rooted conflict about sexuality for those who would give up earthly joys for spiritual rewards.
16. Less publicized, but more subtle in its portrayal of Jesus and the Magdalen is the film "Jesus of Montreal" by Canadian director Denys Arcand.
17. Rushing, Sandra, *The Magdalene Legacy, Exploring the Wounded Icon of Sexuality,* Bergin and Garvey, 1994.

EPILOGUE

1. R. Dowden, The New York Times Magazine, January 27, 2002, pp. 28-31.
2. A. T. Fleming, "Maternal Madness", New York Times, Week in Review, Sunday, March 17, 2002, p.3.
3. Ibid, p.3.

INDEX

Acton, Dr. W. 110, 203, 218, 226
Ambrose, St. 49, 51, 56, 57
Anne, mother of Mary 75, 104
Augustine, St. 37, 47, 54, 55, 56, 57, 58, 59, 69, 90,
136
Augustus, Caesar 46, 53
Beatrice 84, 175
Bernard, St. 82, 85
Boccaccio 80, 177, 208
Brown, Dan 254
Calvin, J. 93, 94, 187, 189, 190, 195, 202
Cana-in-Galilee 25
Clarissa 98, 99
Claudel, Camille 245, 246
Cleland, John 197, 198, 213
Clement of Alexandria 51, 54, 74
Collins, Charles 108
Collins, Wilkie 204, 205, 206
Convertite 185
Cornforth, Fanny 207
Coutts, Burdett 221
Crashaw, R. 192
Crysostum, J. 49
Da Vinci Code 2, 116, 254
Dante 84, 85, 104, 206
Dickens, C. 204, 219, 221, 226
Diderot 97

Digby 168
Dodd, W. 220, 221
Elizabeth, St. 26, 27, 68, 206, 219
Esther 32, 219
Eustochium 72, 95
Ford, John 186, 193, 195
Gentileschi, A. 182
Gentileschi, O. 181
Gregory of Nyssa 49
Gnostic Gospels: 130, 137, 142, 168, 191, 254
______ Bartholomew 81
_______James 66, 68, 69, 120, 121, 122, 132, 202
_______Mary 28, 46, 134, 135
_______Peter 130
_______Philip 70, 132, 135
_______Second Apocalypse, James 132
Sophia of Jesus Christ 133
Helia, St. 73
Hillel 21, 42, 44, 263
Isis 26, 78, 85, 143, 144, 151
Jerome, St. 35, 39, 51, 57, 72, 73, 74, 75, 93, 95, 101, 104, 109
Jesus Christ Superstar 115, 247, 248, 249
Joseph 5, 18, 24, 25, 26, 27, 28, 39, 65, 66, 67, 68, 69, 104, 120, 121, 123, 125, 215
Judith 31, 32, 183
Julian 46, 59
Katuba 33
Kazantzakis 249
London by Midnight Mission 222
Loudon 80
Louverture, T. 18
Luther, M. 90, 91, 92, 94, 188, 189
Magdalene Asylums 227, 228

Magdalene Houses 185, 226
Mary of Bethany 8, 11, 12, 15, 143, 187
Mary of Egypt 151, 152, 156
Martha of Bethany 8, 11, 12, 155, 251
Mill, J. 204
Millais, J. S. 102, 103
Montez, L. 223, 224
Munch, E. ii, v, 233, 234, 235, 236, 237, 238, 239
My Secret Life 212, 213, 240
Orff, Carl 168
Origen 49, 51, 63
Pamela 97, 98, 99
Passion Plays 162, 163 164, 165, 150, 167
Pattmore, C. 101, 102
Paul, St. 8, 9, 19, 41, 50, 57, 58, 74,131, 132, 141, 142, 144, 145, 246
Pelagius 59
Peter, St. 8, 10, 43, 118, 119, 121, 124, 127, 130, 134, 135, 140, 156, 191
Penitentials 79, 80, 81, 108, 154
Richardson, S. 97, 98, 99
Rodin, A. 243, 244, 245, 246
Rosetti, Christina 101, 104, 105, 106, 107, 108
______ Dante, G. 206
______ Maria 105, 108
Rushing, S. 254
Ruskin, John 102, 103, 104, 202, 203, 206
______ Effie 102, 103
Samaritan Woman 6, 7, 8, 188
Sarah, desert mother 74
Savanarola 172, 173
Scorsese, M. 248, 249, 252, 253
Scott, W.B. 106

Seneca 53, 54
Shammai 41
Smolin, M. 261, 262
Song of Songs 32, 243
Southwell, R. 190, 191, 192
Tabitha 10
Taylor, Harriet 204
Tertullian 48, 49, 74, 142
Thecla 9, 74, 142
Titian 171, 179, 180, 181
Voragine 154, 155, 156, 157
Woman taken in adultery 41, 145, 164, 188
Zola, E. 208, 212, 216, 218

ABOUT THE AUTHOR

As a social and cultural historian with special interests in New and Old Testament, Judaism in the first century C.E, and the historical Jesus, Doris Tishkoff is uniquely qualified for a study that transcends the boundaries of specialization. In addition to a Ph.D. in history from Michigan State University, Dr. Tishkoff studied Old Testament at the Hebrew Union Seminary in Los Angeles and connections between first century Judaism and Christianity with Nahum Glatzer of Brandeis University, and also taught Jewish history at Leo Baeck Temple in Los Angeles. In the field of European history she has taught at Oregon Institute of Technology, the University of Oregon, and Franklin Pierce College. Currently she teaches in the History Department at Quinnipiac University in Hamden, Connecticut. Her research and writing includes works on the music and culture of the eighteenth century, the history of sexuality, the history of religion, and women's studies. Known for her lively lecture style, Dr. Tishkoff is at home with both academic and lay audiences.

Printed in the United States
52307LVS00004B/339

7/06